PRESENTED TO:

_____

FROM:

_____

DATE:

_____

GOD'S PURPOSE

FOR

YOUR LIFE

365 DEVOTIONS

CHARLES F. STANLEY

THOMAS NELSON
Since 1798

JANUARY

RESOLVED

Your eyes have seen my unformed substance; and in Your book were all written the days that were ordained for me, when as yet there was not one of them.

PSALM 139:16

G od has a plan for your life that does not change even though your life may take turns that you've never expected. Take that to heart today. The New Year is a time when people review the past and embrace a fresh start. For you, that may carry with it some pain over losses but also hopefulness for what's to come. Be confident in the fact that no matter what the days ahead may bring, God's loving, perfect purposes for your life remain. They do not change. Nothing is a surprise to Him.

The same God who breathed life into you and formed you in your mother's womb loves you enough to plan for your future and be actively involved in all that concerns you. He has promised that if you'll seek Him, you'll find Him, and you will discover His awesome will for your life. And the course Jesus has orchestrated for you is never for your harm, but for your edification, establishment, and encouragement. So begin this New Year by resolving to be focused on Him and trust Him for the path ahead.

Jesus, thank You that this year is in Your plan and is guided by Your hand. I resolve to trust in You. Amen.

ALL THE DETAILS

O LORD, You are my God; I will exalt You, I will give thanks to Your name; for You have worked wonders, plans formed long ago, with perfect faithfulness.

ISAIAH 25:1

When thinking about God's will, it is easy to accept that He has grand plans for the church, nations, and even the world as a whole. But perhaps it is not so easy for you to believe He has plans for you *individually*. That would mean that the sovereign Lord of the universe cares about you specifically—about the intimate details of your life, despite your flaws, failures, and mistakes.

Even if we believe that in our minds, sometimes embracing it when things go wrong is not so easy. We wonder how God could let difficult things happen if He really cares for us.

But Jesus says, "The very hairs of your head are all numbered" (Matthew 10:30). If He would pay attention to how many strands of hair you have, do you think He would be less vigilant about the path of your life? He truly cares about all your details, so entrust them to His hands and count on His faithfulness.

Jesus, I believe You care about my future.
Teach me to love You more and entrust each
moment to Your loving hands. Amen.

A PURPOSE TO ARISE

Indeed, He loves His people; all Your holy ones are in Your hand. They followed in Your steps; they accept and receive direction from You.

DEUTERONOMY 33:3 AMP

What is the reason you get out of bed each morning? Is it because you have a great goal to pursue, a responsibility to fulfill, or some pressure that drives you forth?

Many people face despair as they awake each day because they don't have a vital sense of purpose, direction, and meaning in their lives. Work, relationships, and other earthly objectives cannot always keep us motivated. Without a basic, unfailing anchor of hope, it is easy to lose heart when life doesn't go as planned.

But you were created with a purpose—one that can help you arise each day with hopefulness and can motivate you to endure. What is that reason for your existence? God formed you to love you and to be loved by you. His mercies are new every morning. Because of His presence with you, you have everything you need to be victorious.

So go forth today with that knowledge. Get out of bed with the assurance you are loved, are valued, and have all you need to rise up to all you were created to do and enjoy.

Jesus, You are my reason to rise up each morning and have hope. Thank You for loving me and leading me to abundant life. Amen.

REACHABLE

Trust in the LORD with all your heart and do not lean on your own understanding. In all your ways acknowledge Him, and He will make your paths straight.

PROVERBS 3:5–6

God's will can seem grand and unreachable, can't it? After decades of hearing believers talk about their struggles, I've realized two reasons people get so frustrated with the Christian life: either they don't understand the nature of the will of God, or they don't know how to find it. And if you don't comprehend those two things, you may feel insecure and directionless in your walk with Jesus.

However, take heart today that God is *committed* to your success—the Lord is dedicated to helping you experience Him, the purposes you were created for, and the full expression of your potential. That means His will for you is not unreachable. In fact, He is constantly communicating it to you. If you set your heart to love and seek Him, He will take you there.

So today, don't take the frustrating path of trying to guess God's mind. Rather, seek Him, trust Him to disclose His plans, obey Him, and He will direct your course.

Lord, I want Your will and set my heart to obey
You. Reveal Your will and Your ways to me
so I may walk in Your perfect path. Amen.

ALWAYS HOPE

*Hope in the LORD; for with the LORD there is
unfailing love. His redemption overflows.*

PSALM 130:7 NLT

S ome days you may wonder, *Is there hope for my life?* From everything that has happened, the losses you've endured, the limitations before you, and the mistakes you've made, it can seem like the answer would be no. But if this is where you are, I say to you with confidence: *With God, there is* always *hope, and He has a plan in mind for your tomorrows. Hang on to Him and keep going.*

God knows exactly where you are at this very minute, and He understands your every struggle and disappointment. He is the One who has all the answers you need—and each one is found within His Word. Your life may seem to have hit a low point right now, but He is not going to abandon you—not ever (John 14:18). If you will trust Him, He will continue to work in your life. Then you will see His plan for your life unfold in a mighty way. This is His promise to each one of us.

Jesus, thank You for always giving me
hope! I know that this is not the end of my
journey, but the beginning of something
new You are doing in me. Amen.

THERE IS A PLAN

The plans of the LORD stand firm forever.
PSALM 33:11 NIV

Right now, set your mind on this truth: *Our God is a planner.* He is not a reactor. He did not set this world in motion to be ruled by chance or unchecked forces. Nor did He create you to live without hope and purpose. He has a plan.

What that means is that the joys, challenges, and trials you are experiencing are all by design for your training and edification. True, at times you may sin, and afflictions may arise as a consequence of your choices. However, none of that is beyond the perfect planning, power, and provision of your Savior.

Just think about how carefully God planned your salvation. The Lord strategically unfolded His grand design to send the Savior throughout the ages—through changes in kings and empires—and nothing impeded Him. Then the good news went from the empty tomb to the disciples and from person to person until it reached you.

If you'll think about how precisely the Father carried all this out, you'll realize how deeply He treasures you and how carefully He thinks about your future. So do not fear or be dismayed whatever may come. Trust God's plan.

**Jesus, I know You have a perfect plan,
and none of my circumstances surprise
You. I will trust You to lead me. Amen.**

DO AS HE SAYS

"I will do as You say."

LUKE 5:5

Fishermen with any experience on the Sea of Galilee knew that the optimal time to catch fish was during the night in shallow water. During the day, the fish dove deep, where it was far more difficult to successfully sink nets to catch them. However, when Jesus instructed Peter to fish during the day, he obeyed—even though he was tired and not completely certain Jesus knew what He was asking.

Perhaps you remember a time when God asked you to do something beyond what you thought reasonable. You did not know if what you were hearing was the right thing to do because it appeared so counterintuitive. Maybe you are in such a season right now. Understand without a shadow of doubt that you will never go wrong obeying God.

Peter did as Jesus asked and pulled in so many fish that his nets began to break. The same will be true in your situation. You may not know exactly why God is calling you to do as He instructs, but you can be sure that when you do as He says, you will experience a blessing beyond your imagination.

> Jesus, I will do what You ask. When I
> don't understand the path ahead or Your
> instruction, I will trust You, knowing
> You have never failed me. Amen.

REVEALED BY STEP

None of those who wait for You will be ashamed.

PSALM 25:3

Waiting is difficult, especially if we are expectantly hoping for God to answer our prayers or lead us in some specific manner. This is compounded by the fact that we live in a society that insists on immediate results—instant food, overnight shipping, downloadable resources, and information at our fingertips. If it can't happen quickly, we often will be frustrated—tempted to give up and walk away.

However, experiencing the fullness of God's will is not something that happens immediately. It takes time—often, a lifetime—to see His plan unfold. He may give us an idea as to what His will is, but it takes a life of step-by-step devotion to uncover His complete purpose for our lives. And the truth is, it is His mercy and compassion that limit what He reveals to us, lest we be overwhelmed by discouragement, fear, or—even worse—pride.

Friend, you don't need the whole plan right now. When God instructs you to step forward, just obey Him. Go forward in faith. And as you trust Him, He will provide what you most long for—His leadership into a bright, fulfilling future.

Jesus, in the mountains and valleys, I follow You step-by-step. I will wait on You and trust You with my future. Amen.

JESUS IS THE KEY

An apostle of Christ Jesus by the will of God,
according to the promise of life in Christ Jesus.

2 TIMOTHY 1:1

J esus is the ultimate key to knowing and living out God's will. He is your example of the life of faith in every way (Romans 8:29), and He provides you with access to the throne of grace so you can learn His plan (Hebrews 4:16). His Holy Spirit guides you (John 16:13–14), His prayers empower you (Hebrews 7:25), and His Word provides a light to your path (Psalm 119:105).

I say this because many people believe that God's will is about living by religious or moral rules. At the most basic level, it is—but it is really much more than that. It is about a profound, intimate relationship with God Himself—a relationship that results in a life that overflows with His wisdom, purpose, and power.

The Father has created you with a reason in mind, to fulfill an important role in His kingdom. And it is *in* Jesus, as a person who is saved by Him, and *through* Jesus, as His disciple who is in fellowship with Him, that you discover, understand, and walk in His purposes.

Jesus, You are God's will personified. I fix my eyes on You and know You will lead me in the center of His will. Amen.

YOUR INTERCESSOR

He is able also to save forever those who draw near
to God through Him, since He always lives to make
intercession for them.

HEBREWS 7:25

D o you realize Jesus is praying unceasingly for you even at this very moment? As you read these words, He is speaking out the commands that move heaven and earth so His will can be carried out in your life.

You may feel as though you do not have a friend you can turn to for help and encouragement. However, you do—always. Jesus listens to your every prayer, will never leave or forsake you, and is always your Advocate before God's throne (1 John 2:1). He continuously remains closer to you than a brother (Proverbs 18:24).

As your Savior, He wants the very best for you, which is why He is constantly calling you to know and do God's will (Philippians 2:13). Jesus knows how to lead you so that you will fulfill the purposes for which you were created and glorify Him (Ephesians 2:10).

So today, know you are not alone. Indeed, you have the best Prayer Warrior possible. Listen to Him, trust Him, and be assured that He will never lead you astray.

Jesus, thank You for praying for me and leading me in doing God's will! I trust You. Amen.

SUFFICIENT PROVISION

God is able to make all grace abound to you, so
that always having all sufficiency in everything,
you may have an abundance for every good deed.

2 CORINTHIANS 9:8

What do you do when you know that God has revealed His will to you, but you don't know how it can possibly happen because of your limited resources? This is a question that everyone who follows God faces at one point or another. At such a time, the only thing to do is to obey, step forward by faith, and do as He says. Otherwise, you may miss doing His will and receiving the blessings that He has for you.

Thankfully, you can go forward with the assurance that God can and will provide for your needs in amazing ways as you obey Him (Philippians 4:19). You move forward step-by-step as He commands, and He supplies you provision by provision.

Likewise, God will work through the circumstances of your life to direct you. He will open and close the doors you need each day, moving strategically to answer your prayers and accomplish His purposes. So keep trusting Him and go forward with the faith that you'll have exactly what you need.

Jesus, thank You for providing for me
daily. I confess I am overwhelmed by this
need, but I will trust You in it. Amen.

NEAR

*For me, the nearness of God is my good; I have
made the Lord GOD my refuge.*

PSALM 73:28

D o you ever feel as if God is far from you? Be assured, He is steadfastly near. Do not be disheartened because you don't see Him in your circumstances.

I saw an illustration of this during a photography excursion I took to the Matterhorn in Switzerland. When I got to the great mountain, I was greeted by a snowstorm that unforgivingly persisted for three days. The blanket of snow was so thick, I never even saw the foot of the mountain. On my last night there, I shared my disappointment with the Lord.

The next day, I awoke at 5:20 a.m. and looked out my window. The storm had been swept away, and there was the Matterhorn in all her glory, with a halo of moonlight crowning her. It was as if God said, "See what happens when you wait for Me."

The lesson I learned was that God is always near whether I can see Him or not. He is always at work regardless of what is blocking my view. So always keep watching and waiting for Him. The fog will eventually clear, and what He's accomplished will astound you.

**Lord, You know how my heart longs to see
You in my situation. Open my spiritual eyes
and remove what blocks my view. Amen.**

REST FOR THE SOUL

"Ask where the good way is, and walk in it, and you will find rest for your souls."

JEREMIAH 6:16 NIV

Are you exhausted? Does life's treadmill have you running faster than you can endure? If your answer is yes, you may be chasing earthly security that does not satisfy and causes crisis after crisis. Sadly, when you place your hope in temporal things—money, status, achievements, acceptance, or even the love of your family and friends—your foundation will inevitably crumble. Earthly solutions will not satisfy the deepest needs of your heart and cannot defend against the troubles that arise. Your identity must be based on something greater than what the world offers if you are to stand strong.

As the old saying goes, life is not about *who* you are; it's about *whose* you are. And your exhaustion is evidence that you haven't given yourself fully to God. Your challenge is to get out of the way so Christ can lead you. Because when you finally see how beloved you are and the abundant life He has for you, you will begin to live for God, through His power. That is the way to find rest for your soul.

Jesus, I confess that I am still trying to be in control. Show me Your ways so I may live in Your strength and for Your glory. Amen.

WEAVINGS

You formed my inward parts; You wove me in my mother's womb.

PSALM 139:13

God sees your potential. No matter how young or old you are, your abilities or infirmities—your Creator sees what is possible through your life. You are His masterpiece, a work conceived in grace and love. And if you allow Him to, He will weave the circumstances of your life together in such a way that He receives the glory, and your heart will be full.

For many people, this is a hard concept to grasp because of the messages and setbacks they've received throughout their lives. Perhaps today you see your life as incomplete or without much worth. It could be that physical, relational, financial, or other personal challenges make you feel hopeless. But God views you from a totally different perspective. When He sees you, He sees a person He loves—of worth and great promise.

Take heart that your every frustration and disappointment has a purpose. And your God will weave all these circumstances together for your good if you will love and trust Him. Therefore, do not despair. Instead, trust Him and let Him make you into the person He knows you can be.

Jesus, You know my life and still call me to You.
Thank You for giving me hope and continuing
to work out Your plan for my life. Amen.

PLACEMENT

He guides me in the paths of righteousness for His name's sake.

PSALM 23:3

Have you asked God what He would like to do through you? If not, I encourage you to do so today. Ask Him, "Lord, how do You want me to invest my life?"

You may not realize how profoundly the Lord desires to work and impact others through you. But He does. Jesus is looking for willing vessels who will submit themselves to Him and allow Him to do the rest. Each person who dedicates his or her life to God is given a valuable role to play in His kingdom.

However, do not get bogged down by the question, *What does God want me to become?* Submitting to Him does not necessarily mean a new assignment or becoming a pastor or missionary. Although this may eventually be part of His plan for you, He usually begins right where you are, walking in fellowship with Him each day. He will reveal who He wants you to talk to.

Your Savior will place you in the position He wants you to occupy. Simply trust that when He wants to work through you, He can get you where you need to go and give you all you need to serve Him.

**Jesus, how do You want me to invest my life?
Lead me to do Your will always. Amen.**

ABUNDANT LIFE

"I came that they may have life, and have it abundantly."

JOHN 10:10

W hat is the abundant life Jesus has for you? It is a life rooted in eternity—one that looks beyond your troubles today to a tomorrow full of hope, where Christ is your Leader, strength, joy, and peace. The abundant life means your ultimate goal becomes to live in undisturbed union with Jesus and reflect His likeness—filled with expectancy of all He will do through you forever.

Yes, at times the abundant life means an abundance of tears. But through Jesus' continuing work in you, you eventually reach a place where you know how to face fear, pain, and the pressures this side of heaven. You are sustained by an inner tranquility and joy because you know for certain that your God is faithful, good, and at work in all circumstances. Every end promises unimagined beginnings.

The abundant life is a choice you make day by day to embrace who God created you to be. Becoming the masterpiece God formed you to be is a lifelong process, but it is worth it because of the beautiful, unique reflection you become of your Savior.

Jesus, I want Your abundant life, but I am afraid because of the trials I face. Lead me, my Savior, and help me become the person You envision me to be. Amen.

LISTENING FOR DIRECTION

Teach me how to live, O LORD. Lead me along the right path.

PSALM 27:11 NLT

What is the very best course for your life?

This is a difficult question to answer considering our limited wisdom and vision of the future. We cannot possibly know what challenges will arise on the path before us. This is why one of the most important disciplines we can develop as believers is that of listening to God. He always knows the way that is most beneficial for us.

All too often, however, the Lord's wisdom is muffled by the clamor of daily life. Sometimes we start out walking with God but get so far ahead of Him that we can no longer hear His voice. Perhaps we get busy, prefer doing things our own way, or are lured into listening to others who have their own agenda. At that point, we can lose contact with the only Guide who truly knows the most optimal path forward.

Don't make that mistake. Be alert to the Master's voice as you journey through life. Stay in the Word, walk in the Spirit, be receptive and responsive to God's promptings, and you'll be sure to remain on the right road.

Jesus, I want to travel the very best course for my life, and I know it is found in You. Teach me to hear You and walk in Your ways. Amen.

THE TREASURE OF HIS WORD

Strengthen me according to Your word.
PSALM 119:28

Why is it that I am always telling you to read the Bible? I know this admonition can become repetitive. However, we have such a precious gift in Scripture—the very thoughts and plans of the living God! Therefore, it is important that we take advantage of it.

God's Word is as timely and applicable to our lives today as it was on the day it was first written. In fact, every time I read my Bible, I receive new insights into the character of God and the challenges I'm facing. Often, certain words, phrases, or verses seem to leap off the page in a powerful way—and I know God is bringing something to my attention that is important for me to know.

The same can be true for you. The foremost way that God communicates with you is through His Word. Through it, He gives you comfort, wisdom, strength, direction, and hope. Scripture teaches you to distinguish between His voice and the others that vie for your attention—so you can take the right path and avoid pitfalls.

So take hold of the treasure He has given. Read the Word and listen to your living, loving God.

Jesus, I confess that sometimes my Bible reading is dry. Help me to know You through Scripture. Bring Your Word to life, Lord. Amen.

THE IMPLANTED WORD

Let my cry come before You, O LORD; give me
understanding according to Your word.

PSALM 119:169

D o you believe God can speak to you? I do. There have been times when I've gone to bed with a problem on my mind, and the Lord has awakened me in the middle of the night with a verse of Scripture. At other times, I've awakened in the morning with a particular passage as my first thought. Each time, I knew God was bringing the Word that was already planted in my heart to remembrance to answer the deep questions I had brought Him. He was speaking to me directly about the matters that were troubling me.

This is why reading the Bible regularly can be so powerful. When you face a trial or challenge, God reminds you of His Word—comforting, counseling, encouraging, convicting, strengthening, and leading you.

Would you like to hear God's voice? Do you need His direction? Start by opening your Bible. Plant His Word in your heart, and don't ignore it when He brings it to mind. Then trust God to bring Scripture to your remembrance in very timely ways—right at the moment when you need to make a decision, encourage another person, or solve a problem.

Jesus, teach me how to listen to You
through Scripture. Plant it deep in my
heart and lead me, Savior. Amen.

THE TRANSFORMING WORD

*Establish Your word to Your servant, as that which
produces reverence for You.*

PSALM 119:38

What you may not know about God's Word is the power in it. As you read Scripture regularly, meditate on it, and apply it, the Holy Spirit works through it to change your thought patterns and transform your behavior (Romans 12:1–2). You begin to respond as Jesus responded and reflect His character.

Paul referred to this process of changing you into Christ's likeness as *sanctification* and explained that it occurs "by the washing of water with the word" (Ephesians 5:26). The more you read the Bible, the more it cleanses your mind of sinful thoughts and desires. You begin to want what the Lord has planned for you.

God's Word changes us. That's one thing that separates the Bible from any other book ever written—its transformational nature. You cannot read the very words and thoughts of the living God and not be inspired, comforted, convicted, and, ultimately, changed. The Holy Spirit implants it into our minds and hearts and from it grows the fruit of Christlikeness. Through Scripture, He trains us, gives us wisdom, heals our wounds, and encourages us. The only caveat is that you have to allow Him to work by trusting what He says.

**Jesus, teach me Your Word. Speak to me
through Scripture that I may know You
and grow in Your likeness. Amen.**

WRONG DIRECTION?

You have kept your promise to your servant David.

1 KINGS 8:24 NLT

When God makes a promise to us, at times it will feel like He has us running in the wrong direction to take hold of it. This is on purpose, to grow our character and stretch our faith.

If you recall, David was anointed king over Israel, but it was decades before he actually sat on the nation's throne. During those intervening years, David had many dangerous and disappointing moments to endure, including being hunted by King Saul. This was because before David could do God's will, he had to be trained by adversity—learning to trust God completely, regardless of his circumstances.

Like David, you may be walking through a deep valley and wondering if you are still in God's will and on track for His promise. Remember, God has promised to guide you, and it is His responsibility to fulfill His word. Your job is to obey Him and persevere through the training.

David knew that he would eventually emerge victorious, so he became a man after God's heart and learned to do God's will regardless of his circumstances. You can too. Today, trust that the Lord keeps all His promises—including the ones He's made to you.

Jesus, help me trust You and learn through my trials. I have faith You will fulfill Your promise to me! Amen.

THE ROOT OF YOUR NEED

*Examine me, O LORD, and try me; test my mind
and my heart. For Your lovingkindness is before
my eyes, and I have walked in Your truth.*

PSALM 26:2–3

D o you have unmet needs in your life? Do you wonder why God
has not answered your cries for His mercy and grace?

You are certainly not alone. This deep, internal lack is a major
part of the human condition in our world today and why we see so
much turmoil, conflict, and pain. What drives, fuels, and shapes all
of our external needs is the deficiency in the foundational spiritual
aspect of our lives that causes us to experience a lack of inner peace
with God, others, and ourselves. They are the real, profound internal
needs we face as human beings, and they are not only unmet but are
growing ever deeper and broader.

So today, I challenge you to look past your immediate, external
needs to their roots. Where do they come from? What emotional
or spiritual needs are hidden beneath their surface that continually
remind you of your woundedness? Get those filled, and the external
wounds will heal.

Jesus, I don't know what inner roots fuel these
external needs. Please identify them in me. You
promise to fill these deep needs. Teach me how
You overcome them on my behalf. Amen.

FIXING YOUR THOUGHTS

*"Which of you by worrying can add a single hour
to his life's span?"*

LUKE 12:25

What do you think about most? Is it something you lack, a relationship, or some goal? To what does your mind turn when trouble arises? As a Christian, you may immediately answer, "Jesus." But I challenge you to track your thinking to the actual thoughts and phrases that arise within you.

The reason I say this is because as you seek God's plan, a great deal of the anxiety you feel may be due to thinking about the wrong things. It could be that you are so concerned about what you lack in your life, what others think, or issues beyond your control, that you fail to focus on the very promises and purposes of God that will bring you peace.

You may believe you are being proactive or responsible by fixating about certain details and situations, but you aren't. All you're really proving is that you do not trust God to guide you. The Lord cares more about getting you to His destination for you than you do. Focus on Him—truly fix your thoughts on Him, replacing the messages of worry with His truth—because He will not fail you.

Jesus, I confess that I am surprised by the things I really think about. Help me replace my worrisome thoughts with Your truth. Amen.

CALLED TO SHARE

"Go into all the world and preach the gospel to all creation."

MARK 16:15

There are certain activities that we are told are God's will for every believer, and one of those is active ministry. Every Christian is called to share the gospel with others in both word and deed—and to do so under the leadership of the Holy Spirit.

That doesn't mean that every Christian is called to be a pastor, evangelist, or missionary. Rather, as a follower of Jesus, your call is to ask the Lord to guide your steps daily so you walk precisely where He wants you to. You are sensitive to His leading—to talk to whomever He tells you, to act when He says to, and to refrain when He calls you to wait or to be silent.

This may seem overwhelming to you, and you may feel inadequate talking to others about Jesus. But remember, God created you for the assignments He gives you (Ephesians 2:10). Your task is not to show your brilliance, but to allow the Lord to shine through you.

So do not be afraid. The One who prompts you to speak on His behalf will give you the words you need to glorify Him (Luke 12:12).

Jesus, guide me today and every day to be the witness You created me to be. Give me the boldness and words to lead many to You. Amen.

GET UP AND GET GOING

*"Why are you crying out to Me? Tell the sons of
Israel to go forward."*

EXODUS 14:15

Today, do what you think God is calling you to do—regardless of whether you are sure of His course or not. If the Lord is showing you to take a step of faith, make a call, write a letter, and so on—do it. If He says, "Be still and wait before Me," clear the time and listen for Him.

Of course, you may be wondering, "What if I do so and get it wrong—I don't do precisely what He wants me to do?" Then be assured He'll correct your course and show you what to do. Just as a car that is started and in gear is easier to steer than a car that's parked, a person who is in motion and willing to obey God is easier for Him to position than a reticent person is for Him to get up and moving.

So trust God to lead you to His next place of service for you. He will reveal to you the doors that He wants you to move through, but first you must go through the ones He's already opened.

Jesus, I will go forward and do as You
say—trusting You will correct my course. I
want to do Your will, my God. Amen.

GOD SATISFIES

My soul longs for You, as a parched land.

PSALM 143:6

O nly God can meet all your needs with His infinite power, love, and wisdom. So if you are hoping for someone else to do so, your focus is misplaced. That may be the cause of some of the emptiness you feel. This is because no person, group, or organization is equipped to satisfy you fully—certainly not the deep inner needs that are vital to your sense of wholeness. The reach of human interaction always falls short specifically because there are areas of our lives made to interact with God and Him alone.

However, when you allow the Lord to be your Source of fulfillment, His presence vastly improves your relationships. This is because He understands who you are and what it takes to fill your heart. He heals those areas of woundedness that cause you to react in fear and anger. And He gives you insight into how to love others as He does.

People can and should love and help each other, but no one should ever think they can satisfy the deepest inner hungers of another's soul. But God can. Look to Him, point others to Him, and allow Him to fill you completely.

Jesus, thank You for understanding me.
Be my Source, Lord. Teach me how to
depend on You for my needs. Amen.

GUARANTEES

I will instruct you and teach you in the way which you should go; I will counsel you with My eye upon you.

PSALM 32:8

Today, take heart in these three facts about God's plans for us.
First, God will show us His will. Our Savior assumes responsibility for telling us how to live each day. It is, however, our responsibility to do as He says. If He says move forward, we must comply, trusting Him to orchestrate the circumstances of our lives and provide for our needs.

Second, God is committed to our success. From birth, the Lord has been working the circumstances of our lives together to fulfill the purposes He has for us. He remains steadfast in His desire to teach us how to accomplish everything He created us to do.

Third, God will correct and redirect us when we make a wrong turn. No matter how badly we messed up, God will take the broken pieces of our lives and, with the glue of His unconditional love, He will put us back together. He says without fail, "I will take you, right where you are, and show you how to live out the rest of your life with My help and My strength."

Jesus, thank You for being committed to Your wonderful plan for my life. Teach me to live in a manner that glorifies You. Amen.

GOOD CHANGES

*Weeping may last for the night, but a shout of joy
comes in the morning.*

PSALM 30:5

O ne of the mistakes you and I can make in life is to despair
that our situation will never change—the pains, burdens, and
challenges will continue unceasingly. This can make us feel like God
has forgotten us or doesn't have a good plan for us.

However, changes are inevitable—they are part of our everyday
lives. We may interpret this as negative because change sometimes
means we lose people and things that are dear to us. But what we
must remember is the Lord God is part of our story. In a moment, He
can absolutely transform our situations in ways we never imagined
possible. He did so throughout Scripture for Abraham, Moses, David,
Joseph, and countless others.

On the Damascus Road, Jesus spoke to Paul, and from that
moment on, everything was different (Acts 9:1–19). Paul had been
a critical, unbelieving persecutor of the church. But a few moments
in the presence of the living Lord was all it took to change his entire
outlook, life, purpose, and eternal destination.

God can transform your circumstances as well. So do not despair.
Wait and watch for the Lord to work in what concerns you.

**Jesus, I know You can intervene in my
circumstances and transform them.
I wait in hope for You. Amen.**

What Is Good

*They who seek the LORD shall not be in want of any
good thing.*

PSALM 34:10

O n your heart today may be something that you've been praying about for quite some time, and you are wondering if what
you're asking is okay with God.

There is nothing wrong with having desires—especially if they
are in line with God's will for your life. In fact, at times, you will
have longings that your heavenly Father is eager to meet because they
enhance His plan for you.

Likewise, today's verse promises that you will not lack "any good
thing" as you seek God. But what does that really mean? Understand
that the Lord calls something *good* if it produces a helpful, enriching,
genuinely satisfying, and eternal benefit for you.

Many times, however, we take it on ourselves to define what's
good for us, and we can be tempted to doubt God for disagreeing
with us. But only He can see the full scope of our lives and what is
truly beneficial to us.

Therefore, whether God answers yes or no to your request, take
heart that He is acting in your interest. In fact, He often saves you
from what is just okay so you can enjoy what is truly best for you.

**Jesus, I will trust Your wisdom to give what is
good and withhold what isn't. Thank You for
protecting and providing for me. Amen.**

EQUIPPED FOR GOOD

The God of peace, who brought up from the
dead . . . Jesus our Lord, equip you in every good
thing to do His will, working in us that which
is pleasing in His sight, through Jesus Christ, to
whom be the glory forever and ever. Amen.

HEBREWS 13:20–21

Is there some task God is calling you to accept that appears beyond the scope of your abilities? You tell the Lord, "I can't do this," but you know it is His will for you?

God will call you to undertake difficult assignments because He is teaching you not to depend on your own gifts and abilities. Rather, He wants you to learn to rely solely on Him. He wants to strengthen your faith, grow your character, and transform you into the image of Jesus.

So if you believe God has called you to do something for Him that is too great for you, you're probably right. But understand that He's led you to this on purpose for your good—to build you up and prepare you for even greater things. So do not be afraid no matter how impossible your assignment may appear. Go forward with God, and trust Him to equip you and provide all that you may need.

Jesus, You know I feel inadequate for the task
ahead. But You are more than adequate, and I
thank You that I will see Your power at work. Amen.

SURRENDERED TO HIM

*Offer yourselves as a living sacrifice to God,
dedicated to his service and pleasing to Him.*

ROMANS 12:1 GNT

The Lord doesn't just want things *from* you—He wants *you*. His desire is not merely for you to make sacrifices, but for you to be fully surrendered for His use.

This means it's not just your external acts that need to be put on the altar today. It is not just your tithe, a particular habit, or some treasured object. Your heart—in fact, everything about you—is the sacrifice your heavenly Father requires.

Remember, the Lord says, "I delight in loyalty rather than sacrifice, and in the knowledge of God rather than burnt offerings" (Hosea 6:6). The word for *loyalty* is the Hebrew word *chesed*, and it can be translated as *love, goodness, kindness,* and *faithfulness.* It is love that expresses itself through a godly life and has its root in a relationship with the Father. This is a word closely associated with the character of God, and that's the point—He wants you to reflect His character (Romans 8:29).

God wants His spiritual fruit of love, joy, peace, patience, kindness, goodness, faithfulness, gentleness, and self-control to flow through you (Galatians 5:22–23). To Him, that is always far more important than outward sacrifices.

**Jesus, I am Yours. Teach me to surrender
myself to You fully. Amen.**

FEBRUARY

REFLECTING JESUS

Those whom He foreknew, He also predestined to
become conformed to the image of His Son.

ROMANS 8:29

God's will for your life is for you to look like Jesus—reflecting His character, purposes, and mission. This process of transforming you into Christ's likeness progresses as you present yourself as a holy sacrifice unto the Lord in increasing measure (Romans 12:1–2).

However, the ability to do this hinges on having a good understanding of who God really is. He is the Lord God, the all-powerful and all-knowing Creator of all that exists, the only true and everlasting God, your Savior, who deserves your wholehearted devotion and praise. He not only created you with care but redeemed you in love. And because He gives you both earthly and eternal life, He has a right to work through you as His ambassador, for His glory.

This is not an easy process. But friend, I can testify this is life at its very best. The plans He has for you far outshine what you could ever imagine for yourself. Therefore, trust Him to transform you, be responsive to whatever He asks, and walk in God's will.

Lord, please help me take hold of whatever You want me to understand and however You desire for me to serve You. Help me be like Jesus. I surrender myself to You. Amen.

LEADING IN PRAYER

He teaches the humble His way.
PSALM 25:9

There will be times when you won't know how to pray. Whether it is because of the weariness of your soul or the complexity of your circumstances, you just won't have the words. All you know is to cry out, "Jesus, I need You."

This will feel very vulnerable and unsettling, but do not despair, because this is a good place to be. God is working through you and your situation in a new way that you cannot control or understand; you just have to rely on Him. And He is showing you that He is everything you need—even the One who prays through you.

Romans 8:26–27 promises, "The Spirit also helps our weakness; for we do not know how to pray as we should, but the Spirit Himself intercedes for us with groanings too deep for words; and He who searches the hearts knows what the mind of the Spirit is, because He intercedes for the saints according to the will of God."

Embrace this today by asking the Holy Spirit to give you the words to pray. God is doing a new work in you and leading you into unfamiliar territory. Depend on Him to guide you in His will and deeper into fellowship with Him.

**Jesus, please show me what to pray.
I trust You to lead me. Amen.**

LEADING YOUR WAY

O Upright One, make the path of the righteous level.

ISAIAH 26:7

D o you realize that God rejoices over you and loves you with an everlasting love? You don't have to cower in fear over what will happen tomorrow, because God has gone out before you, clearing the path that you will walk. You can walk victoriously through this life knowing that the Sovereign of the universe is with you, guiding your every step and leading you to places of hope and victory.

Why is it important to understand this truth? Because just as God has a plan for your life, the Enemy would like nothing better than to block you from reaching it. His goal is to prevent you from reaching your full potential, so he will do his best to fill you with fear, doubt, and discouragement. Don't let him succeed.

Instead, once you have checked your course according to God's Word and have taken time to seek Him through prayer, you are ready to step forward. He will unfalteringly lead you in the way that you should go. This doesn't mean that you will never face difficulty. Rather, the hardships you face are tools that God will use to refine you and make your future even brighter. So go forward in hope and confidence.

Jesus, I trust You! Lead me on level ground, Lord; my hope is in You! Amen.

GRANDER VISION

To set free . . . that men may tell of the name of the LORD.

PSALM 102:20–21

A re you ever afraid to approach the Father—reticent to discover what He really thinks about you? Certainly, interacting with holy God can make anyone feel vulnerable. We see this in the story of Isaiah. The moment he came into the Lord's presence, he was overwhelmed by his own sinfulness (Isaiah 6:1–7).

However, as we learn from Isaiah's account, this conviction we feel in His presence is never for our condemnation; rather, it's meant to set us free, make us stronger, and ready us for a grander vision (v. 8).

God holds out His great love for you—working so that you can be transformed by the power of His Holy Spirit, established in your faith, and prepared for the great plans He has for you. So those feelings of conviction you may have are not God condemning or rejecting you—far from it (Romans 8:1)! He always feels love and forgiveness toward you, regardless of what you've done. Rather, your Father is saying your life matters to Him and He sees more in you than you do in yourself. So anytime you fear His presence, remember that! Turn to Him immediately, and experience His love and grander purposes.

Jesus, thank You that Your correction is just that—for refining, not condemning. Send me to do Your will. Amen.

GOD SPEAKS

God . . . spoke long ago to the fathers in the
prophets in many portions and in many ways.

HEBREWS 1:1

One of the greatest areas of frustration for many believers is the ability to hear God. They wonder how someone can truly know he or she has a promise or answer from Him—especially as the days pass without confirmation or circumstances go awry. After all, He is God and we are not. Even in our interactions with other people, whom we can hear with our physical ears, we often mistake their meaning. And the Lord is spiritual—we cannot see, touch, or sit face-to-face with Him. How can we ever be certain that we are hearing Him and not our own hearts?

Yet the Lord is actively speaking to us and wants to communicate with us. He bids us to approach Him and promises to get through to us (Jeremiah 33:3). But understand that *believing* that God speaks to you is both the key and one of the biggest differences between a person experiencing the extraordinary, fruitful Christian life and the one just practicing religion. Therefore, if you wish to know and walk in the Father's will for you, "ask in faith without any doubting" that He speaks in a manner you can hear (James 1:6).

Jesus, I do believe that You speak. Help me to hear You. Confirm Your will to me. Amen.

NOT HEARING DUE TO UNBELIEF

"Do you believe that I am able to do this?"
MATTHEW 9:28

I've often said that listening to God is essential to walking with Him. However, there are times when we think, *I've been listening and can't hear a thing from the Lord.* Why don't we hear Him? Over the next three days we will consider three common reasons for this.

The first is this: *The Lord has spoken, and we can't believe His answer, so we think we heard Him wrong.* This is a faith issue. The inadequacies, adverse circumstances, and lies that are planted deep within us have convinced us that God won't really come through. We cannot see how He will accomplish it, so we disregard what we've heard.

This happened when the people of Israel left Egypt and traveled to the promised land. When they arrived, they discovered residents in the land were numerous and very strong. The Israelites were so frightened by their enemies they gave up without even trying to take hold of their inheritance (Numbers 13).

Don't make their mistake and miss the promise. You don't have to know how God will accomplish what He's promised you—just that He's never gone back on His word. Listen to Him and trust what He tells you.

Jesus, I believe You—I know You can do all You've said. Confirm Your word to me. Amen.

NOT HEARING DUE TO REFUSAL

I delight to do Your will, O my God.

PSALM 40:8

Y ou may believe that you want God's will, but do you really? Or are you set on having Him do things *your* way? Whether you realize it or not, this is often a reason we miss what God is saying to us: *He has spoken, and we don't like His answer, so we refuse to accept it.*

There are times God will call us to do difficult things, such as forgive someone who has hurt us, sacrifice something we care about, or take on a burden that we believe will limit our freedom. We cannot see how this is key to His will being accomplished in our lives, so we ignore what He is saying.

However, realize that just because you disregard God's command doesn't mean it goes away. God does not require you to understand His will, just obey it, even if it seems unreasonable. The Father would not ask it of you unless He saw something important in your life that requires it. And He will not move forward until you do as He says.

So whenever you get stuck hearing from the Father, always go back to the last thing God told you and do it—even if it doesn't make sense to you.

Jesus, I do want Your will. Please forgive me for being resistant. Help me do as You say. Amen.

NOT HEARING DUE TO TIMING

At an acceptable time; O God, in the greatness of
Your lovingkindness, answer me.

PSALM 69:13

A third reason we sometimes don't have an answer from God is because *the Father has not yet spoken.* In other words, the Lord is willing to speak to you, but you may have put artificial time limits on when He should, and He knows that either you don't need the information yet or it will harm you.

This is frustrating for us. At times, we believe we have both a need and a right to know information as soon as we ask for it. But often we must wait because of purposes hidden to us.

Your heavenly Father is always working, but timing is everything for His purposes. In the unseen, He is orchestrating His provision for you in ways, places, and with people you cannot imagine. Therefore, the delays you face in hearing Him are not a denial of His desire to speak to you; rather, they are an integral part of His strategy to arrange all the details and get you positioned for His plan.

Therefore, take heart. God is actively working on your behalf. Don't give up seeking Him. He knows the exact timing for when you need to hear Him.

Jesus, I trust You. I will wait on Your perfect
timing with expectancy and hope. Amen.

ACCEPTING THE CALL

The love of Christ compels us . . . He died for
all, that those who live should live no longer for
themselves, but for Him.

2 CORINTHIANS 5:14–15 NKJV

At times, I've had people come to me and say they think God has called them into the ministry. They ask, "How can I know for sure whether God is calling me to serve Him?" Of course, there are many things I would tell them—such as the need to identify their spiritual gifts and serve Him right where they are while they discern His will.

However, the most telling evidence that you are supposed to serve God in a given area is that deep down inside you have an awesome sense of compulsion. You feel compelled to give your life to Jesus and can't imagine doing anything else but living for Him.

So if you're asking the Father if He's called you to preach the gospel or serve Him in some way, consider whether anything else is even an option for you. Certainly, you may have gifts in other areas. But if you find that your internal drive is set on serving Him and making the name of Jesus known to others, then yes, God is calling you.

Jesus, with all You have given for me, I
cannot conceive of doing anything else
but living for You. I say yes to Your call.
Guide me in serving You. Amen.

YOUR FAITHFUL HIGH PRIEST

It was necessary for him to be made in every respect like us, his brothers and sisters, so that he could be our merciful and faithful High Priest before God.

HEBREWS 2:17 NLT

Do you realize that Jesus sympathizes with you and understands what it is like to be you? Let that incredible thought sink in. It may sometimes feel like no one understands you—your most profound questions, lofty dreams, and deepest hurts. But Jesus does. He has experienced everything that you have—rejection, ridicule, and even hardships within His earthly family. And He has compassion for you.

Even better, Jesus not only knows *why* you do what you do but also *what it will take* to help you walk in His will. As the One who "has been tempted in all things as we are, yet without sin" (Hebrews 4:15), your Savior is well aware of the tactics the Enemy will try to use to get you to step off of God's path and sin. He comprehends why you may cling to unhealthy habits in order to protect yourself. And He has the very best plan—one unmatched by any other on earth—for freeing you and teaching you to walk in His will.

Jesus, thank You for understanding me when no one else does. I praise You for being my wise and loving High Priest before God. Amen.

CHOOSING HIS PRIORITIES

"I know the plans that I have for you," declares the
LORD, "plans for welfare and not for calamity to
give you a future and a hope."

JEREMIAH 29:11

Today, rather than focus on what you desire, turn your attention to what God wants—His plans and priorities for your life. After all, what you long for generally leads to the realization of what you cannot do or be in your own strength. But when you focus instead on what the Lord enables you to accomplish, you know that He assumes full responsibility for your needs as you obey Him.

The reason this change in focus is important is that no possession, relationship, or status we can attain is ever going to heal or fulfill us emotionally or spiritually. Why? Because God made us for Him. Certainly, the Lord wants us to have good relationships with others, but He created us to be in fellowship with Him, first and foremost. When we try to get our needs met apart from Him, our efforts lead only to disappointment, discouragement, disillusionment, and despair.

Friend, only God can fill the emptiness in your heart. Only He is sufficient to meet your deepest needs for acceptance, love, and worthiness. And only as you turn to Him are these needs met, leading you to wholeness. So allow Him to set your path and priorities.

Jesus, I choose Your plans for my
life. Lead me, Lord. Amen.

CHOOSING HIS LOVE

*"God so loved the world, that He gave His only
begotten Son, that whoever believes in Him shall
not perish, but have eternal life."*

JOHN 3:16

The most important decision you will ever make in life is a decision about love—whether or not to receive God's love in salvation. The choices that follow are like it—whether you will love God and, by extension, love others.

However, what you should know about God's love is that it is absolute—divine, eternal, and sacrificial. His care for you does not waver or change over time. He is not influenced by circumstances or situations. His love for you cannot be diminished.

Likewise, whatever we might say about God Himself, we must say about His love—it is wise, powerful, and ever present with us. His love penetrates our deepest wounds and causes us to heal, change, and grow. And if we allow His love access, it will overtake us completely—heart, soul, mind, and strength.

Are you willing? Have you accepted God's love? Have you allowed it to reach into every area of your life and transform you? If not, you should. Because absolutely nothing fills the emptiness like or is better than His awesome love.

**Jesus, I receive Your love and worship
You as my Savior, my Lord, and my
God! You have all of me. Amen.**

MISPLACED EFFORT

"I have loved you with an everlasting love;
therefore I have drawn you with lovingkindness."

JEREMIAH 31:3

Throughout your life, have you ever felt as if you've needed to earn the right to be loved and accepted by others? In this broken world, it's a natural conclusion. However, this type of thinking is actually destructive when you relate to God. This is because your focus is on striving to earn the approval He has already given you instead of simply knowing the One who loves you. The end result of that approach to life is exhausting, self-defeating effort and unyielding frustration. No matter how much you sacrifice, it never fills the emptiness.

Why don't your efforts work? Because Jesus has already declared, "It is finished" (John 19:30). The acceptance you desire has already been provided—and acting as if you need to earn it actually shows disrespect to the gift your Savior has given.

Therefore, friend, stop striving. Look to Jesus, who loves you freely, and seek to know Him. Acknowledge that you don't have to do a thing except receive what He is pouring out to you and praise Him for His great gift. You need never have a love-starved heart again.

Jesus, forgive me for striving. Please show me Your face, help me know Your heart, and teach me to receive Your love. Lord Jesus, I worship You. Amen.

LOVED

We have come to know and have believed the love which God has for us. God is love, and the one who abides in love abides in God, and God abides in him.

1 JOHN 4:16

D o you believe in the love God has for you? Do you trust His love—that it isn't like human love, which is unreliable and may wound you, but is unconditional, and He always works for your good?

The reason Jesus left His heavenly home, took the form of a bond servant, lived an impoverished and sacrificial earthly life, and then died one of the most excruciating deaths in history was to have a relationship with you. That's how much He cares about you, desires to reveal Himself to you, and longs to live with you forever.

You may doubt that today because you know your faults, failings, and every reason why others shouldn't care for you. The pain of rejection can go so deep that accepting God's unconditional love may be a challenge. But that doesn't change the fact that Jesus loves you deeply, eternally, and without fail. You absolutely cannot stop Him from loving you. So stop telling yourself He doesn't. Embrace His love, and love Him in return.

Jesus, sometimes I just don't feel like I deserve You. But You have made me acceptable. Help me know the fullness of Your love. Amen.

LOVE HIM

"You shall love the Lord your God with all your heart,
and with all your soul, and with all your mind."

MATTHEW 22:37

The last few days we've discussed accepting God's love. However, why should we love Him in return? We know it is a command, but He is God—He doesn't need anything we have to offer (Acts 17:25). Why is it important that we express love to Him?

The reason isn't so much for God's good as it is for ours. As we adore Him, we understand how deeply loved we really are and discover who He is making us into. We find that because He created us, He knows our limitations, drives, and weaknesses—and not only cares for us but actively invites us to join Him, giving us meaning, satisfaction, purpose, and hope. We also come to realize that everything He does is for our good.

Finally, as we express affection for Him, He teaches us how to love as He does—how to give and receive love in the most fulfilling, divine manner possible.

So yes, love God. Even if you're not sure how—just open your heart to Him and simply express how wonderful He is and how grateful you are for Him.

Jesus, I love You—You are so worthy of my adoration! Teach me to love You more each and every day. Amen.

CLOSE UNION

*"I am the way, and the truth, and the life; no one
comes to the Father but through Me."*

JOHN 14:6

We may sometimes think of today's verse in terms of salvation, but it is true of the Christian life as well. Jesus wants to be *your* way, *your* truth, and *your* life. In Him and through Him are the Father's will for you.

So we should never mistakenly think, *God's not really interested in teaching me, leading me, or revealing His will.* Yes, He certainly is—more than you can ever possibly imagine (Romans 8:32). Not only is the Lord attentive to the great and impactful circumstances of your life, but He is also observant of details so small they escape your notice. He cares about the burdens, challenges, and conflicts that concern you.

What God wants most from you is a personal relationship where you walk with Him in such close union that you're consistently aware of His presence. Yes, He wants that. In fact, that's why He has given His own Spirit to live within you and direct you.

Jesus, thank You for being my way, my truth, and
my life. Help me fix my eyes on You and trust You
in every circumstance so I can be a reflection
of Your love and grace to others. Amen.

TRUST YOUR LORD

*The LORD will continually guide you, and satisfy
your desire in scorched places, and give strength to
your bones.*

ISAIAH 58:11

When you place your trust in Jesus, you accept Him as your Lord. This new relationship and identity will increasingly necessitate that you abandon yourself to Him and willingly let go of the things that comprise your worldly security and fulfillment.

Your heart may long for financial, social, relational, or sexual fulfillment, or you may wish to dull your pain with food or other substances. But material possessions and earthly solutions cannot fill the deep, unsettling voids that you feel or heal the wounds you have. This is why Jesus told His disciples to "seek first His kingdom and His righteousness; and all these things will be added to you" (Matthew 6:33). Everything you truly need is already yours in Christ.

Giving yourself to Jesus does not mean you lose; rather, it means you are firmly on track for the best life possible. Will it be perfect and trouble-free? No. But your Savior always gives you much more than earthly solutions could ever provide—and what He gives you, no one will ever be able to take away.

Jesus, I want to trust You as my Lord. Thank You
for teaching me how to give every area over to
You and for fulfilling my deepest needs. Amen.

BROKEN FOR FREEDOM

*By His knowledge the deeps were broken up and
the skies drip with dew.*

PROVERBS 3:20

Sometimes when we experience trials, we may erroneously believe that God has rejected us or is punishing us in some way. However, one of the ways the Lord helps us become His disciples is through the process of brokenness.

Brokenness is God's method of dealing with our dependence on anything other than Him for fulfillment and security. No matter how committed we may be to God, we'll always fight the inclination to do things our way rather than His. So Jesus endeavors to bring every area of our lives into submission to His will by permitting times of difficulty that liberate us from false sources of identity—showing us how faulty they really are. Likewise, He works through our trials to transform us into His likeness and give us purpose, equipping us for all He has planned.

Jesus continually breaks down the obstacles within us until we're completely surrendered to Him and trust Him fully. That is why I encourage you to be in God's Word daily. Because through Scripture, Christ speaks to your heart, strengthens you, and encourages you as He sets you free from what keeps you bound. He teaches you the truth that sets you free (John 8:32).

**Jesus, being broken is painful, but I
know You're setting me free. Amen.**

WATCH FOR LOVE

"The Father Himself loves you, because you have loved Me."

JOHN 16:27

Do you realize that God desires to communicate His great love to you on a daily basis? He wants you to know how much you mean to Him and how He delights in having a relationship with you. His love may come to you in the form of an unexpected blessing or provision, a call from a loved one, the kindness of a stranger, a favorite Scripture or song, or a hug from a child. Whatever it may be, each day God has a new way of showing how profoundly He cares for you.

Often, however, we might miss out on the Lord's overtures because we're not looking for them or are avoiding fellowship with Him. We complain about what we lack and become so focused on our problems and burdens that we forget to listen to Him. But when we do, we miss all the reasons He's given us to rejoice—and they are many.

Don't do that; instead, watch for His love. The Lover of your soul never runs out of unique and profoundly touching ways to tell you that He cares about you. So be on the lookout and be grateful. Because there are so many wonderful things He wants to say to you.

Jesus, thank You for loving me! I rejoice in all the ways You care for me. Amen.

FITTING IN

*You watched me as I was being formed in . . . the
dark of the womb.*

PSALM 139:15 NLT

D o you ever try to blend in with others with the hope that
they will accept you? You lay down your unique identity and
strengths in order to belong. It's not only exhausting, but deep within
you, you feel lost and isolated.

Friend, God created you exactly as He wanted you—with your
personality, gifts, and temperament. When you find yourself hiding
your real self in order to fit in with others, you need to stop and ask,
*Why am I so afraid to be myself? What value is this person or group
of people providing that merits denying who I am? What do I think I
will gain by this? And if they truly cannot accept the real me, are they
worth being with?*

Most likely, no matter what advantages that person or group
brings to your life, it won't be worth the cost to your own heart.
Denying who God made you to be means cutting off the flow of
His power and purpose in your life. That damages you, stifles your
creativity, and limits your influence. You end up cutting yourself off
from the very intimacy you desire so intensely. Don't do it.

**Jesus, the way You created me to be is good. Help
me embrace all You formed me to be. Amen.**

HEARING THE WORD

I will hear what God the LORD will say; for He will speak peace.

PSALM 85:8

Whenever you read Scripture, consider what the Holy Spirit may be communicating to you through it. Don't just ask, *How do I solve my problem?* Instead, keep the following prayerful questions in mind.

Lord, what is the context of what I am reading? Help me understand the foundation and heart of what has been written. Are You revealing something about Your character, relationship with me, or provision? Are there attitudes, beliefs, and habits that are undermining my well-being or relationship with You?

Lord, what do You want to communicate to me today? Make those verses and principles stick out, and help me to focus on what You desire me to see. Are there any actions or steps that You are revealing to me through Your Word? How do You desire me to apply what I am reading? What do You desire to accomplish in and through me?

Your heavenly Father will bring things to mind He wants to address in your life. No matter what it is, do not push it aside. Instead, continue pursuing how Jesus desires for you to deal with it. Because that, at its most profound core, is doing God's will.

Jesus, I want to hear what You have to say. Help me understand what You are communicating through Your Word. Amen.

BELIEVE HIM

God has not given us a spirit of fear, but of power
and of love and of a sound mind.

2 TIMOTHY 1:7 NKJV

B elieving *in* God and *believing God* are two different things—
and it is important that you understand the distinction in order
to live the victorious Christian life. Believing *in* God is saying, "I
know God exists." But *believing God* is trusting what He has said
about Himself, about us, and about the relationship He desires to
have with us. This goes beyond our basic salvation to having utmost
faith in Jesus for *every* detail of our lives.

For example, today's verse means having full confidence that
fear does not come from the Lord—confidence, a sense of belonging,
and clarity do. So you can be sure that God is going to give you the
strength, the love, the wisdom to face whatever may come.

Do you believe God today? Do you trust there's no real reason
to fear? Yes, your circumstances may seem overwhelming, but He
walks with you through all of it (Isaiah 41:10). So you can take heart
and have faith that with His help, nothing will be impossible to you
(Matthew 17:20).

God, I know that a great deal of my struggle
is that I don't actually believe You. Help
my unbelief, my Lord and my Savior. You
are worthy of all my trust. Amen.

RECEIVE HIS WISDOM

If any of you lacks wisdom, let him ask of God, who gives to all generously and without reproach, and it will be given to him.

JAMES 1:5

D o you ever find yourself without any sense of direction in your decisions? Do find yourself thinking, *I just don't know what to do*? If so, understand that this is the Lord calling you to listen to Him.

God wants to help you—to be generous in directing you and setting the course of your life. Therefore, if you don't know what to do, the best solution is always to seek the Lord. That doesn't mean you sit and do nothing; rather, you are vigilant for how God is responding to you—for what He is revealing to you and doing in your situation.

Perhaps you'd say, "I've already sought God. He's not answering." But here is the key: you "must ask in faith without any doubting" (James 1:6). Maybe the real issue is that you don't have faith that He will respond to you or that the answer He's given is right.

Friend, God is faithful. Stop doubting. Do the last thing God told you to do, and keep seeking Him. He will show you what to do—and generously at that.

Jesus, I ask for Your wisdom and will trust what
You say. I know You will lead me right. Amen.

INTENTIONAL STORMS

Who then is this, that even the wind and the sea
obey Him?

MARK 4:41

When life's circumstances are chaotic and confusing, we can feel very insecure and frightened. We may ask, "What's going on? Has God lost control?" Perhaps we wonder if the Father has forgotten us or if we've done something wrong.

This was the case for the disciples in Mark 4. Jesus told them to set sail for the other side of the Sea of Galilee. To their surprise, however, a fierce storm arose that tossed their boat violently. Their response? "Teacher, do You not care that we are perishing?" (Mark 4:38).

If we're honest, we would admit that at times we've asked God the same thing. The chaos produces fear in us because no one likes feeling out of control. When those times come, however, we must remind ourselves of one unshakable fact: God has a plan, and He is always in control.

Jesus sent the disciples into the tempest, hushed it for them, and got them to their destination safely. He will help you as well. And as He did with them, Jesus may have allowed this storm to show you just how good, faithful, and powerful He really is.

Jesus, You are God and You are always
in control. I entrust myself and this
storm to Your loving hands. Amen.

GOD WILL SHOW YOU

*Teach me to do Your will, for You are my God; let
Your good Spirit lead me on level ground.*

PSALM 143:10

God will show you His plan when you seek Him. Decide right
now to believe this simple fact today: it is God's character to
reveal Himself and His will to you.

Think about it; if the Lord wants you to walk along a particular
path, then He must assume responsibility for leading you to it and
training you for it. He understands that from your limited, earthly
perspective, the road can become confusing and that the choices you
face are difficult and complex. But as a good and faithful Father, who
perfectly sees what's ahead and what you require to face it, He is more
than willing to help you—and He says so many times in His Word.

In Psalm 32:8, He assures you, "I will instruct you and teach
you in the way which you should go; I will counsel you with My
eye upon you." So as you try to figure out what is best for you—
anticipating obstacles and opportunities you cannot see in a future
that is unsure—don't rely solely on your limited wisdom. Depend
on your loving Father to guide you. He will certainly show you what
to do.

**Jesus, I need Your guidance. I trust You
to reveal the path to me. Amen.**

HEARING GOD THROUGH SCRIPTURE

Your word is a lamp to my feet and a light to my path.

PSALM 119:105

G od wants you to know and do His will; you can be assured that He will make it known to you in His time. However, the main way He reveals His purposes for you is always through Scripture, which is His comprehensive instruction book for living. Meditating on God's Word is absolutely essential for receiving His counsel and illuminating the way you should go.

This is why one of the best things you can do as you read Scripture is to ask, "Lord God, what are You saying to me? How do You want me to apply this to my life? What is it I'm supposed to learn, Father?"

This is because when you present an open, teachable heart, the Holy Spirit will work through Scripture supernaturally to lead you, train you, correct your erroneous thinking, convict you of sin, influence your decisions, or stop you when you are drifting from God's will (2 Timothy 3:16–17). He helps you see the reality of your circumstances and how to handle them in a manner that honors Him.

Jesus, as I open Your Word today, help me hear what You are saying and apply what You desire me to learn. Thank You for speaking to me through Your Word. Amen.

WHY THE WORD?

All Scripture is inspired by God and profitable.
2 TIMOTHY 3:16

As we saw yesterday, the Bible speaks to what the Father desires for us to do and helps us to accomplish it. It is His instruction book for living. But what makes it so powerful is that it is *inspired*— literally, Scripture is *God breathed*. This is how the Lord wrote the sixty-six books through His approximately forty servants throughout the ages—He divinely breathed these books out, inspiring the authors through His Spirit to write them.

The Bible did not originate with people; it came from God's mind, and its principles carry His power. This is why it is still so powerful, even though the biblical authors lived in such a different culture and time than you do. Scripture originates from a Source outside of them and, indeed, outside of time itself (Isaiah 46:10).

This is what makes the Bible like no other book in the world; it flowed from the heart of God rather than man. Thankfully, because this is true, the Holy Spirit can speak directly to your circumstances through it. This is what makes Scripture so *profitable*—it is helpful and advantageous to you because through it, God always steers you to His highest and best for you.

Lord Jesus, certainly Scripture is powerful! Transform and guide me to Your highest and best through Your marvelous Word. Amen.

THE WORK OF THE WORD

For teaching, for reproof, for correction, for training in righteousness.

2 TIMOTHY 3:16

God's Word is both inspired and profitable for all the ways the Lord wants to work in your life. He works through Scripture to:

Teach. Even if there is no one else around to instruct you, God reveals Himself to you through Scripture—His ways, how to follow Him, and how to honor Him in your choices. He also teaches you about yourself, others, how to have healthy relationships, and how to handle every situation in life.

Reprove. Through the Bible, God exposes the attitudes, beliefs, and habits that are undermining your well-being and relationship with Christ so you can change course (John 8:32).

Correct. Through the Word, God also helps you get on the right path, restores you, improves your life and character, and makes you complete as His child.

Train in righteousness. Finally, through Scripture, God trains you by renewing your mind, deepening your faith, healing your most profound strongholds, and transforming you into the likeness of Christ. The work of God through the Word is powerful because, ultimately, He is preparing you for all He will do through you.

Jesus, Your Word is a gift! Thank You for working through it to teach, reprove, correct, and train me. Amen.

THE EFFECT OF THE WORD

So that the person who serves God may be fully qualified.

2 TIMOTHY 3:17 GNT

O ften, I hear people say that they are scared to do God's will because they do not feel suited for what the Lord is calling them to do. They are fearful of being proven weak, unworthy, or incapable. This is yet another reason Scripture is so important to knowing and doing God's will—through it, the Lord makes you fully qualified, complete, and perfectly fit for the tasks ahead.

What the Father does through His Word is to remind you of your new identity in Christ—that you are a beloved child of the almighty God (Romans 8:16), formed as His masterpiece (Psalm 139:13–14), created for good works (Ephesians 2:10), empowered by the Holy Spirit (Ephesians 1:13–14; Philippians 4:13), endowed with every spiritual blessing (Ephesians 1:3), favored with continuous access to the throne of grace (Hebrews 4:16), and called to be a partaker of His heavenly calling (Hebrews 3:1).

Scripture reminds you of who you really are and where your success truly comes from. As Paul writes, "Our adequacy is from God, who also made us adequate as servants" (2 Corinthians 3:5–6). And because of that, you can certainly fulfill the awesome purposes the Lord has created you to walk in.

Lord, thank You for Your Word and for empowering me to serve You through it. Amen.

MARCH

THE EQUIPPING OF THE WORD

*God uses it to . . . equip his people to do every good
work.*

2 TIMOTHY 3:17 NLT

During the last few days, we've seen that the Word is indeed central to knowing and doing God's will. You cannot truly live the triumphant Christian life apart from it. The Lord works through it to equip you—thoroughly furnishing you with everything you need to complete every good work.

At times, the most difficult thing for any of us to do is finish well. We come to points in our lives when we feel we cannot go on or achieve what we have been given to accomplish. The burdens become too heavy, the decisions too complex, the challenges too disheartening, and the road too bewildering. We wonder if we have what it takes to keep going or if we should just give up.

But what the Word does in such times is help us complete the journey. It trains us to keep "fixing our eyes on Jesus, the author and perfecter of faith" (Hebrews 12:2). Through Scripture, God gives us the spiritual food that fuels us, providing the wisdom and energy we need to keep going each day and confront the obstacles that await us on the path.

Jesus, thank You for working through Your
Word to equip me for every good work,
including the length of the journey. I will endure
knowing You are always with me. Amen.

HEARING GOD THROUGH CIRCUMSTANCES

My circumstances have turned out for the greater progress of the gospel.

PHILIPPIANS 1:12

At times, God will speak to you through the circumstances of your life. Your experiences are not random; rather, they are allowed by the Lord for His good purposes. He is continually working in your life to direct you in His will and accomplish it through you.

This is especially important to understand when certain relationships end or your situation turns negative. The Lord operates through the closed doors just as much as through the open ones. We may often become discouraged or confused by the choices and blessings God seems to take away from us. However, if we focus only on what we *cannot* do, we often don't realize the opportunities and blessings He has provided for us.

So do not despair; rather, actively look for how God may be guiding you through your circumstances. Has the Father blocked the road before you in either a temporary or permanent manner? Is it because He has a different path for you? Allow the Father to direct you and speak life into all your circumstances. The right door will be open to you.

Jesus, empower me by Your Holy Spirit
to understand what You are doing
in my circumstances. Amen.

COUNSEL FROM OTHERS

The person of understanding will acquire wise counsel.

PROVERBS 1:5 AMP

There are moments in life when we crave the counsel of a godly friend or loved one. We want someone to walk with us through the difficulties of life and to remind us of all God has provided. There is absolutely nothing wrong with this. In fact, no Christian has ever been called to "go it alone" in his or her walk of faith. We were called to live in community.

With that said, however, you need to be careful about whom you listen to. Most people will have an opinion about what course you should take, but some will point you in the wrong direction. The last person you want to get counsel from is somebody who is actively disobeying the Father.

Rather, it is crucial for you to look to others who are obviously submitted to the Father and obeying Him. Seek out Christians who clearly understand how to listen to God, have strong relationships with Him, and are living in His will. You want someone with whom it is very evident that he or she is walking in the center of His path for them—so they can help you do the same.

Jesus, I want to be wise about who I listen to. Lead me to others who walk with You and will offer wise counsel. Amen.

THE CONTENT OF COUNSEL

Listen to counsel and accept discipline, that you may be wise the rest of your days.

PROVERBS 19:20

When you seek to receive counsel from others, always be careful. As we saw yesterday, you should seek advice only from Christians who clearly understand how to listen to God and who have strong relationships with Him.

Of course, no matter how godly your friends are, never ask them to make your decisions for you. You are seeking the Father's will, not just the next step you should take. The process of discovering His plan for your life is about becoming dependent on *Him*, not on what others think. So instead, ask, "Do you have any insight into what God may be saying to me based on Scripture or how you've seen Him work in your life? What does God's Word say about the decision I am making?"

A godly counselor will be motivated to guide you to the truth—even when it is uncomfortable or it hurts—because he or she will be committed to helping you obediently follow Jesus. So look for people whose desire is for you to have a strong relationship with Christ. Those are the friends who will help you experience life at its best.

Jesus, help me to be wise about who I listen to and the guidance I receive from them. Help me to be more dependent on You, not others. Amen.

THE COURSE OF THE CONSCIENCE

I always try to maintain a clear conscience before
God and all people.

ACTS 24:16 NLT

S hould you listen to your conscience? Each of us has a conscience, whether we believe in Jesus or not—so it's not necessarily a godly compass for us. Nevertheless, under the right circumstances, the conscience can be helpful as we are seeking the Father's plan.

The conscience's main purpose is to protect you—stopping you from proceeding on a sinful course or prompting you to do what is right. The unsettling alarm that sounds within you when you're contemplating a disastrous decision can safeguard you from foolish choices. Likewise, there are times when the conscience reminds you of the right thing to do. So the conscience gives you internal feedback about a course of action, but it's not necessarily meant to direct you.

Rather, our greatest source of guidance is always found in the unchanging Word of God and the guidance of the Holy Spirit. Scripture and the indwelling Spirit work together with the conscience to steer us in the right direction. This is why it's always so important to stay connected to Jesus through the Bible and in prayer. Only a Christ-centered, submitted conscience will be truly helpful.

Jesus, help me maintain a clear conscience
that is godly and submitted to You. Amen.

UNDERSTANDING COMMON SENSE

Live sensibly, righteously and godly in the present age.
TITUS 2:12

C an you really count on your common sense to know God's will? You may be surprised to discover how many decisions for your life fall within what the Father has already revealed to you. For example, it's wise to eat a healthy diet, get proper rest, and exercise—these are all the Lord's will for you.

But the way God can work through common sense goes much deeper than this. For instance, people may drink to escape their problems—only to find they feel worse the next day, and their troubles are still there. Or perhaps people will try to buy their way to a sense of worth, freedom, and acceptability. But they discover that what they've purchased actually makes them feel more emptiness.

So common sense aids you by leading you to realize that you are trying to achieve your goals in the wrong way or with the wrong people. In this manner, common sense confirms that something is not working in a godly, productive manner for you, and you should seek the Lord through His Word and in prayer to learn how to turn your situation around.

Jesus, reveal what is not working in my
life so that I may seek You and learn
the right way from You. Amen.

OBEYING HIS PROMPTINGS

Walk by the Spirit, and you will not carry out the desire of the flesh.

GALATIANS 5:16

When you sense the Lord is moving you in a particular direction or to do something specific, don't try to reason it out. Of course, it is always important to test where your impulses are coming from (1 John 4:1). As today's verse instructs, if your desires are sinful, you know they aren't coming from the Holy Spirit—and vice versa.

But you can always be confident walking by the Spirit—living each moment in dependence on the Holy Spirit, sensitive to His voice, and obedient to His promptings. As you go throughout each day, listen for the Father to speak to you; and when He does, obey Him. For example, you may feel convicted to flee from something that is tempting you to sin, you may be compelled to contact and encourage someone who is hurting, or you may feel led to do something unusually kind for a stranger. Do it.

These are all ways God compels you to act in His will. Just do as He tells you to do—even when you don't understand why. Your Father knows how to direct you in the best way possible, so trust Him and go forward.

Holy Spirit, direct all my steps today. Open my ears to Your prompting and direction, that I may glorify the Savior. Amen.

SEEKING THE PEACE

Let the peace of Christ rule in your hearts.
COLOSSIANS 3:15

Perhaps you've heard people say, "I don't have peace" when speaking about a particular decision. They are referring to the fact that when you are either outside God's will or working against Him, you'll feel spiritual friction. But when you're in the center of God's will, you will feel harmony with Him.

Most of us can point to areas of our lives that cause us stress, unhappiness, and turmoil. But regardless of the situation, we are promised that we can find tranquility in Christ (Philippians 4:6–7). However, the supernatural peace Jesus offers us rests on our agreement with Him. We must be willing to do as He says in His Word.

When you submit your daily choices to Jesus, you are not only in harmony with His Holy Spirit but are safeguarded within His protection, enlightened with His wisdom, and empowered by His strength. The peace you experience can be evidence that you are, indeed, walking in His will. So invite His peace to characterize your life by allowing Him to rule your heart. Jesus will be your assurance and security regardless of the circumstances you face.

Jesus, You know the areas of friction
in my life. Rule my heart and teach me
how to have Your peace. Amen.

TIE IT TOGETHER

*This I pray, that your love may abound still more
and more in real knowledge and all discernment.*

PHILIPPIANS 1:9

How do you make sense of all you're experiencing and understand how God desires for you to proceed? During the last few days, we've looked at several ways Jesus communicates His will to you. As you've seen, He speaks through Scripture, the circumstances of your life, the counsel of godly Christians, your conscience, common sense, promptings, and prayer. He even gives you a feeling of peace and contentment when you walk in His will. And He shows you how it all ties together as you spend time with Him in prayer.

The Lord is able to speak to you clearly and empower you to do whatever He calls you to do. In fact, He orchestrates everything you need—moving people, resources, situations, and even changing you—all to carry out His wonderful will for your life.

However, you do have to *listen* to Him. In your times of prayer, it is necessary to stop talking long enough to hear what Jesus has to say about what He's shown you. Then, once you do, you must actively apply what He's said to your life. Because God *will* reveal His plan when you set your heart to hear and obey what He is saying to you.

**Jesus, I am listening. Show me Your
will and lead me. Amen.**

THE SPIRIT OF TRUTH

"The Spirit of truth . . . will guide you into all the truth."

JOHN 16:13

D o you have anyone in your life who tells you without qualification or disclaimer, "I believe in you—your talents, future, and the plans God has for you"? This is the message the Holy Spirit speaks to you. He indwells you and leads you in the truth so that all the potential and promise the Lord built in you can come to full fruition.

The Holy Spirit is completely committed to building you up to be all God created you to be. The biblical term for this is *edification*—He strengthens, matures, and readies you for service. He continually affirms, "Your life matters to Me." Likewise, He leads you in all truth because He wants to empower you to succeed. He will often reveal to you why certain things are happening, how they fit into the broader purposes of God, and the understanding you need so you can be free.

Therefore, when you're faced with puzzling situations or difficult problems, ask the Lord what to do and what He is teaching you through it. Then give the Holy Spirit room to instruct you. He will not only guide you wisely but will encourage you about the great things He desires to accomplish through you.

Spirit of Truth, guide me. Lead me to become all You created me to be. Amen.

A HEAVENLY FOCUS

The world is passing away, and also its lusts; but the one who does the will of God lives forever.

1 JOHN 2:17

Do you ever think of what heaven will be like? Do you ever consider that the time you spend here is really only a breath in comparison to the eternity you'll spend with God in your new home? This is why I often say that the anticipation of Christ's return should keep us living productively. Realizing that how we behave here on earth sets the stage for how we will live and be rewarded in heaven forever should have a purifying effect on our lives.

As believers, we are citizens of God's heavenly kingdom and therefore are accountable to be ambassadors for the King of kings. When we keep this truth in focus, we will be more committed to act as He intends us to—abiding by the higher standards of our home country so others will want to go there. The hope of heaven should compel us to yield to God's transformational work and serve Him boldly and sacrificially, understanding "this world is passing away" (1 Corinthians 7:31).

So today, consider carefully: are you serving temporary goals here or the Lord's eternal, heavenly purposes? Choose the path that will last. Begin now to serve the eternal kingdom of God.

Jesus, how would You have me serve You? Show me, Lord, and I will obey. Amen.

HUMBLE YOURSELF

A disciple is not above his teacher, nor a slave above his master.

MATTHEW 10:24

Today, remember that you belong to Jesus. When you accepted Him as your Savior, you in essence said, "I want to have a relationship with You, Lord God." And in that, you acknowledged His authority over you.

I say this not to frighten but to comfort you. Jesus wants to lead you and teach you how to do things His way—a better manner than you could ever imagine on your own. However, it is very important that you acknowledge that He is God and you are not. You can stop trying to be strong and sufficient before Him. As James 4:10 says, "Humble yourselves in the presence of the Lord, and He will exalt you." He will teach you how to be like Him—bearing His image, living in His strength, and walking in His wisdom.

So today, let down your guard before God. He is the Lord, the Sufficient One, your Redeemer. It's not only okay to admit that you don't have it all together; it is crucial if you want to take hold of all He has for you.

Lord Jesus, You are God and I am not. I come before You humbly, acknowledging that I am fearful and wounded and I need Your wisdom and strength. Help me, Lord. Amen.

SERVING AND RULING

We are ambassadors for Christ, as though God
were making an appeal through us; we beg you on
behalf of Christ, be reconciled to God.

2 CORINTHIANS 5:20

S ometimes as you're serving God and pursuing His will, you'll find that one of the greatest challenges you'll face is with other people. Always remember that you're called to *serve people* and have *dominion over evil*. So many people get this backward—they're ruling over people and serving the Enemy by imposing their own wills instead of doing God's. Don't fall for that trap.

Your role as a disciple of Christ is to model the way that Jesus lived—a life of love, ministry, forgiveness, sacrifice, humble submission to the Father, and total victory over the power of sin. This is why Jesus admonished you to emulate Him, saying, "Greater love has no one than this, that one lay down his life for his friends" (John 15:13). Yes, you are to have authority over the Enemy—armed with the name of Jesus to withstand the Devil's assaults and resist his temptations. But when it comes to people, you are an ambassador of *reconciliation*—not *condemnation*—calling people to be saved from sin with an attitude of humility. Others will respond to Jesus because of His love flowing through you (John 13:35).

Jesus, allow Your love to flow through me so
others can know You and be saved. Amen.

FREE FROM REGRET

"If the Son makes you free, you will be free indeed."
JOHN 8:36

I wish I hadn't done that. I wish I hadn't made that decision or agreed to that."

Do you ever look back over your life and feel regret? If so, it's likely you've experienced some type of emotional wound—one that may be marked by ongoing guilt or shame. It is understandable. Living in a fallen world, we are bound to make mistakes that leave a painful mark. In fact, the phrase "I wish I had never" is a warning indicator that there is something deep within you that needs to be made right with God.

As a believer, you know you're under the blood of Jesus and forgiven of your sins. And if you've confessed and repented of your transgressions, you know He is faithful to forgive you and cleanse you of all unrighteousness (1 John 1:9). But remember that sin at its core is trying to get your needs met your way rather than God's. There's something within you that still has trouble trusting Him.

Therefore, if you're struggling with regrets today, go to God and ask Him to reveal the true source of your pain. He will not only heal you but teach you to get your needs met His way and with His freedom.

Jesus, only You know how to set me free from these regrets. Lead me to liberty, my Savior. Amen.

TRUE HEALING

O LORD, be gracious to me; heal my soul.
PSALM 41:4

When Jesus healed a paralyzed man who had been lowered through a roof by his friends, the first thing He said to him was, "Son, your sins are forgiven" (Mark 2:5). Jesus—the Lord God, who knew the man better than he knew himself—identified his main issue to be spiritual. Of course, this left everyone around Christ surprised. In their eyes, the paralytic's primary problem was physical.

This goes to show that sometimes we'll seek out Christ for external issues—our health, finances, relationships, or what have you. However, what He addresses as we spend time with Him in prayer is something deep within our souls. This may be astounding to us because we think we know what's causing us pain. But Jesus sees the true root of our woundedness.

Of course, Jesus answers the exterior troubles we bring to Him as well. He empowered the paralytic to pick up his pallet and walk. He does the same for you. However, what's important to understand is your Savior wants you to be healed *fully*—not just on the surface, but inside out. So never ignore what Jesus tells you or pinpoints as the true issue. Trust Him as your Great Physician, and accept His order of addressing your needs.

Jesus, I trust You to address the true root of my pain and heal me. Amen.

LET IT GO

Submit therefore to God. Resist the devil and he
will flee from you.

JAMES 4:7

F riend, is there any issue or behavior that God has pointed out as not belonging in your life but that you refuse to relinquish? Do not continue to struggle with Him—let it go. Whenever you draw a line between you and the Lord over any issue, you are actively choosing disappointment. By refusing to put something on the altar, however large or small it may be, you unwittingly limit your relationship with Jesus and shut out the very Source of your life—missing wonderful things He has planned for you. And because the Father cares for you too much to leave you in bondage to it, He will discipline you.

Nothing pleases God more than your full surrender, and He rewards it abundantly. This is because, more than anything else, your Father wants an intimate relationship with you that leads you to the abundant life. Therefore, search your heart and root out anything that stands between you and Jesus. If there's anything that means more to you than Christ does, it will hinder you from experiencing the fullness of His love. Don't hurt yourself by holding on to it. Let go and invite Jesus to be everything to you.

Jesus, I don't want anything to come between us.
Root it out, that I may be completely Yours. Amen.

INTIMATE LONGING

*Love the LORD your God with all your heart and
with all your soul.*

DEUTERONOMY 6:5

There is absolutely no substitute for personal intimacy with God. Nothing compares with it—it is the key to fulfillment, purpose, and joy. Most people are longing for an exciting and meaningful life, and they're looking in all the wrong places for it: money, prestige, and relationships. Of course, none of those sufficiently fills the void in our hearts. Why? Because that emptiness within us was only ever meant to be indwelt by God's presence.

Therefore, the only thing that can ever satisfy the indescribable longing within you will be an intimate relationship with your Savior. It's important to have goals and relationships, but your primary and most important pursuit should always be to know Christ. Only He can give you the life you long for.

When I think about everything I've experienced in life, my relationship with God has always been absolutely paramount. He has consistently been there to comfort me and bring me through life's trials, however hard they've been. And the gift of His indwelling Spirit has led me in ways above and beyond all I could have asked for or imagined. I know that will be true for you as well. So seek Him and find all you're looking for.

**Jesus, this is what I want—an intimate relationship
with You. Draw me near, Lord. Amen.**

THE CREATOR'S DESIGN

When I consider Your heavens, the work of Your
fingers . . . what is man that You take thought of
him?

PSALM 8:3–4

Have you ever stared in wonder through a telescope—marveling at the universe in which we are so carefully positioned? God's creation is amazing in its vastness and complexity.

It is right to stand in awe of the beauty and intricacy of God's design—of the myriad of interconnecting relationships and systems built into creation. The Lord's handiwork is not haphazard. It operates according to a very detailed and thoughtful order. It is obvious that God has a plan in it all.

And God has a plan for you. Your Creator took just as much care when He formed you and as He draws you into relationship with Him. His design not only encompasses your physical qualities; it also comprises the spiritual realm—how you grow in your faith and character.

So whatever you are facing today, you can have hope. Look at the intricacy, beauty, and wonder of creation. The One who formed it all is also writing your story. And you can have confidence that what He is doing in you is just as marvelously far beyond your imagination.

Jesus, thank You for the intricacy,
beauty, and wonder of Your plan for
my life. I am in awe of You. Amen.

WHAT HE'S GIVEN

"From any tree of the garden you may eat freely;
but from the tree of the knowledge of good and evil
you shall not eat, for in the day that you eat from it
you will surely die."

GENESIS 2:16–17

Whenever we read today's verse, we may be tempted to jump ahead and think of the outcome—Adam and Eve ate the forbidden fruit, which resulted in the fall of humanity.

However, today I ask you to consider how much God *allowed* rather than what He prohibited. He said, "From *any* tree of the garden you may eat freely." We don't know exactly how many trees that was—whether it was hundreds or thousands of different kinds. But the point is, the first couple could enjoy all of it: almonds, apricots, avocados, cashews, cherries, coconuts, dates, oranges, limes, figs, guava, mangoes, nectarines, olives, peaches, pears, pecans, persimmons, plums, pomegranates, walnuts, and so much more. The only restriction was the fruit that would bring them harm.

The same is true for you. You may want to focus on what you cannot have, but that will inevitably lead you to trouble. But victory will come when you focus on all God has given you (Philippians 4:8). Therefore, set your mind to thank and praise Him for all He's provided for you to enjoy.

Jesus, thank You for all the blessings You've given me. I set my mind on You! Amen.

RETURN

They heard the sound of the LORD God walking in the garden in the cool of the day, and the man and his wife hid themselves.

GENESIS 3:8

After Adam and Eve sinned, God still went looking for them. He did not remove His presence from them forever or leave them without explaining the consequences of their sinful actions. Instead, He pursued them, even as they were running away from Him.

God did so with compassion. First, He didn't appear suddenly or blast Adam and Eve to dust. Rather, He made sounds so they could prepare for His arrival. Likewise, the Lord approached them during the cool of the day. This was not for His benefit—the Lord God who formed the sun is unaffected by temperature. Rather, this was for Adam and Eve's comfort.

Understand this is how God approaches you when you sin. He does not leave or forsake you, and He is not wrathful toward you. He has allowed the feeling of conviction in you to prepare you to face Him. And He invites you to His throne of grace when you are ready to come back into fellowship (1 John 1:9). So don't hide yourself; instead, run to Him. Repent and return to your compassionate God.

Jesus, I repent of the disrespect I've shown You. Please forgive me for my sins. Thank You for receiving me back into Your loving arms. Amen.

ENOUGH

A person is not justified by the works of the law,
but by faith in Jesus Christ.

GALATIANS 2:16 NIV

Sometimes you can do all the right things and still feel like the Christian life is not enough. In fact, you can attend church, pray, and even give generously and still feel empty. And if you place your confidence in your own activity instead of God, you may actually be standing in the way of His blessings for your life. Regardless of how you appear to others, God knows whether you are loving *Him* with your service or seeking others' love and approval *for yourself.*

Because your Savior loves you, He works all things for your good and His glory. That means that the circumstances that are painful to you at this moment may be God working to bring you to the end of yourself and ultimately closer to Him. His goals are to love you, lead you to a life that is fruitful and fulfilling, influence those around you, and prepare you for eternity.

Friend, Jesus is enough. The life He has for you is abundant and good. Stop striving to earn it for yourself. Let go and allow Him to lead you to the abundant life.

Jesus, I confess the areas where I am trying to earn
Your blessings. Help me love You more, and let my
service flow from my relationship with You. Amen.

POWER IN IDENTITY

*Know that the LORD Himself is God; It is He who
has made us . . . We are His people.*

PSALM 100:3

Your understanding of *who* you are is the rudder that directs
nearly everything you do. Therefore, you must believe the truth
about who God says you are—a new creation (2 Corinthians 5:17),
His child (1 John 3:1), redeemed (Galatians 3:13), capable (Philippians
4:13), worthy (1 Peter 2:9), and wanted (Romans 8:15–16).

Knowing your identity in Christ and all He has created you to
be can transform any performance-based notions you may have into
the absolute assurance of self-worth based on God's infinite love.
You are the creation of His hands—nothing about you is a mistake.
His imprint is on you, and He wants you to be a reflection of His
glory and character in a world that needs to hear His good news of
salvation.

The Lord will reveal why you were created as well as His assignments for you in this life (Ephesians 2:10). And when you understand
how beloved you are and the greatness of your purpose, you will be
energized to live for God through His power.

᚛

**Jesus, I continue to struggle with feelings of
insecurity and low self-esteem. Help me to fix
my eyes on You instead of myself, because
it is in You I learn who I really am. Amen.**

REFERRED HEALING

O Lord my God, I cried to You for help, and You healed me.

PSALM 30:2

Sometimes we may wonder why the pain and emptiness in our hearts may persist, even though we've sought the Lord and have tried to obey Him. We know Jesus is the Great Physician and can help us. So why doesn't He?

Our problem, however, arises in the areas we will not allow Him to touch or we're not aware require His healing. Often, this is because we don't realize where our issue really originates. For example, you may have an ache in your jaw. So where would you go? Most likely to a dentist, right? But at times, discomfort in the teeth is actually a precursor to a heart attack. In medical science, this is called *referred pain*. The *source* of the problem is not in the same place where the hurt is presenting.

If you've wrestled repeatedly with a pain in a certain area of your life and you've found no relief, it may be that you've been focused on the wrong source. Ask God to reveal what to do and obey Him even when He doesn't make sense. Don't be surprised when He calls you to make a change that seemingly has nothing to do with your problem but that provides the relief you long for.

***

**I will obey whatever You say.
Heal me, Jesus. Amen.**

KEEP TRUSTING

"Call upon Me in the day of trouble; I shall rescue you, and you will honor Me."

PSALM 50:15

When things are going your way, trusting the Lord is easy. But when painful trials come into your life, leaving you frustrated, confused, anxious, or in despair, do you still trust Him? In the face of adversity, many people wonder, *Does God really love me?* And they conclude that a truly caring Father would not allow such difficulty to touch their lives. Often, they question whether He is even willing to do anything about their circumstances.

But today, be assured that your Savior is not only able but also willing to fulfill every single promise He's given you in Scripture. Even when you cannot understand why He would allow certain situations to occur, there are three essential truths that you can cling to, no matter what: (1) God is perfect in His love for you. (2) The Lord is infinite in His wisdom. (3) Your heavenly Father is all-powerful—completely able to accomplish all that concerns you.

So when you face struggles, always remind yourself that Jesus has your best interest in mind. No matter what happens, your unconditionally loving, all-wise, all-powerful God has you in His hand and will work all things together for your good as you walk with Him.

Jesus, I know You will rescue me. Thank
You that I can trust You regardless
of my circumstances. Amen.

WALK IN FAITH

As you have received Christ Jesus the Lord, so walk in Him.

COLOSSIANS 2:6

W alking in Christ refers to the dynamic relationship we are to have with the Lord. Just as it's impossible to make progress while standing still, believers are either moving forward in their Christian life or falling backward. The key for maturing in faith is found in today's verse. How did you and I receive Jesus as our Savior? By faith (Ephesians 2:8–9). We trusted Christ's provision on the cross. The Christian life is to be "walked"—or lived out—in the same way.

Many people walk by their sight and feelings; but allowing our physical senses to guide us spiritually doesn't work, because we'll never have all the information we require. But God does. Therefore He wants us to trust Him daily for whatever needs we may have.

This is why followers of Jesus Christ are commanded to "walk by faith, not by sight" (2 Corinthians 5:7). We must take one step of faith after another, not knowing exactly where He will lead us but trusting that our omniscient, loving God has our best interest in mind. So walking in faith means trusting Jesus for every circumstance and believing He will lead us right every time, without exception.

Jesus, help me walk with You every day, confident that You lead me to life at its very best. Amen.

WHEN WE FAIL

If we are faithless, He remains faithful, for He
cannot deny Himself.

2 TIMOTHY 2:13

As Jesus was arrested and taken to trial, Peter denied knowing Him three times (Matthew 26:69–75). Undoubtedly, this was a very low point in the disciple's life. However, if we're honest, we can relate to feeling such intense fear and confusion that we doubt God—even renouncing what we know about His loving character, unfathomable wisdom, and resurrection power that can set everything right.

Certainly, Peter felt his faith failure as deeply as you and I might. But what we need to see is that Jesus did not deny knowing him—and He doesn't reject us either. While God doesn't want us to yield to temptation, He knows we're not perfect, and there'll be times when we stumble. But He doesn't want our failures to define us. Instead, He wants us to set our focus on Him.

After the resurrection, one of the first things Jesus did was to reassure Peter of His eternal love and purpose. God's plan for Peter's life had not changed—and it does not for you either. You remain a beneficiary of His endless grace and eternal love. Therefore, if you've failed, do not give up or be discouraged. Jesus will never give up on you. Let Him restore you.

Jesus, thank You for not giving up on me! Restore me and help me walk in Your will. Amen.

RECONCILED

We were reconciled to God through the death of
His Son.

ROMANS 5:10

G od's initial plan for us was one of intimate, loving, and unbro-
ken fellowship. But when Adam and Eve chose to eat of the
forbidden tree, for the first time in their existence, they knew what
it meant to sin, to feel spiritually and physically exposed, and to feel
unworthy in the Father's presence. They felt the way every person
after them has, and they did what every person has tried to do at
some point—they tried to hide from God.

However, the Lord acted with mercy toward Adam and Eve,
making them tunics of animal skin to cover their nakedness (Genesis
3:21). And in making that clothing, He shed blood, foreshadowing
the sacrifice that would be necessary to restore the fellowship their
sin had destroyed—the death of Jesus on the cross (Romans 5:12–17).

God gave Adam and Eve a perpetual reminder—a sign as close to
them as their own skin—that even as they walked out of the garden
of Eden into a fallen world, the Lord loved them and designed them
to live abundantly. And that's what Jesus has given us—because He
loves us, He's given us everlasting life and restores our fellowship
with the Father. So stop running from Him. Love your God.

Jesus, thank You for loving me so much!
Help me know and love You more. Amen.

ACCEPT WHAT HE'S GIVEN

He made you alive together with Him, having
forgiven us all our transgressions.

COLOSSIANS 2:13

When Jesus cried out, "It is finished!" from the cross (John 19:30)—He meant it. The price of your sin was paid in full. There is absolutely nothing you can add to the salvation He's given you. And Christ has not only forgiven your sins but has also blessed you with all the benefits of being His beloved child. All you have to do is accept what He has provided by faith.

This is important to understand as you walk in God's will. You're not doing so to earn God's favor—you already have it. Likewise, you aren't doing so to secure your place in heaven. Jesus has done that for you. Rather, you seek His plan because that's the way to take hold of all Christ has done for you.

Jesus, through the power of the Holy Spirit within you, empowers you to be all God has created you to be. You can find all the strength, hope, and love that you'll ever need in Him as you abide in His resurrection power. So don't be afraid of what you lack. Continue to take hold of the new life you've been given so you can know what it means to be fully alive.

Jesus, thank You for making me alive
and blessing me. To You be all the
honor and glory in my life. Amen.

SPIRITUAL ISSUES

"That which is born of the Spirit is spirit."
JOHN 3:6

Nicodemus went to see Jesus at night because Jesus was considered by many of Nicodemus's peers to be nothing more than a low-class, itinerant preacher. But Nicodemus felt compelled because he saw that Jesus had real answers the other rabbis did not have. So Nicodemus approached Jesus with what he thought was an intellectual inquiry—a question that he hoped Jesus could answer.

Jesus, however, perceived that what Nicodemus really needed and wanted was a genuine relationship with God. So Jesus, understanding this could only happen if Nicodemus was born spiritually, addressed the underlying root.

We all need to be saved—to be born with a new, living spirit that can interact with the Lord. So how does that occur? Understand, salvation isn't gained by doing good, by joining a church, or by being baptized. Rather, you are saved by accepting that Jesus' death on the cross was sufficient to forgive your sin and give you a new spirit that is able to relate to God.

Whatever difficulty is on your mind today, it is spiritual at its root, whether you realize it or not. You need Jesus. Therefore, let Him take care of your deepest spiritual need, and the rest will follow.

Jesus, even though my issues appear earthly, I know they're spiritual. Help me, Lord. I need You. Amen.

SAVED IN ALL THINGS

He who did not spare His own Son, but delivered
Him over for us all, how will He not also with Him
freely give us all things?

ROMANS 8:32

It's never popular to talk about the depth of our destitution and despair before Jesus becomes our Savior—that we're lost, spiritually dead in our transgressions (Ephesians 2:1), separated from God (Ephesians 2:12), and on track for the lake of fire (Revelation 20:15).

However, it's necessary to think about these things in order for us to appreciate what we've been given and realize the heart with which the Father provided it. God understood the depth of our spiritual poverty and rescued us because of His great love for us. Jesus gave His life because we're precious to Him. But if He sacrificed so much for us, how is it that we doubt Him in other areas of our lives?

Today accept that Jesus knows what is best for you, and He is directing you to take hold of it. He sees beyond what you do to what would truly satisfy your heart and help you experience His abundant life. Therefore, accept that He not only saves you eternally but also redeems you *fully*. And if you will trust Him, you will see Him deliver you in a wonderful way.

Jesus, thank You for sacrificing so much
for me. I trust You in all things. Amen.

WITH YOU IN TRIUMPH

"I am not alone, because the Father is with Me."
JOHN 16:32

When we face chaotic circumstances, we may lose our sense of hope. We may feel that as our earthly security crumbles beneath us, we are likewise on the brink of perishing.

This was true for the disciples as Jesus was arrested and sent to the cross. Not only was the hope they had in Christ seemingly squashed, but they also felt the intense pressure of being persecuted because of their association with Him.

But with the crucifixion, God had an awesome, eternal plan that He was bringing to full fruition. This is why Jesus expressed the peace of knowing the Father was with Him. Jesus wanted His disciples to have the confidence that God was with them and was succeeding in His purposes regardless of how the situation appeared temporarily. He desires the same for you.

God was in control and victorious in all that happened at the cross, just as He is in what you experience now. The Father is with you in your chaos. Trust that the One who defeated the grave never leaves you and is able to show you His resurrection power.

Jesus, thank You that I can have hope in
You no matter how my circumstances may
appear. You are always with me. Amen.

APRIL

YOU HAVE GRACE

By grace you have been saved through faith; and that not of yourselves, it is the gift of God.

EPHESIANS 2:8

Some days, you may just need some compassion—someone who understands your struggles and sympathizes with your hurts. But realize that when you accept Jesus as your Savior, you experience God's grace—His benevolence toward humanity, given without regard to merit on our part. In other words, Jesus not only comprehends your pain firsthand and empathizes with you (Hebrews 2:17), but He goes beyond that to give you blessings you don't deserve at all.

Grace is a word that remains a mystery to many people, including Christians. This is because deep down, we realize we deserve death. This is why we often question our worth and adopt destructive habits. We are subject to the consequences of the fall, such as stress, emotional turmoil, toil, pain, disease, hardship, and aging. All this takes a toll.

But out of His infinite heart of love, God has provided a means for you to receive life—to experience what He originally created you to enjoy. This is why Jesus died in your place—so that you might live. That's grace. You have the compassion you long for. Take hold of it and the life your Savior died for you to have.

Jesus, thank You for Your amazing grace and love for me! I praise You! Amen.

TAKE HOLD OF FREEDOM

Only in that way could he deliver those who
through fear of death have been living all their lives
as slaves to constant dread.

HEBREWS 2:15 TLB

M any people miss God's very best in life because they refuse to remove the chains of sin that Christ has already unlocked for them. Each day they try to make it through the best they can and pray they'll be able to bear the shame they harbor.

Friend, if this is how you are living the Christian life, you are missing the point of what Jesus accomplished for you. When Christ rose from the dead, He conquered every single power in opposition to Him—sin, death, and all demonic forces—not merely at that time, but forever. There is nothing left to rule over you except your loving, wise, and gracious God. Sin no longer owns you; your debt has been paid; and you no longer bear shame, because you've been given a new identity as a child of the Most High.

The Father wants you to embrace the liberty and joy purchased for you by the blood of Jesus. So today, take hold of the fact that you have been released and have everything you need to overcome. Jesus, your triumphant Commander-in-Chief, has given you the victory! Rejoice in Him and embrace the freedom you've been given.

Jesus, thank You for setting me free! Help me take hold of all You've given. Amen.

CELEBRATING THE RESURRECTION

Death is swallowed up in victory.

1 CORINTHIANS 15:54

Perhaps you wonder why we take time to celebrate the resurrection every year. The main reason, of course, is that Jesus Christ, our Lord and Savior, is *alive*! Really think about that.

Jesus died, went to the grave, and conquered it. He defeated death *forever*! No other religious leader in history can make such a claim—all remain mastered by death. But the One we love, follow, and serve *overcame* it! And because Christ rose from the grave, we and all our believing loved ones will too—we will enjoy eternal life with Him in heaven (John 14:1–3).

But we also celebrate the resurrection because the One who saves us is actively available to help us—*always without fail*. Having lived like us, Jesus understands our fears, failings, and sorrows. We know that if He defeated the grave for us, how much more will He help us with whatever we face with that same resurrection power. Absolutely nothing will be impossible for Him to overcome on our behalf.

Certainly, that is cause for celebration every day!

Jesus, You are alive! You are not just a historical leader; You are right here with me—defending and providing for me with Your resurrection power. I praise You, my living Lord! Amen.

WALK IN VICTORY

"The Son of Man is to be delivered into the hands
of men, and they will kill Him; and . . . He will rise
three days later."

MARK 9:31

Regardless of what you face today, you can walk in victory because Jesus is your example, and His Spirit lives in you. After all, how could Christ possibly bear the scourging, the crucifixion, the weight of all our sins, the grave, and still remain victorious? It was because Jesus had an eternal perspective—He knew the resurrection was a completed fact even before it had occurred. And after three days, Christ rose to walk in victory—and to share that triumph with you.

Through the presence of the Holy Spirit, God gives you strength, power, and assurance as well. The Lord promises to work through every frustration, trial, challenge, and obstacle to move your life toward triumph—toward your own resurrection.

One day you will see the wonder and splendor of God's work and understand the purpose behind each of the troubles you've faced. Like an artist blending both dark and light colors to achieve a beautiful portrait, He will work in your life to create a masterpiece. So have hope and walk in victory.

Jesus, You are victorious! And if You can defeat
the grave, You can and will overcome the trials of
my life. Thank You, Jesus—I walk in victory! Amen.

ALREADY LOVED

"As the Father has loved me, so have I loved you.
Now remain in my love."

JOHN 15:9 NIV

Today, realize that God loves you fully and completely—as much as He can ever possibly love you. He accepts you unconditionally, enjoys spending time with you, and even likes you as a person. You are His child. He warns you against sin because it hurts you, and He doesn't want to see you wounded. But whenever you sin, He stands ready with open arms to forgive you (1 John 1:9).

You cannot be saved any more than you have already been by Jesus—He has completely redeemed you. When Jesus died on the cross and rose from the grave, He paid the entire penalty for your sins—there's no more sacrifice required. You were utterly forgiven the moment you accepted Jesus as your Savior. There's nothing more you need to do to earn God's approval.

So then why live a godly Christian life? First, to say, "Thank You!" for the great gift Jesus has given. Second, to show Him love in return. Third, to be His representative to this lost world. But also so you can take hold of all the blessings God has already given you.

Jesus, thank You that I don't have to
earn Your approval. Help me live a
life that glorifies You. Amen.

ETERNALLY SECURE

*These things I have written . . . so that you may
know that you have eternal life.*

1 JOHN 5:13

Every year during Easter, we focus on the sacrifice of Jesus at
Calvary. From His atonement springs our blessed assurance of
eternal life. Many people who trust Christ as their Savior know they're
saved but are not certain about their eternal security—the work of God
that assures us that our redemption is permanent. They believe their
deliverance can somehow be forfeited through wrong actions.

However, if our salvation is based on *anything* other than the
completed work of Jesus Christ on the cross, then we'll find ourselves
on shaky ground, with lots of doubts. This is why some believers
attempt to involve themselves in the redemption process by their
good works or right behavior. Sadly, they are always prone to wavering faith because they feel they must continuously earn the Lord's
goodwill in order to get to heaven.

Friend, is this you? Remember that God's grace in redemption
is a *gift* (Ephesians 2:8–9). If you add a single work requirement to
it, then it's no longer given to you freely; it is payment for services
rendered. That's not how God works in your life. Absolutely nothing
can revoke what He's given you. Accept that He's made you secure.

**Jesus, thank You that my salvation is
eternally secure! What an awesome
gift You have given! Amen.**

A BASIS FOR LOVE

Walk in love, just as Christ also loved you and gave Himself up for us.

EPHESIANS 5:2

On a daily basis, God may bring people across your path who you may find to be troublesome and irritating. However, He does so as a reminder to you: "I love those who are difficult to care for. I love even when others seem unlovable."

In this, you may feel some uncomfortable conviction. After all, you know the ways you feel unlovable and unworthy. You have flaws, failures, and quirks that annoy or anger others. In fact, you may be more like those whom you dislike than you'd care to admit. But Jesus still loves you and died for you—just as He did for them. What Christ did for you on the cross, He did for your worst enemy. It's when you humbly accept this fact that you can begin to love others as Jesus does.

So when you encounter someone who antagonizes you, ask Jesus to give you His love for him or her. Remember the grace He's given you, and thank Him that He's willing to manifest the fruit of His Spirit through you (Galatians 5:22–23). Then watch what He does through your willing heart. You may very well see the power of God work through your change in demeanor.

Jesus, help me see those I dislike with Your eyes, and let Your love flow through me. Amen.

CELEBRATE THE VICTORIES

They go from strength to strength [increasing in victorious power].

PSALM 84:7 AMP

Have your doubts kept you from experiencing the fullness of God's blessings? Each of us has faced times when we were not sure of the Lord's involvement in our circumstances. We have wondered if we could trust His promises, and we've even questioned the efficacy of the Christian principles that we've applied to our lives. Yes, the Lord has come through on important issues in the past, but our pervasive concerns make us wonder if He will continue.

Understand that the Lord wants to give you promises you can cling to whenever you face a challenge. He will also give you small victories along the way because He knows that your lack of trust in His ability will lead to feelings of unrest and anxiety. So when He gives you a blessing—even a small one—don't ignore it because of the bigger issues. Rather, rejoice fully, knowing it is a foretaste of the triumph to come.

So embrace the Lord's goodness. Lay aside your doubts. Place your trust in the unlimited ability of your all-knowing God, who loves and understands you completely and will never allow you to experience defeat. Because He will never let you down.

Jesus, thank You for the victories You give me along the way. I rejoice in Your ever-present help. Amen.

SOW OBEDIENCE

Do not be deceived, God is not mocked; for
whatever a man sows, this he will also reap.
GALATIANS 6:7

Do you have a choice before you today that is difficult? Obey God no matter how challenging it may be. At times, you will find that submitting yourself to the Lord's authority will involve choices that could result in rejection, loss, or hardship, and it will require courage for you to do as He asks. However difficult your circumstances may be, respond to them with confidence in the One who empowers you to do His will. Has God ever made a mistake, been too late, or proven inadequate? No! Our heavenly Father is all-powerful and consistently faithful. You can trust Him to lead you in the best way.

Always remember that you will reap what you sow, more than you sow, and later than you sow. When you obey God, you will always get His best. It may take time, but you will see His provision. However, when you don't obey the Lord, life may seem easier temporarily, but eventually, it will turn out to be much harder. So demonstrate your trust in God by complying with His will. When you do so, you will certainly reap the rewards He has designed for you in ways above and beyond your imagination.

Jesus, I will obey You no matter how difficult it is, always trusting how You lead me. Amen.

KEEP MATURING

Leaving the elementary teaching about the Christ,
let us press on to maturity.

HEBREWS 6:1

Why don't we become perfectly mature Christians instantly upon accepting Jesus as our Savior? The truth is that though we have been born again with a new, living spirit, we must develop the capacity to experience and trust God fully.

Consider a newborn baby. That baby has the full capacity to become a unique and special adult—with the potential to walk, talk, make decisions, solve problems, and demonstrate thousands of other skills. But the newborn doesn't manifest these abilities immediately upon birth. Instead, intellectual aptitudes develop as the child matures physically; other capabilities are established like building blocks. Many skills are learned through what is modeled, while others require intentional practice.

The same is true for us spiritually. God has given us the Holy Spirit to help us grow and take full advantage of all the spiritual blessings He has already given us. But the process takes time, teaching, training, and, often, trials. The Lord knows not only what we need but also what we are able to handle. This is why it is so important to trust Him to lead us and to keep pressing forward when we encounter growing pains.

Father, thank You for growing me up in the faith. I will trust how You raise me. Amen.

POWERFULLY HIS

I can do all things through Christ who strengthens me.

PHILIPPIANS 4:13 NKJV

A re you aware of the power that is available to you in Jesus? He makes His authority, strength, and wisdom available to you whenever you need it. In fact, His Holy Spirit indwells you, which means that everything Jesus is will always be present with you—empowering you for every task and challenge.

The problem is not with what Jesus gives you; rather, it is what you submit to Him. In order to enjoy the life and power He promises, you must set your heart to be united with Him completely. This is why Jesus prayed, "I am praying . . . that they will all be one, just as you and I are one—as you are in me, Father, and I am in you. And may they be in us so that the world will believe you sent me" (John 17:20–21 NLT).

Have you set your heart to be one with Christ—to continuously give more of yourself to Him and to glorify Him in the world? It is a glorious privilege to reflect Him and enjoy all the blessings He has given. Give yourself to Him wholeheartedly—in heart, word, deed, and mission—and experience His resurrection power.

Lord Jesus, I am Yours. Show me how to be one with You completely so that I may glorify You and others may know You. Amen.

EMBRACE HIS PATH

You shall walk in all the way which the LORD your
God has commanded you, that you may live and
that it may be well with you.

DEUTERONOMY 5:33

Can you recall the last time you were tempted to do the opposite of what you knew the Lord wanted you to do? Deep inside, you understood what was right, but a debate ensued in your mind: *Does God really want me to give that up? Surely, that's not really important to Him.* Such thoughts arose because the Enemy knows that if he can entice you to ignore God, you will dishonor the Lord and impede His good purposes for you.

Realize that disobedience sends the message that you know better than God does when it comes to governing your life. However, the Father's directives for you spring from His deep care for you. He asks for your obedience not because He is a strict taskmaster but because He doesn't want you to destroy yourself or miss the great future He has for you. When you reject what He tells you, you're really rejecting His love.

While God's eternal love for you never changes, your sin certainly disrupts your fellowship with the Savior. Don't let that happen. Make the right choice. You never lose when you obey Him. So submit to God and choose the way of wisdom and blessing.

Jesus, You know the best way for
me. I will obey You. Amen.

HE WILL

"All things are possible to him who believes."

MARK 9:23

There are things you will bring to the Lord that you'll wonder if He really wants to help you with. You know He can do anything, but you're not certain He's really willing to alleviate your burden. This was the case when a father brought his demon-possessed son to Jesus. He wanted to see his son restored, and he knew Christ had the power to do it. He said, "If You can do anything, have compassion on us and help us" (Mark 9:22 NKJV). Jesus said He was willing. So the father said, "Lord, I believe; help my unbelief!" (v. 24).

Perhaps you understand this father's honest exclamation. He humbly admitted that, while he believed in Jesus' ability, there were still some concerns interfering with his faith. The same may be true for you. You trust Jesus, but your fears and doubts about yourself get in the way.

Realize that Jesus doesn't expect you to be perfect. Be honest with Him about your fluctuating faith, but always remember that His power doesn't ebb and flow along with your confidence in Him. Regardless of how you feel, God is always in control. He is trustworthy even when your ability to trust wavers. Therefore, set your heart to believe Him.

Jesus, thank You for always being able and willing to help me. I believe; help my unbelief! Amen.

TESTS AND PROVISIONS

There He tested them.

EXODUS 15:25

After the people of Israel were freed from their bondage in Egypt and had their miraculous escape through the Red Sea, they began encountering challenges such as the need for water. One might wonder why God would allow a lack in such a basic daily need after giving them such an amazing deliverance. Yet God revealed the reason for this to Moses—He was testing the people's faith.

Soon after, however, God led Israel to Elim, where there were twelve springs of water and seventy date palms. Of course, the numbers twelve and seventy were meaningful—with Israel being composed of twelve tribes and having seventy elders. Each tribe had its own spring and each elder his own source of food. Therefore, Elim was a place of not only abundant provision but also providential significance. God was showing Israel that He would care for them perfectly.

This is true for you as well—especially as you encounter your own needs. The Lord's hand is not too short to provide for you, and He has not forgotten about you, but He wants you to trust Him in the unknowns. So take whatever lack you may face as an opportunity for God to reveal His perfect provision.

Jesus, I will trust You with my needs
and all the unknowns even when I
cannot see a way through. Amen.

UNSEEN NEEDS

He entered into heaven itself to appear now before God on our behalf.

HEBREWS 9:24 NLT

At times there may be an inner restlessness or yearning within you that you cannot define. In fact, it may be so subtle and so consistent that you learn to live with it. But the truth of the matter is that something is broken or missing within you—it's just not right. And every time you try to assuage it, you miss the mark and end up feeling worse.

The good news is that Jesus brings every need you have to the Father—even ones you do not realize are there. He is well aware of your inadequacies, limitations, and faults. He comprehends the wounds and behavioral patterns that drive you. He realizes where your motivations and yearnings originate. He recognizes the best way to help you grow. And out of His deep love for you, Jesus brings it all to the Father.

There is no prayer that Jesus prays on your behalf that goes unheeded or unanswered by the Father, because He and the Father are one (John 10:30). So even though at times you have no idea what to pray, you have no reason to fear. Jesus is already helping you. He takes action on your behalf, for your good, in order to meet your need.

Jesus, thank You for praying for me and for meeting my deepest needs. Amen.

ACCEPTED COMPLETELY

*Accept one another, just as Christ also accepted us
to the glory of God.*

ROMANS 15:7

The inner drive for acceptance—either from ourselves or from others—can lead us down dangerous paths. We can engage in destructive behaviors with the desire to prove ourselves valuable, desirable, capable, or worthwhile. It never begins that way, of course. Initially, we may engage in activities and habits that are quite harmless to bring out the best in ourselves or show ourselves worthy. But when one thing after another fails to address our deep inner need, we can become addicted to that which covers over or dulls our pain rather than heals it.

Friend, understand that at the core of what you feel is ultimately a deep need to be accepted by God. You must understand that you were created by the Lord with purpose and excellence (Psalm 139:13–16). You don't have to run from your mistakes, because He forgives you of them through Christ's death on the cross. And regardless of your past, you have a good, worthwhile, and wonderful future.

So right now, repeat to yourself: "In Jesus, I am accepted by God. I am who He wanted me to be. I have purpose and worth." Stop doubting your value and seeking significance through sin. Instead, embrace who He created you to be.

Jesus, thank You for accepting me. Help
me take hold of Your love. Amen.

IMPEDIMENTS

Our soul waits for the LORD; He is our help and our shield.

PSALM 33:20

Many things can impede us from embracing God's will, but I want to tell you about two very common ones.

Setting our focus on the things of this world rather than Jesus. We become so attached to worldly issues of status and identity that we lose the bigger picture of what Christ wants to accomplish through us. Then, when God doesn't give us what we erroneously think gives us worth, we become discouraged and are tempted to sin (James 1:15). This is always disastrous.

Taking a shortcut around God's planned route. We get tired of waiting for the Lord and either rush ahead of Him or go in another direction altogether. But remember, timing is everything to God. He will not change His mind about His plan for you, because He has training and blessings that He wants you to enjoy.

Today, if you are tempted to doubt God's plan or timetable, stop and ask Him to speak to your heart and encourage you as you wait. The Lord wants you to finish the course that He's set before you and be victorious in this life. So set your heart on obeying and honoring Him, because that is the unimpeded path to life at its best.

Jesus, speak to my heart. I set my eyes on You and wait, trusting Your plan and timing. Amen.

BLIND SPOTS

*The secret things belong to the LORD our God, but
the things revealed belong to us.*

DEUTERONOMY 29:29

D o you ever think to yourself, *I just cannot figure out why things
don't work out for me?* All of us have blind spots—places in our
lives where we unknowingly undermine ourselves. While there are
many things about this life that we will never know or understand—
some things are reserved for God—the Lord desires to teach us so
much. As we interact with Him daily, He reveals principles and patterns to us about how we function, relate to others, and need to grow.
However, this means we must be willing to focus on Him and obey
Him as we read Scripture and pray—and not just expect a quick
answer or a simple reply.

If you are frustrated about your life or about circumstances you
are facing today, take time to be alone with the Lord in prayer. Ask
Him to reveal His understanding about your situation and the patterns of behavior in you that have exacerbated it. He wants you to
walk in His good, acceptable, perfect, and victorious will for your
life. So set your heart to learn what He has for you. Because when
you do, you won't be disappointed.

**Jesus, reveal my blind spots to me and how to be
free of them so I can walk in Your will. Amen.**

BATTLE-WON FAITH

I come to you in the name of the LORD of hosts.

1 SAMUEL 17:45

We all know the story of the young shepherd boy who slew the giant. David stood before his formidable foe with no sword, armor, or battle experience. Biblical scholars speculate that Goliath, the mammoth Philistine warrior, stood somewhere between nine and twelve feet tall and weighed several hundred pounds. He was heavily armed, and the sight of him struck terror into the hearts of Saul's army. By all rational accounts, David was no match for his challenger.

The secret of David's success, however, was not in his own ability, but in his willingness to trust and obey God. Likewise, David realized that what he learned in one situation would help him with whatever he faced in the future.

The same is true for you. God has a plan to develop your faith as well—deepening your dependence on Him. You may be facing what seem to be enormous trials and difficulties. But knowing how to respond properly to these challenges is critical to your spiritual growth. So like David, declare that your battles belong to the Lord. Allow God to take your trust and grow it into a strong and mighty faith in His name—one that has the ability to conquer any foe.

Jesus, my battles belong to You! In Your name I triumph! Strengthen my faith and lead me to Your awesome victory. Amen.

In Control

The mind of man plans his way, but the LORD directs his steps.

PROVERBS 16:9

Stop to consider the truth of these statements:

- You cannot make another person love you.
- You cannot always have your way in every situation.
- You cannot own everything you want to.
- You cannot do everything perfectly every time.
- You cannot persuade everybody to think the way you do.

If we are honest with ourselves, we will admit we don't like the fact that we can't control these things. But here is the good news: *God is in complete control.* He alone is omniscient, omnipresent, and omnipotent. He alone rules all creation. And He loves you so much that He always brings good out of everything you face.

So when someone doesn't love you or think like you do, when you don't get your way, when you don't own something or do a task perfectly, you can take heart. It's okay because your God is still in charge. And He is working everything for your good.

Jesus, I will praise You in my setbacks, losses, and lack of control. My life is in Your hands, and I trust You with it. Amen.

TAKE THE STEP

My steps have held fast to Your paths.
PSALM 17:5

What is holding you back from doing God's will? Do you realize when He is calling out to you? As you pray, it may be that you sense a prompting to take a certain course of action. But perhaps it scares you or doesn't make sense.

Often, people say no to the Lord because they are waiting for the big picture of God's will instead of walking with Him step-by-step. So they wait and resist His promptings because of their fears of the unknowns. Sadly, if you ignore God in the small things long enough, you will develop a resistance to His voice. Don't let that happen.

Although there are times that God reveals His ultimate goals—such as making Abraham into a great nation (Genesis 12:1–3)—more often than not, God walks with us step-by-step. Remember, the Lord didn't tell Abraham where he was going—only that He would lead. Abraham had to obey one step at a time just like we do.

So if God's will is confusing or intimidating you today, return to the most recent time you heard Him clearly and obey whatever He instructed you to do. That one act will open the door to taking hold of all He has for you.

Jesus, I want to do Your will. Remind me of the last thing You told me to do and empower me to go forward. Amen.

GOOD NEEDS

I call to You when my heart is faint; lead me to the
rock that is higher than I.

PSALM 61:2

Understand today that God has not placed the needs that you are experiencing in your life so that you'll feel like a defective or incomplete human being. Rather, your needs exist to compel you to seek the Lord. They help you understand that Jesus must be an intimate and integral part of your life in order for you to succeed. You can rely on Him to make you the whole, productive, and effective person He created you to be, and that happens within the greater purposes He has for you on this earth.

Your needs, in other words, are the key to unlocking your true potential. By requiring you to overcome your challenges through the power of the Holy Spirit, they help you access the strength, power, and wisdom Jesus has made available to you. And when you do so, you are transformed—prepared for all He has planned in advance for you to accomplish (Ephesians 2:10).

So do not lament your needs. Rather, thank God for them. And whenever you experience an area of lack that causes you anxiety, let it drive you to the throne of grace and to your loving Savior (Hebrews 4:16).

Jesus, thank You for working through my needs to make me into who You created me to be. Amen.

LET HIM LEAD

When pride comes, then comes dishonor, but with
the humble is wisdom.

PROVERBS 11:2

Do you realize that it was pride that caused Satan's fall from heaven? God had given him a beautiful countenance and had created him to lead worship, but this wasn't good enough for the Enemy. Instead of exalting the Lord, Satan wanted to be the one extolled. Instead of submitting to God's authority, he wanted to rule. And because of it, the Enemy lost everything.

The same is true for us. Every act of sin is an act of rebellion against God, and it all comes from our desire to lead and not follow. The Enemy tempts us to question God's goodness and authority—suggesting we've not received all that should be ours. Thinking we know better than the Lord, we depart from His path, seeking our exaltation and forgetting how much God has blessed us. This is why pride is such a destructive force—it leads us away from true fulfillment to personal ruin and deep loneliness.

However, you can prevent pride from controlling your life. Ask God to reveal to you any areas of arrogance in your life and humble yourself before Him by letting Him lead you. Then worship the Lord, because certainly He will lift you up (James 4:10).

**Jesus, I repent of my prideful ways and submit
to Your leadership. You are the only One
worthy of all my worship and praise. Amen.**

REJOICING OVER YOU

*The LORD your God is in your midst, a victorious
warrior . . . He will be quiet in His love, He will
rejoice over you with shouts of joy.*

ZEPHANIAH 3:17

You are God's masterpiece, and He has given His Word as a
testimony to the love He has for you. The Lord rejoices over
you, though He knows your life is still in the process of becoming all
that He has planned—though you are not yet what you will be. But
He continues shaping your life and conforming you to the image of
His Son because of the wonderful things He sees in you.

Take that to heart today as you encounter feelings of rejection
and loneliness, conflict with others, and other relational challenges.
Amid the uncertainties and pressures surrounding you, Jesus is
your victorious Warrior—at your side to strengthen and encourage
you. Therefore, forgive those who've hurt you, confess your sins,
and embrace the identity you have in Christ—beloved, accepted,
redeemed, competent, and wanted.

Instead of striving to live up to others' standards, live for Jesus.
The Holy Spirit will lovingly teach you to live in a manner pleasing
and honoring to God, which is life at its best.

Jesus, thank You for accepting me and being my
victorious Warrior. I can make it through knowing
You love me and have a vision for my life. Amen.

ABIDE

*"I am the vine, you are the branches; he who abides
in Me and I in him, he bears much fruit, for apart
from Me you can do nothing."*

JOHN 15:5

Years ago, I fell victim to the trap of fretting, rushing, and striving. At the center of my life was the belief that to succeed in the Christian life, I had to work hard to please God. Finally, I came to a point of burnout—I was completely empty.

But as I meditated on John 15:5, I discovered that it was not *my* responsibility to strive or work for anything. My part was to submit to God and allow Him to live His life through me. With this discovery, an enormous weight was lifted and the energy and strength that are available in Christ became mine.

If you are running on empty, I pray you will take this message to heart—in abiding is the life and hope you desire. Through seeking Jesus and resting in Him, you discover that God is actively conforming you to His will and likeness as you listen to Him (Philippians 4:13). He sharpens your talents, purifies your mind, and empowers you for service to His kingdom.

Therefore, stop striving and abide. God is responsible for making your life a powerful vessel of His grace. Your job is to let Him.

**Jesus, I submit to You completely.
Teach me to abide in You. Amen.**

A GRANDER WORK

*I am confident of this very thing, that He who
began a good work in you will perfect it until the
day of Christ Jesus.*

PHILIPPIANS 1:6

D o you realize that the Lord's vision for you has implications that impact His kingdom both on earth and in heaven? God's will for your life has ramifications not only for you as an individual but also for others—the scope of which you cannot possibly fathom because they continue on into eternity.

This is the reason the process you face after you accept Christ as your Savior is one of refinement and of transformation. God chips away at the rough edges of self-will and earthly bondage to reveal all He created you to be. He brings you to greater wholeness so that you might reflect Him to others.

That is why it is always so important that you cling to Jesus regardless of the trials that arise, and yield yourself to His will even when it is difficult. Your life matters—to God and to those who will find Him and grow in Him through you. So do not resist what the Lord is doing. Realize there is a much bigger picture, and take heart.

Jesus, thank You for influencing other
people in an eternal manner through me.
I cling to You as You refine me, and I say
yes to Your good purposes. Amen.

DEFEAT DISCOURAGEMENT

I call upon the LORD, who is worthy to be praised,
and I am saved from my enemies.

PSALM 18:3

O ne of Satan's primary weapons against the believer is discouragement. The Enemy works on our emotions, trying to
persuade us that we're not worthy of God's love, plan, or blessings.
He tells us that the trials we experience are evidence that the Lord has
rejected us. He seeks to make us feel defeated because if he can make
us give up, he will have neutralized a potential vessel of Christ's glory.

However, understand that all the Enemy has are smoke and mir-
rors. God's love for you is unconditional and eternal, based on what
Jesus did for you on the cross. Absolutely nothing can separate you
from His love (Romans 8:38–39). Likewise, Satan can never really
defeat the Lord or His purposes for you. Your Enemy is a defeated
foe, and he can only *try* to undermine your confidence. But you don't
have to let him.

Friend, disappointments are inevitable, but discouragement
is a choice—because you've already been promised the victory
(1 Corinthians 15:57). So trust God, your ever-present help, strength,
and victorious Deliverer—no matter how things look. Jesus has never
let you down and never will.

Jesus, I choose to trust You despite
discouragements and trials. Thank You
for giving me the victory. Amen.

THE GIFT OF PEACE

*The steadfast of mind You will keep in perfect
peace, because he trusts in You.*

ISAIAH 26:3

S ome people have lived in a state of stress for so long, they cannot remember what it's like to have God's peace. Feelings of anxiety permeate their thoughts, and they cannot conceive how they will make it from day to day.

However, this was never the way the Lord intended for us to live. Peace is a gift that God gives each one of us—a fruit of His Spirit that He wants to characterize our lives (Galatians 5:22–23). Because of this, the tranquility we feel—or lack of it—acts as God's umpire in us. When we have a true sense of calm within, we know that we're in the center of His will. If there is a lack of peacefulness, something is wrong.

Therefore, if you're feeling stressed and unsettled today, stop and ask God to reveal what's going on and give your burdens to Him (Philippians 4:6–7). He may lead you to take a step of faith, comfort you in your sorrow, call you to be courageous in your troubles or to surrender your cares to Him (Psalm 55:22). And when you do, the tranquility will follow. So regardless of what you face, allow His abiding presence to give you peace.

**I need You, Lord. I cast my cares on
You. Please be my peace. Amen.**

THE UNSEEN VIEW

The LORD gives wisdom; from His mouth come
knowledge and understanding.

PROVERBS 2:6

The reason your situation may appear confusing is because you may be relying on your limited understanding of it (Proverbs 3:5–6). But when we rely only on human knowledge, we end up getting into serious trouble. We must take into account that God is working in the unseen—in the spiritual realm that we cannot perceive—and engineering resources that we don't even know exist.

Why would the Lord allow these things to be hidden from you? It is because He wants to stretch your faith by having you seek Him in them. You see, the Father doesn't want you to be confined to a day-in, day-out earthly existence. Instead, He wants you to learn to live on the higher planes with Him—where you're growing spiritually, you're taking hold of His blessings, and you're becoming a powerful ambassador for His kingdom.

God cares about and provides for you to a level that is beyond what you can imagine. He is interested in every aspect of your life—even ones you do not perceive. So take time to ask the Lord to show you the direction you need to take, and expect Him to answer. He will make sense of your circumstances and show you the way forward.

Jesus, teach me to view my circumstances from
Your perspective. I submit to You in them. Amen.

GIVE LOVE

"Give, and you will receive. Your gift will return to you in full—pressed down, shaken together to make room for more, running over."

LUKE 6:38 NLT

D o you need love today? Of course, the first place we should always go is God. But sometimes what we need is "Jesus with flesh on." We yearn for other people to show us compassion and care.

However, understand that the way you are going to have your need for love met is not by demanding love, but by giving it. Pouring out love to others readies your soul to receive it in a supernatural way. Therefore, find a place where you can serve others in the name of Jesus. Get involved in an outreach ministry that is assisting people, and care about them for who they are. Then, even before you get out of bed in the morning, ask the Lord to give you the compassion, wisdom, and strength to do at least one thing every day that will be beneficial to another person. You don't have to take on the world. Simply demonstrate to others that they matter to God.

You have nothing to lose and so much to gain. So today, trust God to help you, and then make an effort to do something to help or show love to another person.

Jesus, open my eyes to others' needs, and help me to love them as You would. Amen.

MAY

STAY FAITHFUL

*A book of remembrance was written before Him
for those who fear the LORD and who esteem His
name.*

MALACHI 3:16

There came a time when the Jewish people were speaking harshly
against the Lord, saying, "It is useless to serve God" (Malachi
3:14 NKJV). The people were praising those who were disobedient and
proud rather than seeking revival and restoration. When a nation
turns against the Lord, it can be difficult to stay faithful.

Perhaps you understand that pressure as you watch society drift
away from God. But the Lord asks that you continue to walk with
Him and submit to His will. You may think at times that He is asking
a great deal from you because of the cost of being a Christian. But
in the context of all He gives you now and in eternity, He really asks
very little. In return for your imperfect, sometimes wavering obedience, He gives you everything you have: life, health, relationships,
protection, provision, wisdom, talent, spiritual giftedness, creativity,
resurrection power, and a new spirit with which you can fellowship
with Him. And He calls you His child and His special treasure.

Yes, life may be challenging when others turn against the Lord.
But He is always worth following, regardless of the price. So do not
fear. Stay faithful and obey God.

**Jesus, I will follow You no matter how difficult
it gets, because I trust in You. Amen.**

RECEIVING HIS ACCEPTANCE

I have no greater joy than this, to hear of my
children walking in the truth.

3 JOHN 4

God is always in a stance of acceptance toward you. Anytime you are ready to turn to Him, He is ready to receive you. He loves you as you are, without qualification. Certainly, He wants you to walk in His ways and love Him in return. This is not because He wants to control you, but because the Father—in His perfect and unlimited wisdom—realizes He has the best path for you now and in eternity. He encourages you to walk in His will for *your* sake, not His.

This is illustrated in a story I heard about a boy who was adopted when he was ten years old. He was having difficulty feeling accepted by his new family until the day came when his father said to him, "Here are your chores." The boy said, "When I was given responsibilities just like all the other kids, I knew I was really part of the family."

The same will be true for you. Part of walking in God's acceptance will be embracing His assignments for you. This is not because you are earning His love, but because you will see your special, irreplaceable, and fulfilling place in His family.

> Jesus, thank You for accepting me. Help me walk in
> Your will and be a vital part of Your family. Amen.

ALL YOU NEED

Even though I walk through the valley of the
shadow of death, I fear no evil, for You are with
me.

PSALM 23:4

O ur heavenly Father is available to us at all times. He is never too busy to hear our prayers. Rather, He delights in having close, intimate communion with us. Whenever we're willing to spend time with Him, He draws near to us.

I recall a time I was feeling overwhelmed by the problems I was facing, and I was particularly lonely. I began to pour out my heart to God, telling Him how I felt and how miserable I was. Suddenly, it seemed as if the Lord Himself was standing next to me—I had no doubt He was there. His presence was tangible, although unseen. It was as if the Lord spoke to my heart: *You have Me. Am I not enough for you?*

I responded, "Yes, Lord, You are."

He is enough for you as well. No matter how you may feel, how you've been rejected by others, or how much you hurt, you always have the Lord. He is sufficient for whatever you need. So don't ignore the One who can truly fill your heart. Call out to Jesus and let Him be all you need.

Jesus, thank You for always being with
me and being exactly what I need. I
cling to You, my Savior. Amen.

OUR ADVOCATE

If anyone sins, we have an Advocate with the
Father, Jesus Christ the righteous.

1 JOHN 2:1

So you've messed up again. You've sinned. You've done what God has commanded you not to do. How can you possibly face Him?

Whenever we sin, we may feel like we've failed and that God couldn't continue to love us. However, this is when we must take heart and realize all Jesus has done for us. Jesus is not just our Savior; He is also our Advocate. When He redeemed us, He knew we could not live perfect lives. This is why He took on human flesh—to experience as we do the pressures you and I face. Therefore, He understands how deeply our wounds and fears can affect us and why we sometimes turn to sin to ease our pain. However, Jesus also knows that our iniquity is never the solution for our hurts and anxieties—it can only deepen the despair that is already there.

Jesus defends us even when we fail Him (1 John 1:9). Why? Because He died to make us free and is committed to finishing the job.

So when you sin, don't be afraid. Turn back to the Savior and repent. Run back to His loving arms, and allow Him to liberate you completely.

Jesus, I confess my sin to You and run back to You. Teach me to live in Your freedom. Amen.

DOMINION OVER DEMONS

Greater is He who is in you than he who is in the world.

1 JOHN 4:4

At times I hear people talking about demons, and I am amazed at the power they ascribe to them. While I certainly believe in demonic power, I'm not afraid of it. I am in union with One who is so far greater than all the forces of hell put together that there truly is no comparison. The Devil is unequal to the Lord and always under His dominion. The Enemy will never win a victory over Him, because the Lord is always exceedingly more powerful and wiser.

Therefore, as believers, we should not give as much credit to spiritual forces of evil as we often do. Yes, they can exert influence over us, which is why we must take every thought captive to Christ (2 Corinthians 10:5). We must also stay under the umbrella of God's protection by obeying His commands so they will not gain a foothold in us. But demons are within the confines of God's authority and cannot harm us in any way that is beyond Him to overcome.

So do not be afraid. Submit to Jesus—the One who has conquered sin and death—and you will be safe in His care.

Jesus, You are greater than any force on earth or in heaven. Keep me in the center of Your will and under Your protection. Amen.

DON'T DEBATE THE DEBATER

Where is the debater of this age? Has not God made foolish the wisdom of the world?

1 CORINTHIANS 1:20

Yesterday, we discussed the fact that the Lord has dominion over the forces of evil and will always be victorious. To take hold of this, we must understand that the way the Enemy undermines us is that he will debate with us about whether what God has said is true. He does so to tempt us to doubt the Lord (Genesis 3:1–3).

At this point, it's important that we do not underestimate the Enemy's effectiveness as a debater. Satan has argued with the greatest minds throughout history since the world began and has often won. His goal is to get us to overthink a matter until we are utterly obsessed and confounded by it. We can't sleep. We cannot get away from it. It's in every thought—every conversation. It is then he can confuse us to the point we no longer trust the Father.

Don't fall for his trap. Stop trying to figure everything out, because all you're really doing is debating the Enemy—and he's much better at it than you are. Instead, resist him by quoting God's Word and expressing your trust that the Lord always leads you to victory (Proverbs 3:5–6).

Jesus, I will not lean on my understanding,
but trust You completely, knowing You
always lead me to triumph. Amen.

USEFUL

The sacrifices of God are a broken spirit; a broken
and a contrite heart, O God, You will not despise.
PSALM 51:17

A t times, we might feel disqualified from serving God because of our past. However, remember that Moses killed an Egyptian, but the Lord delivered Israel from Egypt through him. David committed adultery with Bathsheba and had her husband, Uriah, killed, but God made him king over Israel. Mary Magdalene was once filled with demons, but Jesus trusted her to tell His disciples about His resurrection. Saul was a vicious persecutor of the church, yet the Lord worked through him as the apostle Paul to take the gospel to the Gentiles.

The difference in these people's lives was this: when they had an encounter with God, they said yes to Him. They were willing to turn from their sinful ways to doing things as He said. They didn't remain the people they once were. They chose instead to order their lives after God and follow His plan for them.

The same can be true for you. God doesn't call the equipped—He equips the called. He works through fallen, broken people to show His glory. So turn from your sin and follow Him. Trust Him to make something awesome of your life like He did for them.

Jesus, thank You for forgiving my
failures and transforming my life into
a vessel for Your glory. Amen.

POWERFUL POTENTIAL

With great power the apostles were giving
testimony to the resurrection of the Lord Jesus, and
abundant grace was upon them all.

ACTS 4:33

D o you realize that God has given you great potential? The possibilities for your life are vast. The majority of people don't realize what the Lord could do through them, and because of that, they greatly underestimate the potential within them. As a result, they shortchange themselves, achieve less than they could, and fail to dream big enough dreams.

But you can take hold of all God created you to enjoy. And that's not limited to how you can achieve great accomplishments. Rather, you can experience the spiritual depth and power of Moses, Joshua, and Elijah. You can take hold of the fulfilling, fruitful, history-changing relationship with the Lord that few people experience—not because God limits His availability, presence, or authority but because so few commit themselves to knowing Him in such profound intimacy and fellowship.

You don't have to miss all of that—you can take hold of all that God has for you. The Lord is infinite, and when He pours Himself into you, you take on His power, wisdom, and strength. There is no limit to how He can multiply your efforts to accomplish His purposes.

Jesus, I want all You have for me! Teach me
to love and serve You, my Savior! Amen.

PERFECTED THROUGH LOVE

If we love one another, God abides in us, and His love is perfected in us.

1 JOHN 4:12

Perfectionism is the attitude that tasks must be done faultlessly at all times in order for a person to be acceptable—and it's a terrible trap. The trouble with perfectionism is that, first, it misplaces a person's worth in their achievements rather than the identity Christ has given us. Second, perfectionists are usually so focused on their goals that they alienate their relationships. Finally, perfectionism is simply unsustainable—no one can be flawless 100 percent of the time.

If you find yourself trapped by perfectionism, you may feel stressed, tired, and broken. But understand that Jesus has already been perfect on your behalf. Now, what He desires for you is simply to enjoy a deeper relationship with Him and to join Him in His purposes—humbly loving the lost and hurting in His name.

God doesn't expect you to be perfect; in fact, He knows you can't be. What He wants is for you to rest in His love and show His love to others. So stop putting standards on yourself that He never intended—you're actually missing His purposes completely. Instead, let go of your perfectionist tendencies, be transparent in your brokenness, and let His love flow through you.

Jesus, I know that to minister to others, I don't need to be perfect, just loving. Let Your love flow through me. Amen.

CONTINUE TO TRUST

God causes all things to work together for good to those who love God.

ROMANS 8:28

God could have stopped what happened to you, but He didn't. After all, the Lord is all-powerful—everything in creation is under His authority. And because He did not intervene, there are doubts plaguing your thoughts. You know Jesus loves you, but now you wonder what that really means. You trust His promise to provide for you, but the unknowns are so great that fear has infected your heart. All you know at this point is that there are more questions than answers.

Sometimes there are no easy solutions, especially when the pain is profound. However, what we can know for certain is that our heavenly Father is good and loving. Absolutely nothing touches our lives without some benefit—however cloaked in mystery it may be at the moment. God wants to teach us, refine us, and transform us into His image. He does not forget or forsake us; rather, in all things He is readying us for His greater blessings.

So do not lose heart today. Do not give in to your doubts. Hang on to the truth that God is still involved in your life and you still matter to Him. And trust that somehow He is working all of this out for your good—because He undoubtedly is.

**Jesus, I don't understand it all,
but I will trust You. Amen.**

SUBMITTING THE REINS

For Your name's sake You will lead me.

PSALM 31:3

I have ridden a number of horses that seemed to sense what I desired with just a small motion on my part. They were well-trained, obedient, and lively in spirit. Riding them was a joy. On the other hand, I've had a couple of horses that were impossible. They didn't do what I wanted no matter what I tried. Some were stubborn because they'd never been trained properly, but others were that way because when they were broken, their spirits were damaged.

As I would spend time with these noble creatures, I would often think of the parallels with how we respond to God. When we are sensitive to and submit to the Lord's promptings, life is a joy even when we are plodding through rough terrain. But when we are stubborn and resistant, everything—even the easiest trails—becomes difficult.

Today, are you being sensitive to the Lord's promptings, or are you fighting Him? God wants you to join Him on this great adventure of life. He knows the best way to take and how to navigate the obstacles in a manner that won't break your spirit. Whether the ride is a joy or a trial is up to you. Let Him have the reins.

Jesus, I submit the reins of my life to You. Make me sensitive to Your promptings so I can obey You completely. Amen.

CHOOSING HIS WILL

"Your kingdom come. Your will be done, on earth as it is in heaven."

MATTHEW 6:10

The Holy Spirit will continue to work in your life until you come to the place where you can say, "Not my will, but Yours be done, Lord. My life is in Your hands. Whatever You want, I'll do." God brings us to the point where we can submit every aspect of our lives to Him—our relationships, ideas, feelings, desires, and dreams—knowing He leads us to life at its best.

The Lord's purpose in this is never to hurt us but to help us accept that His way is exceedingly, abundantly, and overwhelmingly better than ours. Because when we do so, we will have an eagerness and an enthusiasm for doing God's will—one with the energy, hopefulness, endurance, and faith that moves mountains for the sake of His kingdom.

So do not despise the Lord's training or resist Him. God's desire is to mold and refine you so He can work through you. And the challenges in your life have been given because the Holy Spirit understands what it takes to bring you into submission in a way that ultimately builds you up. His goal is to set you free to be who He created you to be—with His wisdom, power, energy, joy, enthusiasm, and vision.

Lord, I want Your will. I know Your way is always exceedingly, overwhelmingly best. Amen.

TWOFOLD HEALTH

In his illness, You restore him to health.

PSALM 41:3

I once heard a doctor describe his work as having a twofold nature. Part of his work was to clean out what didn't belong—cutting away diseased tissue or ridding the body of infection. The second aspect of his task was in assisting the healing process—helping the body to build itself back up. He would—through medication or rehabilitation—create an environment where the body could be strengthened.

In the Christian life, both cleansing and building are necessary for the healing process to be completed. The Holy Spirit will use conviction and chastisement to cut away what doesn't belong in your life now that you have a relationship with God. This is painful because what He removes is often something you rely on for earthly comfort, security, or worth, but is actually undermining your spiritual health. Once you have submitted to this cleansing process, however, He then builds you up—giving you the strength, courage, and endurance to embrace the fullness of God's plan for you.

Are you in one or both of these phases? Is the Lord setting you free from bondage and building you up for service? Do not fear. Your Great Physician knows exactly what He is doing to make you a healthy, fruitful member of the body of Christ.

**Jesus, thank You for healing me spiritually.
You are, indeed, my Great Physician. Amen.**

WAIT WITH HOPE

My soul, wait in silence for God only, for my hope is from Him.

PSALM 62:5

Today, declare your certainty that God is working everything together for your good. The last thing your heavenly Father wants you to do is to despair or passively hope everything will work out. Unfortunately, many people do just that—they skeptically wait for the Lord to open a door, complaining the whole time.

Instead, use the waiting moments of your life to pray and know God better. Praise your heavenly Father for all He has done in the past and what He is doing in the future. Likewise, use this time to prepare by actively applying Scripture to your life and helping others know Him.

Because God has a plan for your life, you can know for certain that He is using even the most trying circumstances of your life to ready you for His greater goals. As you walk with Him, He is molding and shaping you to fulfill His purposes, which fit you perfectly and will satisfy your soul. From your perspective, it may look like you are way off course, but you can know for certain that from God's vantage point, you are right on track and following His pathway. So speak out in faith that what He has for you is good.

Jesus, I trust You are working everything together for good! Amen.

A HINDRANCE OF SELF-WILL

*"Seek first His kingdom and His righteousness, and
all these things will be added to you."*

MATTHEW 6:33

I s there a driving goal in your life that takes God's place in your heart? Perhaps it's to attain a certain level of status or have a certain kind of relationship. You know what it is because it consumes your thoughts, prayers, and sleepless nights. Sadly, it may also be blinding you to God's plans.

At the core of this is *self-will*—the uncontrolled impulse inside us that demands our own way. So when considering the pursuit of God's will, we must be aware that our minds may be so overtaken with our own goals that we've become insensitive to the Lord's promptings. Don't let this happen.

God wants to meet the deepest desires of your heart. Yes, He may have a different way to satisfy your soul than you've chosen. But take heart; He is not insensitive to the longings in you—and, in fact, answers them more fully than you can imagine. However, realize that He is also vigilant to ensure that nothing else takes residence on the throne of your heart—which is His rightful place. So make God your driving goal, and leave the rest to Him.

**Jesus, reveal any self-will that's hindering
me, and take Your rightful place on
the throne of my heart. Amen.**

THE HINDRANCE OF UNWISE COUNSEL

Blessed is the man who does not walk in the counsel of the wicked, nor stand in the path of sinners.

PSALM 1:1

Are you aware of the either subtle or overt ways your friends and loved ones direct your life? Whether you realize it or not, the people around you will influence your choices and will always have an opinion when you have a decision to make. The problem is that they probably know even less of what God's will is for your life than you do. They sift what they see in your life through their own personality, needs, values, and perspective. So you cannot rely on other people to discover the Lord's plan for you.

Can you call on godly friends for wise counsel about what the Bible says concerning your situation? Of course you can. But you must be very wise about who you allow to speak into your life. The ungodly influence of others can lead you to wrong decisions and even away from the Lord's path for you.

So when there are forks in the road and you don't know what to do, you cannot take a public vote among your friends or family members concerning your course of action. You have to listen to God.

Jesus, please reveal and protect me from unwise counsel. Lead me in Your way, Lord. Amen.

DETECTING FAULTY COUNSEL

The thoughts of the righteous are just, but the
counsels of the wicked are deceitful.

PROVERBS 12:5

How can you detect bad advice? It is easier than you may realize. Unwise counselors generally make either little or no mention of God or twist His message to suit their ideas. Their guidance will be based on what they think and what's acceptable in the culture rather than on what the Lord has taught is wise and true. In fact, unwise advisers may suggest a course of action that is far from biblical.

Likewise, imprudent counselors may recommend reading material that is non-Christian or criticize the godly people you know. In addition, you may notice an absence of prayer in your interactions with them. Remember, their goal will not be to help you find God's will or submit to Him in your decisions. Rather, they may wish to tell you what you want to hear in order to win your confidence and approval, to make you dependent on them, or even to control you.

So be careful to avoid counselors with an ungodly lifestyle. This applies to both professionals and friends—nonbelievers and Christians. If someone is not living in submission to Christ, it's doubtful that he or she will be able to give godly advice.

Jesus, sometimes bad advice is so subtle that
it's difficult to recognize. Please reveal it to me,
and help me obey You in all things. Amen.

KNOW HIS WAYS

Show me Your ways, O LORD; teach me Your paths.
PSALM 25:4 NKJV

One of the reasons we sometimes miss how the Lord is working in our lives is because we don't really know God and His ways. Maybe you would say, "I've received Jesus as my Savior. Surely I know Him. What more is there to understand?" But if you only know Jesus as your Redeemer—and not as your Great Physician, Lord of lords, Good Shepherd, High Priest, Mighty Warrior, and all the other ways He ministers to you—there will be a great deal you're missing about His will and how He operates. Even worse, you may not trust Him as deeply as you should because you don't truly know His character and how profoundly He cares for you.

Remember, knowing God's will means understanding how *He thinks* about your situation. This makes learning about Him and His principles absolutely crucial to your pursuit of His plan. The less you know about Him, the less you'll know how to listen to Him, which in turn means the less you're going to hear from Him. But the more you understand about Christ and who He is, the more you'll be able to perceive His activity in your circumstances. Therefore, set your heart to know Him.

Jesus, I want to know and love You more. Show me Your ways. I put my hope in You. Amen.

THE HINDRANCE OF UNBELIEF

They were not able to enter because of unbelief.
HEBREWS 3:19

Do you trust that God speaks with you about every area of your life? Do you truly believe that He still communicates today—that He interacts with you personally and helps you with the issues you care about deeply?

We may all desire to respond, "Yes, absolutely!" to such questions. Perhaps we would even agree Scripture provides us with moral guidelines for living. But there are many Christians who don't truly believe that God speaks, and they show they don't by their actions. When the Father communicates with them personally about some crucial matter of their lives, they do not obey Him. They ignore His promptings—either because it's too costly or because they're afraid. But at its core, this is unbelief—doubt concerning the Lord's character and wisdom. And it's a sin.

Friend, it may be very challenging when what God reveals to you does not make sense or frightens you in some way. But just because you do not comprehend or like the Lord's plan doesn't give you a right to doubt it. The Lord God is speaking to you. If you want to walk in His will, you'll have to push past your doubt and fear and step out in faith.

Jesus, help me trust You even when it's costly and I am afraid. Amen.

THE HINDRANCE OF UNWORTHINESS

Your hand shall lead me, and Your right hand shall hold me.

PSALM 139:10 NKJV

D o you ever find yourself thinking, *Why would the Lord ever speak to me? I'm not someone who merits His direction. Why should I think God's going to say anything to me?* Understand that your feelings of inferiority can hinder you from hearing the Lord. You may not think this has anything to do with God's will, but it does. If you have a poor self-image and don't understand your identity in Jesus, you can block yourself from receiving what He has for you.

This may seem unfair, and you may think, *I cannot help how I feel about myself.* However, this is really about how you see Jesus and why it's so important that you accept who you are in Him. The reason Christ gives you His Spirit to indwell you is for you to have an active, vibrant relationship with God. He makes you worthy of His love and concern. Certainly, He has a great deal to say to you—about every detail of your life!

So stop doubting. Accept that the One who died for you wants to communicate with you. He loves you and has a great deal to say about all He's created you to be.

Jesus, thank You for making me worthy and speaking to me. I will listen to You. Amen.

THE HINDRANCE OF BUSYNESS

The upright will dwell in Your presence.

PSALM 140:13

Are you so busy serving God that you don't actually have time to spend with Him? We all make choices when constructing our schedules—and often, we may show that the Lord is actually our last priority by how much time we set apart for Him.

This can happen to anyone. I've even known pastors who have stayed so busy "serving the Lord" they couldn't tell you when their last quiet time was or when they last heard from Him. Certainly, they may have prayed for others or read the Bible seeking out a sermon, but that's not the same as having deep, intimate fellowship with the Lord. Sadly, these ministers fill their lives with so much activity that they don't have time to seek Him. And if they don't have a moment to bow before Him and understand His will, then they really never know what He actually desires for them to do.

But you see, it is only what is done in obedience to God that lasts and makes a truly enduring difference. So if you are not consulting the Father about what He wants you to do, then much of what you are running after may be for naught. Don't make that mistake. Invest in what endures by spending time with God.

Jesus, I bow before You to listen. Speak, Lord; Your servant is listening. Amen.

WHAT REALLY MATTERS

"I want you to show love, not offer sacrifices. I want you to know me more than I want burnt offerings."

HOSEA 6:6 NLT

I n Luke 10:38–42, Jesus went to visit a family He loved—Lazarus, Mary, and Martha. When He arrived at their house, Mary stopped everything she was doing so she could learn from Him. Martha, however, was distracted by all that was still to be done, so she kept working. She also felt slighted that Mary wasn't helping with the chores.

In a culture that valued hospitality as theirs did, Martha's reaction was understandable. She wanted her home to be as comfortable and welcoming to Jesus as possible out of respect for Him. However, when Martha complained about Mary, Jesus replied, "Martha, you are worried and bothered about so many things; but only one thing is necessary, for Mary has chosen the good part, which shall not be taken away from her" (Luke 10:41–42).

From their story, we learn that God's expectations for us may be very different from the ones we have for ourselves. Yes, He wants us to serve Him. But His even greater desire for us is that we spend time with Him because He knows that our effective service flows from our moments of profound, intimate communion with Him.

Jesus, I set my heart on You. Speak to me, help me love You more, and lead me to serve as You desire. Amen.

THE HINDRANCE
OF BITTERNESS

Lord, deal kindly with me for Your name's sake;
because Your lovingkindness is good, deliver me.
PSALM 109:21

Do you have unhealed resentment toward God? Do you ever think to yourself, *These horrible things happened to me, but where was God? Why didn't He protect me?* When you experience difficult trials, deep roots of fear and bitterness can take hold that you mistakenly attribute to Him. Consequently, your God-directed anger can become one of the greatest hindrances to your knowing His will. He may speak to you out of love and kindness, but if unforgiveness rules your heart, you'll find it difficult to believe what He says.

But friend, your God is not cruel toward you. He is loving, kind, sacrificial, and wise. Yes, He may have allowed painful circumstances to touch your life, but He didn't necessarily *cause* them, and He certainly did not intend evil. Likewise, He wouldn't have permitted the trial to affect you if there were no benefit in it for you. Therefore, soften your heart toward Him and allow Him to speak to you. Your God wants to heal you with His loving-kindness. Don't turn Him away. Rather, invite Him to bring light to the darkened places.

Jesus, please root out my anger. I know
You are loving and kind to me. Amen.

THE HINDRANCE OF HARBORED SIN

Our old self was crucified with Him, in order that
our body of sin might be done away with.

ROMANS 6:6

D o you realize that harbored sin is one of the greatest hindrances to hearing the voice of God? Don't just dismiss that as something you know. Take it seriously. Habitual sin clouds your mind—dulling you from hearing what God has to say to you.

Of course, we all sin and fight battles with temptation. However, there comes a point when we pass from *committing* a sin to *harboring* it—embracing it as part of who we are and what we're entitled to. This happens as God addresses something in our lives and we ignore Him. He tells us, *This is hurting you. But I want to set you free and truly meet that need in your life. Let go of this destructive habit.* You know exactly what that is because it immediately comes to mind. But you've become enslaved to it—you refuse to let it go.

That harbored sin is clouding your vision, dividing your mind, and distracting from the abundant life your Father desires for you. He has better for you. So let go of that sin, get the accountability and help that will usher you into freedom, and trust God to fill your needs in a more profoundly satisfying way than you've ever imagined.

Jesus, I repent. Help me to be free. Amen.

PRUNED

"Every branch that bears fruit, He prunes it so that it may bear more fruit."

JOHN 15:2

At times there will be people, privileges, and blessings that are removed from your life without explanation. Suddenly, they're gone, and you may wonder if you've done something wrong or if God is punishing you. However, take heart; Jesus told us in advance that each fruitful believer would be pruned for greater effectiveness. He cuts out the extra branches, refocusing our lives to be even more productive for the sake of His kingdom.

One area where we may experience this pruning is in places of past woundedness. Whether we realize it or not, we may be loving others with damaged emotions, drawn to unhealthy situations, and even destructive to ourselves—all issues that keep us from embracing the Lord's purposes for us. So God reveals our harmful attachments by cutting them out of our lives and showing us how detrimentally important to us they were.

The pruning process is not easy, but it is necessary. God loves you too much to let you live in bondage or miss His plan for you because of old wounds. So He will prune you in order to heal you. Don't resist Him. Understand that this is for your good and will lead you to more fruitfulness than you ever imagined.

Jesus, thank You for cutting out what doesn't belong in my life and for healing me. Amen.

PERSEVERE

Be sober in all things, endure hardship, do the work
of an evangelist, fulfill your ministry.

2 TIMOTHY 4:5

Today, persevere. Do not give up, no matter what happens. Continue to seek God and His will for you. You do so by realizing that the difficulties you encounter do not automatically mean you're supposed to change direction. The hardships you endure may delay you in reaching your goals, but they aren't necessarily a dead end for you. During your moments of defeat, God is teaching you something that will help you succeed later on. Paul didn't interpret the tragic events of his life as a reason to stop pressing forward. He knew what God was calling him to do and was committed to accomplishing it. You must be as well.

Also, do not confuse experiencing setbacks with being a failure. Your mistakes, losses, challenges, and defeats are only temporary; they do not define who you are. Instead, look to the Lord to determine the truth about your identity: a forgiven child of God who has an eternal purpose and hope.

Through the power and wisdom of His Holy Spirit indwelling you, your heavenly Father will give you the ability to stay on course. So do not give up. Draw near to the Lord and allow His power and love to sustain you.

Jesus, help me keep pressing forward even when trouble arises. I want to honor You in all I do. Amen.

A KIND WITNESS

*"You shall be My witnesses . . . even to the remotest
part of the earth."*

ACTS 1:8

How did you come to know Jesus as your Savior? Many people have accepted Christ due to the kind and loving influence of a Christian friend or coworker. This is why it is so important to treat others with respect and acceptance. You never know when you will be able to share the gospel with them, and you want your relationship to be an open door that God can work through.

Of course, this may be challenging, especially because unbelievers sometimes operate with such contrasting standards and values to Christians. Despite such differences, however, remember that the most important thing about a person is whether or not they know Jesus. God is responsible to change sinful behavior, but your witness in another person's life may have everlasting implications. This doesn't mean you must condone ungodliness, but you also aren't accountable to change it.

Everybody needs the Lord—even people who seemingly resist all your godly overtures. But keep on expressing the love and grace of God through your words and deeds. The Lord will work through you to change other people's lives in a wonderful, eternal way.

**Jesus, love others through me, and help
me lead them to Your wonderful salvation
through my words and deeds. Amen.**

LIGHT YOUR WORLD

"Let your light shine before men in such a way that they may see your good works, and glorify your Father who is in heaven."

MATTHEW 5:16

L ight has always been a symbol of life and important for survival. In ancient times, Israelite women checked their lamps throughout the night, making sure the light stayed strong and sent the message, "All is well."

However, we must never underestimate the importance of the spiritual light Christ shines through us as His followers. Jesus wants our lives to be like powerful lamps, sending out evidence of His presence and a beacon to those in darkness. When people see you, they should see the light of Christ and be drawn to God.

So consider, can those around you see Jesus through your words and behavior? Does your life make others want to know more about the Lord? Perhaps your life is not what it should be at the moment. Maybe you're discouraged, feeling inadequate, or defeated by the circumstances of your life. But remember that Jesus fuels your lamp—He is the One who shines through you and reminds you, "All is well." So make sure your light stays strong by turning to Him for the strength and wisdom you need. Because He is the Light of life and He wants to illuminate the world through you.

Jesus, may others see Your light in me and know You as their Lord and Savior. Amen.

ALL FROM HIM

You rule over all, and in Your hand is power and might; and it lies in Your hand to make great and to strengthen everyone.

1 CHRONICLES 29:12

D o you know how to receive strength when the going gets tough or your future appears to be in jeopardy? Do you know how to enter into rest when all your earthly hope fails? If you don't, then find comfort in today's Scripture. It provides a wonderful reminder that every good thing comes from God (James 1:17). Therefore, when troubles arise, immediately focus on Him.

The Lord is all-knowing and all-powerful, so you know that everything needed to overcome your circumstances is available in Him. Likewise, He is the Good Shepherd, who is gentle and compassionate in nature and intimately involved in the lives of His people. Because He loves you, He gathers you close and carries you when you are too weary to walk.

Finally, remember that your God is the Supreme Ruler of all creation, and everything you're experiencing has already been factored into His great plans for you. So when your problems seem insurmountable, submit them all to God, who is available to you, powerful, compassionate, and wise.

Jesus, thank You for giving me Your strength. You are always my hope regardless of what happens! Amen.

PREPARED FOR BLESSING

Blessed is the man whom You instruct, O LORD,
and teach out of Your law.

PSALM 94:12 NKJV

G od has a good purpose for every situation and stressor you encounter. This may appear odd to you today if your life is especially busy, painful, or out of control. But understand, there are no coincidences with Him. He is the Architect behind every blessing that comes your way—and many times that begins with helping you understand how weak you are on your own. This is why you don't have to wonder if God truly has a plan for your life. He does—to a detail you cannot begin to conceive.

So that extra assignment, that painful reminder, that conflict, that added challenge—none of it is a surprise to Him. In times of trial and sorrow, take heart that He has allowed your difficulties to bring some deeper understanding of Him to you. He is in the midst of blessing you with the development of your character, faith, hope, and some good gift that will remain with you forever.

The Lord your God is preparing you for a blessing—not necessarily in a material sense, but spiritually and emotionally. So don't despise the pressures and trials; rather, embrace them with His grace. And keep watch for all He will do for you.

Jesus, I trust You. Thank You for the blessings
You give me through these trials. Amen.

THE RELATIONSHIP OF FAITH

Without faith it is impossible to please Him, for he
who comes to God must believe that He is and that
He is a rewarder of those who seek Him.

HEBREWS 11:6

Through years of walking with God, Abraham developed the ability to see beyond his immediate challenges to the Lord who had great plans for him. He knew God could overcome any obstacle. So when the Lord commanded Abraham to sacrifice his son Isaac on the altar, Abraham did not complain or cower in fear. He trusted that the Lord had important purposes for the request. Abraham believed God—that He would accomplish everything He had promised (Genesis 15:6).

In Abraham's life we see two things that are essential to living a faith-motivated life. First, we must believe that God exists—that He is real, true, and trustworthy. Second, we must believe that He is faithful to do what He's promised us. Through our intimate relationship with Him, we are fully convinced of His holy and loving character—that He acts only for our good.

If you've been trying to work up your faith and have failed, it may be because you are building it on the wrong foundation. Faith is not a goal you can work to achieve. It comes as you relate to God personally and see who He is. So grow your faith. Know Him and believe.

Jesus, I believe You. Help me to know
and love You more. Amen.

JUNE

MORE THAN ADEQUATE

"That they may believe that the LORD . . . has appeared to you."

EXODUS 4:5

Every one of the great saints in Scripture—Abraham, Moses, Joshua, David, Peter, Paul, and so on—felt inadequate for the tasks the Lord gave them. On their own, they knew they were unable to accomplish what He was asking of them. But they also knew "with God all things are possible" (Matthew 19:26).

Take Moses, for example. Even though the Lord miraculously called him from the burning bush, Moses was fearful he could not successfully deliver the people of Israel from Egyptian bondage. His timidity was not only in confronting the powerful Egyptians. Moses was certain the Israelites would reject him as well. He said, "What if they will not believe me or listen to what I say?" (Exodus 4:1).

You may feel inadequate to accomplish all God has called you to do. But take heart—you are completely insufficient, but *He is more than sufficient*. The challenge you face exists to reveal *His* awesome existence through you. And when the Lord has given you success and gained His triumph, everyone will know it was God who was with you the whole time. He will get the glory and you will have the victory.

Jesus, I go forward with faith. I know You are more than adequate for this task and deserve all the honor and glory. Amen.

FREEDOM IN FORGIVENESS

*"If you forgive others for their transgressions, your
heavenly Father will also forgive you."*

MATTHEW 6:14

Is there someone you need to forgive today? If you're having
trouble, remember the benefits forgiveness gives you.

First, pardoning the other person is the only way to overcome
the negative feelings that are keeping you captive. You give God the
opportunity to replace your resentment and hurt with concern, pity,
or compassion. Second, the Lord can help you accept the person who
wounded you without feeling the need to exact retribution. He gives
you understanding into why they acted as they did—an appreciation
for their situation and the underlying issues that caused their behavior. He helps you take them as they are—just as Jesus does for you.
Third, resentment can cause us to be self-centered—focused on our
wounds rather than on loving others. Through forgiveness, God can
refocus us to minister to and care for others.

Forgiveness is a process that can be painful; however, you cannot
afford to hold on to an unforgiving spirit. You must forgive others
and find out what it means to be really free. If you'll persevere and
keep your eyes on the One who forgave you, it will be a liberating
force like nothing else you've experienced. So forgive.

**Jesus, I choose to forgive today as You have
forgiven me. Increase my love and understanding
for the ones who have hurt me. Amen.**

DON'T AVOID HIM

Though we are overwhelmed by our sins, you
forgive them all.

PSALM 65:3 NLT

After disobeying God, Adam and Eve found themselves in a terrible place. Their first reaction was to run and hide because of their fear and feelings of unworthiness. They avoided God. Instead of coming to Him to reestablish their relationship, they evaded any interaction with Him. Finally, when He confronted them with eating from the Tree of the Knowledge of Good and Evil, they refused to accept responsibility and blamed each other for the transgression.

We can read Adam and Eve's story and see everything they did wrong. However, if we're honest, we'll admit we do the same thing. When we sin, instead of acknowledging and confessing it, we frequently look for ways to hide from God, avoiding the issues He wants to address in our lives. And when we do come before Him, we often shift the blame to others. However, we're each responsible for our actions, regardless of the circumstances or who else is involved.

Don't let guilt or shame keep you from the Lord. Just as He sought out Adam and Eve to restore fellowship, He seeks you. Stop hiding. Turn to Him, accept responsibility, and receive His forgiveness. No good ever came from running from Him.

Jesus, reveal my sin to me so I can repent. I know
You set me free by Your forgiveness. Amen.

PRAYING HIS WILL

This is the confidence which we have before Him, that, if we ask anything according to His will, He hears us.

1 JOHN 5:14

Do you long to pray more effectively? So often we hear requests to the Lord to provide, protect, or bless. But there is another very powerful way to pray. When you use Scripture to speak to God, your appeal contains His own divine authority.

Consider Colossians 1:9–10: "We have not ceased to pray for you and to ask that you may be filled with the knowledge of His will in all spiritual wisdom and understanding, so that you will walk in a manner worthy of the Lord, to please Him in all respects, bearing fruit in every good work." Whether you pray this for yourself or for others, you know you are praying in agreement with Christ. He wants to give our seeking hearts enough information to trust and follow Him, so we will conduct ourselves in a manner that exalts Him.

Therefore, when you go before the Lord, open Scripture—which you know are the very thoughts and words of God—and allow it to guide you in understanding His plans and purposes. Then you will be able to intercede with confidence, knowing you are praying in His will.

Jesus, lead me to the Scripture You desire me to pray, and may Your will be done in my life. Amen.

WINNING THE BATTLE

Our struggle is . . . against the spiritual forces of wickedness.

EPHESIANS 6:12

It is important for you to realize that there's always a spiritual conflict raging around you, so you can battle sin effectively and live in a manner pleasing to the Lord.

The struggle you face exists in three areas. *First, you have an internal enemy.* Ever since the fall in the garden of Eden, our hearts have been bent away from God. This means you will always be tempted to do wrong as long as you remain in your earthly body. Thankfully, the Holy Spirit continuously draws you toward the Lord. *Next, you have an external enemy,* which are the ungodly beliefs and philosophies of the world (1 John 2:15). As a believer, you're called to be salt and light to those around you without allowing their ways to influence you or distract you from Christ. *Third, you have an accursed Enemy—the Devil.* Satan's desire is to replace God as the lord of your life and dishonor Jesus through you. Resist him by always exalting the Savior.

Successful soldiers understand their enemies in order to defeat them. Therefore, be aware of what you face in this spiritual battle. Stand firm in Christ by arming yourself with God's Word.

Jesus, spiritual enemies require spiritual weapons. Protect me and teach me to exalt You in all things. Amen.

LIVING IN VICTORY

*I press on toward the goal for the prize of the
upward call of God in Christ Jesus.*
PHILIPPIANS 3:14

D o you want to live in the victory Christ has given you? If you
hope to finish well, you must exhibit the following traits.

Courage, being willing to risk failure. Though it's natural to want
to appear strong and capable, God delights in empowering you in
your weaknesses, so He gets the glory. *Confidence*, knowing that even
when God calls you to a task beyond your ability, you can move
ahead because He will enable you to do His will. *Commitment* in the
journey, understanding that the Lord promises to guide you, provide
whatever is needed, and strengthen you along the way. *Persistence*,
realizing that the road you're traveling is full of distractions, opposition, and obstacles that'll tempt you to give up, but that Jesus is
worth your endurance. *Focus*, forgetting what lies behind and pressing forward to what lies ahead because of who it is that calls you
(Philippians 3:13–14).

The key to success in this race is an all-consuming desire to
honor Christ and reach the goal. So don't give up or settle for the
immediate gratification the world offers. Understand the prize that
awaits you, and press on.

Jesus, help me live in Your victory—with courage,
confidence, commitment, persistence, and
focus—so You can receive the glory. Amen.

CONSTANT ACCESS

This was in accordance with the eternal purpose
which He carried out in Christ Jesus our Lord, in
whom we have boldness and confident access.

EPHESIANS 3:11–12

Wouldn't it be wonderful if you could call your pastor or a trusted Christian counselor at any moment for whatever concerns you? We all long to have someone we respect, who is wise and godly, to ask about the questions on our hearts, run our ideas by, and who would always help us make decisions. Thankfully, we can have that kind of relationship with Jesus, who is with us at every moment.

Jesus is continuously available to you in whatever it is you may need. He has lived a pure and blameless life on earth, understands the pressures and temptations you face, and knows how to help you overcome it all. Likewise, He knows what heaven is like—what it will require of you and what it will take to prepare you for it. And the best part is that He is both sitting at the right hand of the Father and He is also present with you always through His Holy Spirit.

In other words, Jesus offers you counsel that is better, wiser, timelier, and more insightful than anyone else ever could. So rejoice in the access you've been given, and enjoy it often.

Jesus, thank You for saving me and giving me counsel. You are so good to me! Amen.

STEP OUT IN FAITH

I did this so you would trust not in human wisdom
but in the power of God.

1 CORINTHIANS 2:5 NLT

One of the things that can hinder us from taking hold of God's will is when we have an aversion to taking risks. We prefer to play it safe by gathering as many facts as possible, analyzing our options, and stepping out only when we're reasonably certain of the outcome. We don't want to experience loss or heartache, and we're afraid of looking foolish or incompetent, incurring financial difficulty, or facing physical danger. From a human viewpoint, eliminating uncertainty makes sense.

But from God's perspective, calling us to step out from our comfort zones is absolutely necessary to our growth in the Christian life. Of course, from His viewpoint, there is no real uncertainty, because He has control over all things.

Is God asking you to step out in faith in some manner that doesn't make sense to you? Remember that your spiritual maturity will be hampered if you refuse to submit to God. The Lord understands your fears and timidity, but He still expects your obedience. Therefore, step out in faith and watch what He does to grow your relationship with Him. Certainly, He'll never let you down.

Jesus, even when I don't understand, I will obey You, knowing the center of Your will is the safest place to be. Amen.

COMFORT IN DARK SEASONS

You light my lamp; the LORD my God illumines my darkness.

PSALM 18:28

From one day to the next, Joseph lost almost everything—his family, home, and freedom (Genesis 37). How stunned and rejected he must have felt when his brothers sold him and he was taken to Egypt as a slave. No one would have blamed Joseph for feeling devastated.

Life is like that at times. Sudden changes usher us into dark seasons where we feel as if we've lost everything. We don't understand God's purposes and may even wonder if He's abandoned us. But the Lord didn't forsake Joseph, and He is not rejecting us either. Even as a slave in a foreign land, Joseph experienced God's favor. And from his life, we know that a key to walking through dark seasons is to embrace the Lord's constant presence with us.

Friend, because of the indwelling Holy Spirit—given to you permanently at salvation—you belong to Jesus forever. No circumstance, suffering, or loss can separate you from His love (Romans 8:38–39). You are not alone in this dark time. So give thanks for Christ's promise to be with you. Because He will sustain you in difficulty and will lift you up in due time, just as He did for Joseph.

Jesus, You comfort, guide, and sustain me in the dark seasons. I know You will deliver me, and I praise Your wonderful name. Amen.

OVERCOMING THE SILENCE

*Oh, what joy for those whose disobedience is
forgiven, whose sin is put out of sight!*

PSALM 32:1 NLT

Have you ever experienced a time when God was silent toward you? Most of the time, when the Father is quiet, it is because there is something within you He's already pointed out that He wants you to deal with. Notice, I said "most of the time." This does not always apply. But usually, when someone is having trouble hearing the Lord, it is because there's something He's already told you, and you've ignored Him—sweeping the issue under the rug and refusing to deal with it.

If this is the case, understand it is important that you address the issue because it is crucial to your spiritual health. You are only hurting yourself by refusing to give up your addiction, sinful actions, or destructive coping mechanisms.

When I have experienced such times and dealt with the attitudes or behaviors in question, God's will became crystal clear to me. The same will be true for you. Therefore, the wisest thing you can do is pray the prayer below and obey whatever He reveals.

Jesus, search my heart. Show me what is
blinding me to Your will. And give me the
strength and wisdom to turn away from the
sinful attitudes that are preventing me from
following You in complete obedience. Amen.

VOICE YOUR GRATEFULNESS

*"He who offers a sacrifice of thanksgiving honors
Me; and to him who orders his way aright I shall
show the salvation of God."*

PSALM 50:23

Giving thanks and making a positive confession of faith in God can be a powerful force in your life. This does not mean speaking boastfully or claiming the Lord's deliverance apart from His expressed will for your life. Rather, voicing your gratefulness to God for His faithfulness and provision is an indication of your submission to His will regardless of your hopes or expectations.

Life may not be turning out the way you thought it would. You may be struggling with your circumstances. However, because you serve a risen Lord, you know that no matter what you face in this life, God is greater and will ultimately deliver you. He will bless you as you seek Him. He will guard, protect, and lead you to a place of fruitfulness and hope. Therefore, you always have cause for praise.

With this in mind, take time to exalt and worship God today. Tell Jesus you trust Him to carry your burdens and help you through every difficulty. Give Him thanks for every blessing you can think of. Because your God will never fail you, and praising Him will pave the way for your deliverance.

**Wholeheartedly I thank and praise
You, Jesus, trusting You to always
lead me the right way. Amen.**

COMPLETE OBEDIENCE

*"If anyone serves Me, he must follow Me . . . If
anyone serves Me, the Father will honor him."*

JOHN 12:26

True obedience to God means doing *what* He says, *when* He says, *how* He says, *as long as* He says, *until* what He says is accomplished. Unfortunately, this concept is sometimes lost on us. We can rationalize partial obedience—which is actually disobedience—to the point of missing God's best blessings.

So if you are wondering why sometimes—though you try and try—your life still doesn't work out, the answer could be how submitted you are to the Lord and His purposes. If you're experiencing spiritual frustration, there may be an area of disobedience in your life that you have not addressed. Perhaps God has asked something of you, and in response, you have ignored Him or done only part of what He requires—in your timing and way rather than His.

Consider your ways carefully. Is there a particular area of your life that the Lord is continually bringing to your attention? When you go to Him in prayer, does the same issue surface repeatedly? If the Lord addresses something in you, don't continue doing it *your* way instead of *His*. Submit to Him. Because when you do, everything else will fall into place.

Jesus, I want to obey You. Reveal
where I have fallen short so I may
submit to You completely. Amen.

IN PROGRESS

Having been freed from sin and enslaved to God,
you derive your benefit, resulting in sanctification,
and the outcome, eternal life.

ROMANS 6:22

No matter how you've messed up, realize that you are a work in progress. God is molding you into a person with whom He wants to live and fellowship forever. Because of this, you have the hope that you are not going to be the same person tomorrow that you are today. If you continue to walk with God, you will be more like Christ—with more of His character, grace, wisdom, and power. Your mistakes are not your identity; who He is making you into is who you were always meant to be.

Jesus is writing His story into your life. He is building eternal value into you—replicating His character, preparing you for good works, and establishing His kingdom in you. So your mistakes are not the end. You are still in progress.

You may not like who you are today, and that's okay. Because God is at work in you—transforming you and preparing you for a life you are going to love. Therefore, don't give up or give in to disheartenment. You have every reason to live and have hope. Cling to Him and trust that the best is still to come.

**Jesus, thank You for seeing value in me,
transforming me, and making me Yours. Amen.**

FAITHFUL IN ALL

"He who is faithful in a very little thing is faithful also in much."

LUKE 16:10

God can absolutely revolutionize your life. Regardless of whether that means a change of career, location, relationship, or situation—the Lord can work supernaturally in your circumstances. However, you must be willing to do what He says—in His timing and way. Are you willing to trust Him wholeheartedly?

Hymn writer John H. Sammis expressed it like this: "Trust and obey, for there's no other way to be happy in Jesus, but to trust and obey." Let me add that there is no such thing as joy apart from Jesus. Without a right relationship with Christ, you will never have the contentment, peace, or assurance you were created for. Nothing else in this world can ever truly satisfy as He can.

So to become a wholly surrendered disciple of Jesus, you must begin by obeying Him in every aspect of your life, however small it may appear. Unless you say yes to the seemingly little instructions from the Lord, you will never really know what your life can be or what wonderful blessings can be yours. Why risk losing when you can be certain of winning? Obey God and leave the consequences to Him.

Jesus, I want to be obedient and faithful to You even in the smallest things. Lead me in every way, my Lord. Amen.

STEP-BY-STEP

The Lord directs the steps of the godly. He delights in every detail of their lives.

PSALM 37:23 NLT

There will be moments in your walk with Jesus when He will only show you the next step instead of disclosing the entire plan to you. You will feel like saying, "Lord, what are You doing? How are You going to work this out?"

But this is the way the Lord operates. He gives you sufficient light in order to travel to the next point on His road map. When you reach that place, He gives you the next clue on the journey. This is the way He teaches you to be fully dependent on Him. If He showed you the full story and how to do everything at one time, you'd run off, doing your own thing. Next thing you know, you're stepping off a cliff, because you think, *I've got this.*

That's why the will of God usually comes a step at a time. He knows that we would bypass the very obstacles and challenges that prepare us and make the journey successful. But we simply cannot lose doing what God wants us to do, when He wants us to do it, and in the manner He says to proceed. This is the most certain way to success.

Jesus, thank You for teaching me to depend on You. I will trust in You step-by-step. Amen.

ACKNOWLEDGE THE GIVER

*"Bring the whole tithe . . . test Me now in this . . . if
I will not open for you the windows of heaven and
pour out for you a blessing until it overflows."*

MALACHI 3:10

G od asks only that you obey Him, and when you do, He joyfully opens the floodgates of blessing for you. We see this
principle illustrated when the prophet Malachi spoke to a generation
of Hebrews who had turned away from the Lord. They were no longer
obeying God or bringing their sacrifices to the temple. As a result,
the entire nation was suffering. So Malachi called the people back to
obedient giving with this word from the Lord. God asked them only
to obey His commandments and give one-tenth of their produce—a
tithe—to Him. He gave back a blessing that was so great, they could
not contain it.

This principle applies to us as well. God is the One who gives us
all we have. He doesn't take from us or draw authority by asking for
sacrifices. The exact opposite is true. The Lord gives us His power,
resources, and wisdom freely, and it is when we acknowledge it and
honor Him as God that He generously pours out blessings from His
infinite storehouse in heaven.

Jesus, I know everything I have comes from Your
hand. I commit my tithe, talents, and time to
You. Thank You for providing for me. Amen.

WAIT IN FAITH

Rest in the LORD and wait patiently for Him.
PSALM 37:7

S ometimes the days, weeks, months, and even years can pass without an answer from God about something very dear to us. And if you're in such a season, I encourage you to take heart and don't give up hope. Understand that waiting on God's timing is not only one of the most profitable lessons you will ever learn as a believer, but one of the most necessary. I have petitioned God on many occasions and received only silence as an answer. At times, it seemed as if I waited forever for a response. But however long the wait, God has *always* come through for me. And it was through those times of waiting He taught me to trust Him more.

Yes, waiting is one of the most difficult things you'll do as a Christian because there is always that underlying doubt that the Father will answer your prayers. This is especially true when others are receiving what your heart desires. However, God has very important reasons for having you wait, and they are—without exception—*always* for your benefit. Do not doubt God. Keep trusting and waiting because He will lift you up in due time and give you beyond what you imagine and what you truly need.

Jesus, I wait for You, trusting that the delays are not denials but are important for Your purposes. Amen.

PREPARATION TIME

I will wait on Your name, for it is good.

PSALM 52:9

David was only sixteen when he was anointed king of Israel; yet he did not take the throne until he was thirty. Certainly, there were moments when David must have thought God had forgotten him. However, everything the Lord promised David came to pass, but it was only after He had thoroughly trained David to serve Him.

Likewise, what you are praying for may be God's will for you, but He must prepare you for it in His timing. Think of it this way: if you assemble a model airplane, you must first wait for the glue to dry before launching your aircraft. Perhaps after two hours, the glue looks nearly set, but not quite solid. Because you're eager to get started, you take your plane outside and hoist it into the air. Sadly, before it gains altitude, it comes crashing to the ground—pieces falling everywhere because it just wasn't ready.

The same is true for the blessings God has for you. Your spiritual maturity is the glue that holds them together. If you take hold of them before the Lord deems you ready, everything may fall disastrously apart. So don't grow impatient. God has not forgotten you—He's simply making you ready. Learn to wait on Him with grace.

**Jesus, I know You will not forget me. I trust
Your timing and preparation. Amen.**

NO MORE FEAR

There is no fear in love; but perfect love casts out fear.

1 JOHN 4:18

If you fear God's mistreatment, then you don't really know how much He loves you and has given for you. The Father cares for you deeply and unconditionally. He allows challenges in your life so He can teach you to walk more closely with Him, free you from bondage, and develop your character. Challenges are never for your harm—not ever. Rather, when God touches something in your life and there's fear or anger there, it's because there's a deep wound that requires healing. He works in those painful areas for you to be fully free of whatever is destroying you.

How do I know this? Because that is who God is. He not only saves you but also completely liberates you from enslavement to sin and the suffering it causes you. Think about it: Has the Lord ever poured out His wrath on you when you've expressed anger to Him? Do you know why He doesn't? Because your Savior understands the deep and excruciating hurt you feel (Hebrews 2:17–18). He realizes the wounds that your experiences have caused in you. He has compassion and mercy toward you and works for you to be healed of the pain that plagues you.

Jesus, I know that everything You do is good. Thank You for loving me and setting me free. Amen.

GOD OUR FATHER

See how great a love the Father has bestowed on us,
that we would be called children of God.

1 JOHN 3:1

Do you fully understand what it means to have God as your Father? Understand regardless of how your earthly dad treated you, the Lord God is greater—more loving, compassionate, wise, and powerful—and He is exactly what your soul longs for.

You can see exactly the type of Father God is to you by reading the Gospels and discovering the character of Jesus. Jesus was always kind, caring, astute, and gracious. He healed all who came to Him—ministering to their hearts as well as their ailments. He held little children tenderly and blessed them. He always had time for people, always invited them to join Him, and always had wise counsel for them. Likewise, we know Jesus is sacrificial in His love for us. He died on the cross for you—so you could have a relationship with Him forever.

When you take a profound look at Jesus, you'll form a genuine picture of who God is as your Father. So ask the Lord to help you understand how much He truly loves and cares for you. Certainly, He will reveal Himself to you and be the Father you need.

Lord, I want to fully understand what it
means that You are my Father. Teach me; I
want to know and love You more. Amen.

THE TURNAROUND

You meant evil against me, but God meant it for good in order to bring about this present result, to preserve many people alive.

GENESIS 50:20

T he God you serve loves to turn seemingly hopeless situations around completely. Take Joseph, for example. He was sold into slavery by his brothers and dragged off to Egypt. Joseph gained some prominence there, but due to the unfair and false accusations of another, he spent years in an Egyptian prison.

To many, it may have appeared that God had forsaken Joseph. Rejected by family, enslaved, and imprisoned, what hope could he possibly have? To the unknowing eye, his was a useless, wasted life.

But God looked on Joseph and saw someone who stayed faithful despite the trials. Joseph honored the Lord and served others with godly devotion. And when the time was right, God turned everything around by raising Joseph up to lead Egypt, second in command to Pharaoh himself.

Likewise, there may be aspects of your life that feel hopeless. The most important thing you can do is to remain faithful to Jesus. Because when you do, you invite the Lord to be glorified in your life. So don't lose heart, but honor God. He can and will turn your situation around in ways you cannot imagine.

Jesus, You can turn anything around! Thank You for working all things together for my good! Amen.

A MINISTER OF COMFORT

He comforts us in all our troubles so that we can
comfort others.

2 CORINTHIANS 1:4 NLT

You've heard repeatedly that God causes all the circumstances of your life to work together for your good and His glory. But do you truly believe it? Sometimes it is difficult. If a trial is sufficiently unexpected or painful, it can leave you wondering why God allowed you to face such turmoil.

The only way to deal with the suffering positively and proactively is to view it through the eyes of God. So ask Him to help you see your circumstances from His perspective. Everything won't be completely clear, but you'll have confidence that the Savior who redeemed you will not abandon His work in your life.

Always remember that you are the beloved child of the living God. If sorrow touches your life, the Lord knows all about it and catches your tears (Psalm 56:8). Yet He is strong enough to take your pain and loneliness and produce something worthwhile out of them. He will use the adversity you've experienced to help you reach out to others who have been hurt and are struggling. He will take your pain and tragedy and use both to mold you into a wise and caring minister of His comfort.

Jesus, thank You for working through my pain to
make me into a minister of Your grace. Amen.

THE SPIRIT LEADS

My spirit within me seeks You diligently.

ISAIAH 26:9

Once you've turned to God and accepted His salvation, He begins to transform you by the power of His Holy Spirit into a new creature—one who bears the nature of Jesus. You have been completely forgiven of all your sins, and you've been changed spiritually—from death to life. This allows God's Spirit to indwell, lead, and mature you.

At times, when the Holy Spirit is actively working in you, it may actually feel as if there is something unsettled in your relationship with God. This is the Holy Spirit stretching your faith, helping you transition from an evidence-based relationship with the Father to genuine, spiritually grounded trust in the steadfastness, trustworthiness, and faithfulness of God Himself. Likewise, the Holy Spirit will convict you of sin in an ongoing way as a means of leading you to freedom and transforming you into the likeness of Jesus.

Therefore, don't be discouraged if you feel God's promptings or restlessness in your spirit. He will never leave you or lead you astray. Rather, He is calling you deeper into relationship with Him and to the abundant life. Therefore, obey the Holy Spirit. He will help you receive and take hold of the Lord's wonderful will for your life.

Holy Spirit, transform me! Increase my faith and love for You, and lead me in Your will, Lord God. Amen.

GO TO HIM

Come close to God, and God will come close to you.
Wash your hands, you sinners; purify your hearts,
for your loyalty is divided between God and the
world.

JAMES 4:8 NLT

God is not like the person you reach out to repeatedly but who never answers you back. He is not the delivery service that loses your letter or package. He is not the family member who refuses to interact with you. Rather, He says, "You will seek Me and find Me, when you search for Me with all your heart" (Jeremiah 29:13). The Lord God *wants* to grow in a loving relationship with you and guide you along the path of life.

This means the problem of fellowship usually comes from our side. So why don't we draw near to our Savior more often? Many times, it is because we fear what it will cost us. We know that by approaching holy God, we will be convicted of our sinfulness.

Friend, don't hold on to the things that are destroying you at the expense of the relationship that will truly satisfy your soul. Turn to Jesus, find freedom from what holds you in bondage, and experience the life you were created for.

Jesus, thank You for drawing close when I call. Help
me give up whatever holds me captive so I can
enjoy the abundant life You've given me. Amen.

MOURNING AND GLORY

"If you believe, you will see the glory of God."

JOHN 11:40

There are times when life won't make any sense. In fact, your understanding of how things *should* work may be so shattered by circumstances that the pain will be overwhelming. Naturally, you'll wonder where God is and why He's allowed it all. Take heart that your Savior cares when you hurt. Just as Jesus wept at the tomb of His friend Lazarus, He does so when you're confused and in pain.

However, if you recall the story of Lazarus, Jesus allowed Lazarus to succumb to his illness so that He could do the greater miracle—raising Lazarus from the grave (John 11:1–45). Likewise, God is permitting the circumstances you're facing in order to show His resurrection power in your life.

This season of mourning and difficulty will not last forever. But understand, important things are happening in the unseen. God is not only preparing you but orchestrating facets of your situation to demonstrate His faithfulness to you.

Therefore, don't give up or lose heart. Jesus has an awesome plan. Your responsibility is to stay focused on Him, allow Him to guide you, and be willing to obey Him in every situation. He will take care of the details and show you His glory.

Jesus, thank You for showing me Your glory in every situation. Amen.

ASSURANCE IN OBEDIENCE

Teach me Your way, O LORD; I will walk in Your
truth; unite my heart to fear Your name.

PSALM 86:11

G od is always calling you to step out in obedience. While doing so may create uncertainty in your life, there are some things of which you can be confident.

First, being challenged to grow in your faith is a necessary part of your relationship with God. The Lord will work through situations where you feel doubt, inadequacy, or fear as opportunities to mature your trust in Him. But you can proceed with confidence because, second, you can count on God's presence. The relationship you have with the Lord is absolutely permanent, and His promises are sure. So when He calls you to venture out, you can obey because He's right there with you. Third, the Holy Spirit will enable you to do whatever He calls you to do. His power and wisdom are yours. When you're weak, He strengthens you. When you falter, He steadies you. And when you fall, He picks you up.

So consider: what is God asking of you? Remember that when He says to step out amid uncertainty, you can rely on Him to be with you and equip you. Therefore, say yes to the challenge, thank Him for the opportunity, and trust Him for the journey.

Jesus, I want to obey You in all things. Give me
the courage to do whatever You ask. Amen.

SAFE PASSAGE

He caused the storm to be still . . . He guided them
to their desired haven.

PSALM 107:29–30

T he storms of life can make you feel off course and unsure of
your direction. This was certainly the case for the disciples as
they sailed on the Sea of Galilee and ran into a battering gale. They
couldn't gauge their direction and doubted they would survive.

Yet during that storm, Jesus showed His ability to protect the
disciples even as the tempest whirled around them. Often during
the storms, we are convinced that the elements will sink us—just as
Peter was when he stepped out of the boat. However, the One who
directs the wind and waves can stop their effect on us and rescue us.
Likewise, Jesus demonstrated His sovereignty—that He was fully in
charge of every detail of what the disciples were experiencing. In
this you can take heart: Jesus knows exactly how fierce the storm is,
where you are, and where He wants to take you.

The One who died in your place because of His awesome love is
the One who holds your future, controls the direction of your life,
and won't let you down. So turn to Him in the storm, trust Him, and
have confidence that He'll bring you to your destination.

Jesus, I trust You in the tempest. Thank You for
bringing me safely to the right destination. Amen.

WISDOM IN WAITING

Lord, for what do I wait? My hope is in You.

PSALM 39:7

Waiting on God can be difficult because time is so central to our lives. As creatures who have a beginning and end, we can find the passing days frustrating and even fearful. However, we must trust that the Father sees the bigger picture of our lives and knows exactly how to direct us with perfect skill and timing.

That's why the Lord sometimes withholds the blessings He desires to give you for a season. He knows that what may be a tremendous gift for you later would actually undermine and even destroy your life now. So He works in time and the circumstances of your life to prepare you for it. His delay is not a denial—simply your caring Father's desire to protect His child.

Therefore, as you wait on God, nurture your relationship with Him so you can hear His direction. Also, trust the Lord's judgment. He knows far more about what you desire than you do. So be obedient to Him. Because if you try to make something happen apart from God, you're headed for disaster. Never forget He's actively walking with you, and even when He withholds an answer to your prayers, He's looking out for your best interests.

Jesus, I wait on You, trusting Your great wisdom.
Thank You for Your wise and perfect timing. Amen.

PREPARED FOR THE PROMISE

You are the God of my salvation; for You I wait.

PSALM 25:5

Perhaps at one point or another you've wondered, *If God is all-powerful, all-knowing, and if He loves me unconditionally, why doesn't He meet my needs? Why are there gaping holes not only in my life but in my heart?*

Let me assure you that the Lord is indeed committed to meeting all your needs (Philippians 4:19). God promised He would. Of course, the value of any commitment is based on two things: first, the *ability* of the Promise Maker to fulfill His words, and second, His *integrity*—His character to follow through on what's been promised. We know the Lord certainly qualifies on both counts. He has the wisdom, power, and ability necessary to fulfill His pledges to us. He is also holy and trustworthy—God has always done what He has said He would do.

So why the delay? Sometimes the holdup is us. The only times in Scripture when the Lord has held back His provision are times when His promises were conditional, and humanity's behavior was an intervening factor. Therefore, either He may be working on your ability to receive what you need, or it may just not be time yet. But hang in there. Don't give up on God. Continue seeking Him and trusting Him to provide in due time.

Jesus, I don't understand the persistent needs
in my life, but I will trust You in them. Amen.

VICTORY IN BATTLE

The battle is the LORD's.

1 SAMUEL 17:47

Whatever battle you face today, take hold of the truth that God can lead you to victory. You may go through times of failure. Life may not always turn out the way you planned. But ultimately God will be glorified, and you will be blessed as you trust Him.

Every challenge you face presents an opportunity for God to display His wisdom, power, faithfulness, and love to you. So instead of yielding to thoughts of fear or failure, make a commitment to trust Him. How do you do so? First, recall past victories—all the times He's helped you in the past. Second, search your heart to make sure everything is right with God. Third, make the conscious effort to reject discouragement and strengthen yourself with His truth. Fourth, recognize the real nature of the battle, which is spiritual. Fifth, respond to the challenge with a positive confession of your faith in the Lord. Finally, rely on God's power for success.

Once you've spent time with the Lord and know that it's His will for you to enter the battle, you can count on the victory. You can face any circumstance with confidence and hope because it is God's strength, wisdom, and power that will ultimately lead you to triumph.

Jesus, this battle belongs to You, and I know You will triumph! Amen.

JULY

SHOWING GOD

Hope that is seen is not hope; for who hopes for what he already sees?

ROMANS 8:24

D o you have a preconceived idea about how God is going to meet your needs? Throughout the years, I've encountered a number of people who have explained how they believed the Lord should answer their petitions. This is always a path to disaster because God's ways are higher than ours, and He rarely acts in a manner we can predict. And when the Lord didn't comply with their plans, they grew angry and disheartened with Him.

But understand that God's purpose in allowing you to face a challenge or need is, first, for you to learn to rely on Him. Second, it is for others to see the Lord's power and presence in your life so they'll be drawn to Him. If He responds to you in a manner you can figure out or any person can replicate, where is the glory for Him? No, He must show Himself to be almighty God—beyond what anyone can accomplish in human strength or wisdom.

Therefore, today, stand before the Lord and declare, "I trust You completely to meet my needs in Your timing and according to Your methods." Have faith in Him even when you can't figure Him out. And allow Him to be glorified through you.

Jesus, show Yourself to be God in my situation. I have faith in You. Amen.

THE REAL NEED

After desire has conceived, it gives birth to sin; and
sin, when it is full-grown, gives birth to death.

JAMES 1:15 NIV

Name the problems that plague our world, and you can trace them back to underlying emotional or spiritual needs in people's lives. Whether it's substance abuse, poverty, broken families, crime, or violence—every destructive condition grows out of profound internal needs that are first manifested in the heart.

People react to the circumstances that they believe are the source of their unmet needs but that are often only symptoms. For example, a person may think that money will alleviate the problems and dissatisfactions he has in life, and he may respond to that perceived need in a manner that is unhealthy, ungodly, and ultimately unsatisfactory—with anything from workaholism to theft. But in reality, the deep inner need he is really feeling might be for respect, personal worth, or security. That is an oversimplification, but you see the pattern. That person will be answering the wrong question about what really fills his soul.

Friend, don't make that mistake. God not only reveals the true source of your need but satisfies it beyond imagination. Seek Him and trust Him to be all you require.

Jesus, the truth is that I need You. Please help me see past my perceived needs to the deep inner cry You want to satisfy in me. Amen.

TRAINING TO WIN

Do you not know that those who run in a race all run, but only one receives the prize? Run in such a way that you may win.

1 CORINTHIANS 9:24

During times of difficulty, you may have some trouble keeping your perspective. This is because trials can wear you down, producing weariness and discouragement that distracts you from your objective. Therefore, at such times, understand that there's nothing wrong with asking the Lord to help you keep your eyes on the goal.

This was true in the lives of people throughout Scripture. Joseph, David, Jeremiah, and Paul all faced similar periods of pressure that tested their spiritual and emotional endurance. However, they were able to keep their spiritual focus by consistently seeking the presence of God. They found victory and hope in worshiping Him even when trouble abounded on every side. You can as well.

So when you face times of difficulty, no matter how great the temptation, do not give up. Remember that you are like an athlete in training and are being prepared for God's higher purposes. So keep going by strengthening your focus on Jesus, because He will certainly lead you to a mighty victory.

Jesus, help me to keep focused on You in times of trouble and train me for Your purposes. Thank You for leading me to triumph. Amen.

IN HIS HANDS

The Most High is ruler over the realm of mankind.
DANIEL 4:17

When we look at the current state and the future of the world, we may be tempted to become disheartened. However, the chaos we see is an important reminder for us to focus our hearts on God. When the Lord looks at us, does He see a people of prayer?

Jesus is our sufficiency for meeting the challenges of the world today and tomorrow. Yes, as believers, we should be educated about what is going on, engage in active citizenship, be lights in our communities, and be examples of God's loving grace to others. The Lord expects us to live orderly, prudent, and pure lives as members of our society. However, we are told very clearly that "He controls the course of world events; he removes kings and sets up other kings" (Daniel 2:21 NLT). He does what we cannot with the direction of our nation.

Therefore, there is no reason for fear about what will happen in the future. Rather, we must commit ourselves to prayer—humbling ourselves, seeking His wisdom, and repenting of all that displeases Him (2 Chronicles 7:14). He will equip us for whatever may come and be our security, complete provision, and total defense.

Lord, teach me how to pray for this nation, and help me to be Your light in a community that needs Your guidance and salvation. Amen.

EXTENT OF BLESSING

The LORD longs to be gracious to you, and therefore He waits on high to have compassion on you.

ISAIAH 30:18

Your behavior doesn't determine your relationship with God, but it often determines the degree to which He can bless you. Take the case of the young woman who was very angry that a bank hadn't given her a loan she wanted. "I need that money," she insisted. "If I go into default on my house and car, it's the bank's fault." She refused to accept that she had terrible credit and was too great a risk for the bank. Her lack of funds wasn't the bank's fault—it was hers because of unhealthy financial habits.

Likewise, there will be times you have such destructive habits and behaviors that God cannot bless you. However, if you accept responsibility for your sins and their related consequences, you can then turn to the Lord and ask Him to help you change the patterns of behavior that are undermining your well-being. You can say to God, "Please help me not to do that again. Show me how to walk in Your ways. Give me the courage and strength to obey You so my life can improve."

The Lord always honors that kind of prayer. So take responsibility and let Him transform you into a vessel for blessing.

Jesus, teach me to walk in Your ways, and transform my life. Amen.

OBSTACLES

I will make . . . rugged places into plains. These are
the things I will do.

ISAIAH 42:16

Today, there may be some kind of obstacle standing between you and your heart's desire. You have prayed for so long, only to find this barrier to your progress. The temptation will be to grow angry and bitter over its presence. However, my challenge to you today is to thank God for it. The Lord would not have allowed it in your path if there was not some good purpose for it.

Perhaps the obstacle is revealing something about the person or thing you have desired for so long—some trait or complication that awakens you to problems or challenges you did not previously realize were there. It could be that the hindrance has revealed some issues in your own heart that you must get right with God. Or it may be that through it, the Lord is teaching you more about Him, His ways, and His plans for you.

Whatever the case, you know you can trust your Savior with your life and with whatever it is that hinders your progress. Therefore, even if it hurts, give thanks for that obstacle today, and ask God to reveal Himself through its presence on your path.

Jesus, I give thanks to You for this obstacle. Thank You for what You will reveal about me, the desire of my heart, and Yourself through it. Amen.

GIVE TO RECEIVE

No one can receive anything unless God gives it from heaven.

JOHN 3:27 NLT

Many people miss out on the blessing of God's abundance because they do not attribute their blessings to Him and withhold areas of their lives from Him. They refuse to give Him anything that would constitute a true sacrifice—their financial resources, possessions, time, or talents. Some do this out of ignorance, others out of rebellion, others out of a lack of trust that the Lord will meet their needs.

However, if you truly want to be blessed, you must be generous toward God. As in all other areas, the degree to which you open yourself to the Lord in giving is the degree to which you open yourself to Him for receiving. As we read in 2 Corinthians 9:6, "He who sows sparingly will also reap sparingly, and he who sows bountifully will also reap bountifully."

Why does God ask us to be sacrificial and generous to His work? I believe that it is because our resources are a reflection of ourselves. Our giving reveals the degree to which we trust God to supply what we need. But always remember that the more you give yourself to Him, the more you will be able to embrace all He has for you.

Jesus, I want to obey You. Help me to be generous toward You with my time, talents, and treasure. Amen.

GOD-CENTERED

*Delight yourself in the LORD; and He will give you
the desires of your heart.*

PSALM 37:4

Much of the theology we hear today is self-centered and self-seeking: "Lord, I want You to heal me, prosper me, bless me, and protect me in all the ways I ask." However, we are not at the center of the universe. On the contrary, God is the Creator, Sustainer, and Sovereign of all things, and He requires that we serve Him.

We are highly presumptuous when we demand that the Lord do our bidding as if He were our errand boy. The proper relationship with God is one in which we put ourselves in a position to do *His* bidding. When we look to the Lord in any other way, we make ourselves god—which is actually a form of idolatry. This occurs when we do not seek His presence as much as we seek to control His provision. We care more for what He gives us than we do Him, which means we are worshiping the blessing instead of the Blessing Giver.

Don't make that mistake. Yes, it's fine to have desires, but always remember you belong to God. Serve Him. Do as He says. Make Him your focus and delight, and everything else will follow (Matthew 6:33).

**Jesus, I belong to You, and I live to serve You.
Help me to see You first in all things. Amen.**

IT'S IN THE ATTACHMENT

"The branch cannot bear fruit of itself unless it abides in the vine, so neither can you unless you abide in Me."

JOHN 15:4

You know that serving God is not about effort but about allowing Him to shine through you. But how does that happen? The key is in your attachment to God. This is why Jesus talks about your relationship with Him in terms of a vine and branch. The health and productivity of the branch is completely dependent on its attachment to the vine.

In the same way, the more you seek to know God and to rely on Him, the more He reveals Himself to you. The more He discloses Himself to you, the more you reflect Him to others. You don't have to work it up or strive to perform good works on God's behalf. Instead, you trust the Lord to bring to you the people He wants you to minister to and to pour His power and wisdom through you into their lives.

The firmer you're attached to Jesus, the more His life can flow through you. So get into His presence, connect yourself to Him, and seek to know and love Him more. Before you know it, His power will flow through you supernaturally—just as He always meant it to.

Jesus, help me to be so attached to You that when people look at me they see only You. Amen.

IN HIS WILL

It is God who is at work in you, both to will and to work for His good pleasure.

PHILIPPIANS 2:13

Today, do not be afraid. The circumstances before you may seem confusing at best, painful and destructive at worst. But understand that you have absolutely everything you need to walk in God's plan for your life—the Holy Spirit who lives and works within you and His Word to direct you. The Lord is constantly prompting you to remain in the center of His will and is faithful to adjust your path when you begin to drift—even when you don't realize it. Likewise, He protects you in supernatural ways as you walk in His plan, so that everything works together for your good and His glory.

Therefore, you do not have to grieve or struggle to know God's will, you do not have to manipulate your circumstances to make His plan happen, and you don't have to fear when something goes wrong. Rather, employ your energy in exhibiting faith and walking step-by-step with Him, being confident that He is actively working in the unseen on your behalf (Isaiah 64:4). Because you can be certain that when your heart is inclined toward Him, He uses all the resources at His disposal to accomplish what concerns you (Psalm 57:2).

Jesus, thank You for leading me in Your will. I will trust You regardless of what happens. Amen.

IDENTITY IN JESUS

In Christ Jesus I have found reason for boasting in things pertaining to God.

ROMANS 15:17

When you lack a strong and positive identity, it can be absolutely devastating. Even the most minimal conflicts and criticism can undermine your confidence. When your value is based on other people, achievements, possessions, or power, only disappointment, insecurity, frustration, and anxiety can result.

However, as a believer, your identity and worth are completely established on who Jesus says you are. And you are forever loved, empowered, and accepted by Him. Yes, it is true that you are a stranger in this world because of your association with Christ. That means that people will not always understand you or what God has called you to accomplish. However, remember that all things in this world are temporary—including the standards by which you are judged. But when God says you are His beloved child, that is forever. Likewise, what He accomplished through you is eternal.

Your value, competence, and favor do not come and go based on circumstances or the opinions of others, because you are in Christ. You have become so intimately connected with Jesus that you take on His identity. Don't take this gift for granted or forget it when others are cruel. Rather, thank God for it every day.

Jesus, my true identity is in You. I rest in who You say I am. Amen.

YOUR INTERCESSOR

The Spirit Himself intercedes for us.
ROMANS 8:26

When you don't know what to pray, the Holy Spirit does so for you, according to God's will. He intercedes for you in full agreement with the very purposes for which the Lord created you.

According to Isaiah 11:2, He is the *Spirit of the Lord*, which means that everything He does will be consistent with God's plans and character. He is the *Spirit of wisdom*—He helps you to live out what is right in the Father's sight and conforms you to the image of Christ. He is the *Spirit of understanding*—He gives you supernatural discernment into your circumstances. He is the *Spirit of counsel*—He advises you, showing you what to do in every situation and bringing to remembrance everything Christ taught you (John 14:26). He is the *Spirit of strength*—which means He enables, empowers, and equips you to do God's will. He is the *Spirit of knowledge*—He provides the inventiveness and resourcefulness for the tasks He directs you to accomplish. And He is the *Spirit of the fear of the Lord*—He teaches you how to honor, respect, and obey the Father.

So when you're praying, be confident that you have exactly what you need to interact with God—the Holy Spirit, who communicates to you and for you.

Holy Spirit, thank You for teaching me how to pray and for interceding for me. Amen.

WITH YOU

Be gracious to me, O God . . . for my soul takes
refuge in You.

PSALM 57:1

As David fled from his home and ran from King Saul into the wilderness, he understood true loneliness. His despair went beyond the isolation of leaving his loved ones behind. Rather, he was driven into the solitary wasteland of En Gedi, with no provision or place to lay his head. This was when he cried out to the only One who would never abandon him—the Lord God.

Perhaps you've experienced a loneliness as profound and all-encompassing as David's. However, even before you were born, the Lord knew that you would encounter this season and has a plan for leading you through it. He is as close as you will let Him be. Just like David, you have the privilege of calling out to God, asking Him to be the Friend, Protector, and Provider you need.

Therefore, instead of giving in to despair, go to Him. Jesus promised you that He would not leave you as an orphan but would come to you through the presence of the Holy Spirit. The Spirit seals you in Christ (Ephesians 4:30)—never abandoning you, but always reminding you of God's perfect provision and presence.

Friend, the Lord is with you. So just like David, take heart. And know better days are ahead.

Jesus, thank You for Your constant presence
with me. I take refuge in You. Amen.

Combating Burnout

Whatever you do, do your work heartily, as for the
Lord rather than for men.

Colossians 3:23

I f you've ever experienced burnout, you know what it is to be overly stressed and depleted of physical and emotional energy. This can happen in your profession, but it can also occur as you do ministry if you don't understand the nature of the service God desires of you.

The Holy Spirit empowers you to do whatever the Lord calls you to do. If you fall into the personal performance trap, however, it won't be long until you run out of strength. You'll never be able to please everyone or sustain all the spiritual onslaughts. Likewise, some believers make working for a church or ministry organization an end in itself—with recognition, personal gain, and power as the real incentives for their service. But the Lord will not share His glory with anyone—even those who claim to represent His name.

However, when your service is an outflow of your personal relationship with Jesus, the Holy Spirit gives you guidance, comfort, and confidence. Therefore, if you're feeling burnout, ask God to sift through your motives and reveal any problems. The Lord—not people—is the object of your service. So work for Him and let Him fuel your ministry.

Jesus, You are the One I serve. Search me, Lord,
and reveal anything that doesn't glorify You. Amen.

A PERSONAL COMMISSION

"Go into all the world and preach the gospel to all creation."

MARK 16:15

J esus called us as believers to "make disciples of all the nations, baptizing them in the name of the Father and the Son and the Holy Spirit, teaching them to observe all that I commanded you" (Matthew 28:19–20). Although we accomplish many tasks as the church, our primary message to the world is the gospel of Christ. Everything else we do is an extension of that primary goal—helping people to grow in the salvation Jesus has given.

The good news we proclaim is superior to every worldly philosophy, political ideology, or self-improvement plan because it meets the greatest need of every human heart: reconciliation with the Creator. Although the message is always the same, methods of making it known are as many and diverse as we are—and we've been given spiritual gifts, talents, and abilities to carry out the Great Commission Jesus gave us.

Some Christians think that talking about Jesus is only for pastors, missionaries, or other ministers. But the Lord has a wonderful, unique, and specific way for you to serve Him as well. So tell your friends and family what Christ has done for you. The limiting factor is not God's ability to use you but your availability to His call.

Jesus, show me how to serve You, and give me boldness to proclaim Your gospel. Amen.

TRUST YOUR DEFENDER

God granted Daniel favor and compassion.

DANIEL 1:9

I f you've read the story of Daniel, you know he was a young Hebrew man who obeyed God even when it was costly to him. Daniel had been taken captive to Babylon—a nation that worshiped pagan deities—and was forced into the service of King Nebuchadnezzar. As such, Daniel was given royal cuisine that had been first dedicated to idols—food that the Lord had prohibited the Jewish people from consuming. So Daniel had to decide whether it was better to obey God and risk angering this cruel foreign king or to disobey the Lord and please Nebuchadnezzar.

At face value, the question for Daniel was about food, and he could have rationalized that he was a servant and had no choice. But the real issue was allegiance to God, so Daniel resolved to honor the Lord regardless of what it cost him. And God blessed him for it.

Today, you may face difficult decisions about following God despite pressures from others. You will be tempted to do what is expedient to protect yourself. But remember the Lord is your true Defender. So be like Daniel and obey God's commands despite how fearful the challenge. Because when you honor Him, He will certainly prove Himself faithful.

Jesus, I know You are my Mighty Warrior and True Defender. I will obey. Protect and vindicate Your servant, Lord. Amen.

THE KEY TO OBEDIENCE

"If you love me, obey me."
JOHN 14:15 TLB

More than likely, you have many keys in your life—keys to your home, car, and even your desk. But have you ever thought about having the key to God's heart? It was given to you by Jesus when you accepted Him as your Savior.

Often, people believe that access to the Lord's favor comes through performing pious acts, following a prescribed schedule of religious disciplines, or making tremendous sacrifices. However, the key to God's heart is *obedience that flows from love*. This may seem a lot like the previous list, but it is inherently different because of the source of its motivation. Instead of performing a collection of obligations for the purpose of staying right with Him, Jesus wants you to relate to Him personally and to submit to Him out of love and respect. He wants what you do in service to Him to flow from your intimate relationship with Him, not a sense of earning His goodwill.

So spend time with Him and say yes to whatever He asks out of reverence for Him as God and out of your profound gratefulness for all Jesus has done for you. You'll find not only that you have the key to His heart but that He has the key to yours.

Jesus, I do love You and want to obey whatever You ask. Help me courageously and lovingly submit to Your will. Amen.

CONFIDENT PRAYER

*"O Lord God," I cried out; "O great and awesome
God who keeps his promises and is so loving and
kind to those who love and obey him! Hear my
prayer!"*

NEHEMIAH 1:5 TLB

D o you really see God as being able and willing to handle all
the challenges you bring before Him? Nehemiah did. Upon
hearing about Jerusalem's devastated condition, he mourned, fasted,
and prayed for God's intervention, trusting that the Lord would help.

Nehemiah used three Hebrew terms demonstrating what he
believed about God's character. He called Him *Yahweh*, the living
One who is absolute in faithfulness; *Elohim*, indicating the Lord's
infinite power; and *Adonai*, which means "ruler over all." Nehemiah
was bringing his request before the throne of grace with full confidence in God. And the Lord answered Nehemiah's prayer in a
powerful way. He gave Nehemiah favor with King Artaxerxes, who
sent Nehemiah back to Jerusalem with all the resources he needed
to rebuild the city.

The Lord worked a miracle for Nehemiah, and He can do so
for you as well. So approach Him with complete confidence that He
will hear and answer your prayers. Remember that He is absolute in
faithfulness and infinite in power.

**Jesus, I truly believe that You can and will help
me. Hear my prayer, my awesome God! Amen.**

A Gift in Progress

*Every good thing given and every perfect gift is
from above, coming down from the Father of lights.*

JAMES 1:17

God gives us what He knows will bring us great pleasure and joy, even though we in our finite understanding may not know fully what we need or desire. Take heart in that reality today. The Lord is proactive in meeting our needs. He creates, orchestrates, and engineers the solutions that will further His plan for our lives and satisfy our souls.

So you should never think that God is surprised by the needs or challenges you are experiencing—not even for a second. On the contrary, the Lord knows you far better than you will ever know yourself. He knew this situation would arise in your life long before you were ever conceived in your mother's womb. And from that time, He's planned how He would bless you through it. That's right—*bless* you. This may appear to be a trial at this moment, but this is a vessel through which your heavenly Father desires to give you a gift.

So today, thank the Father for whatever circumstances you find yourself in—no matter how difficult—knowing that He has a good plan for them, and His blessing is on its way.

Jesus, thank You that You have planned
good to come from all of this. I trust
You and praise Your name. Amen.

IN THE WAY YOU HEAR

You will call, and the LORD will answer.
ISAIAH 58:9

Do you ever fear that as you are seeking God, you may not be able to hear Him? If so, remember: God has spoken to people at different times, with various methods, and in diverse manners throughout history (Hebrews 1:1).

Think about it: God communicated to Moses from a burning bush, which not only caught Moses' attention but also showed him God could do the miraculous (Exodus 3). Likewise, the Father spoke to Joseph through dreams (Genesis 37:5–9), to Elijah in the "sound of a gentle blowing" (1 Kings 19:12), and to Joshua through the mighty "captain of the host of the LORD" (Joshua 5:14). He spoke to each one in a special way—according to whom He was speaking to and what He was revealing. He is not limited in how He communicates His plan to us either.

The God who knit us together in our mothers' wombs knows the best way to get our attention and declare His will to us. The Father knows what we can handle, what we are prepared to hear, and the best way to reveal it to us. Therefore, do not fear a failure to hear; rather, rejoice in His ability to speak.

Jesus, I am so grateful that You speak to me in the way I can hear. I rejoice in Your loving-kindness to me. Amen.

SET YOUR MIND

Set your minds on things above, not on earthly things.

COLOSSIANS 3:2 NIV

How do you overcome heartbreak? How do you break free from something you know the Lord wants you to let go of so you can heal? How do you deal with the confusion when there are so many unanswered questions in your mind? Of course, it is the power of God that does that in you. And you invite His healing influence into your life when you actively set your mind on Him.

Therefore, as thoughts of that person or situation arise, it is important for you to refocus your concentration on Christ. This is why in Philippians 4:8–9 Paul wrote, "Whatever is true, whatever is noble, whatever is right, whatever is pure, whatever is lovely, whatever is admirable—if anything is excellent or praiseworthy—think about such things. Whatever you have learned or received or heard from me, or seen in me—put it into practice. And the God of peace will be with you" (NIV).

If you want the peace that Jesus offers you, you have to allow Him to rule your thoughts. Through your worship of Him, you will find the healing, answers, and freedom that your heart is longing for.

Jesus, help me turn my thoughts to You. As fear and pain creep in, help me remember that You are guiding me and won't let me down. Amen.

GOOD PLANS

You do not know what your life will be like tomorrow.

JAMES 4:14

Today's verse is an admonition to those who make plans about the future. James says, "Come now, you who say, 'Today or tomorrow we will go to such and such a city, and spend a year there and engage in business and make a profit.' . . . Instead, you ought to say, 'If the Lord wills, we will live and also do this or that'" (James 4:13, 15).

Some might take this verse as an undesirable warning because they have a vision for the future and objectives for how everything should play out. But really, it is a positive reminder that God is in every tomorrow. So even though we do not know what will happen, He is already there, and it is His will that comes to pass.

Take that to heart today if your future is full of unknowns and your sources of security have crumbled. You don't know the good plans that the Lord has for your future. So seek His will, rejoice in His perfect provision and wisdom, and hold on to hope about tomorrow. Because you know the Lord's will is good, acceptable, and perfect (Romans 12:2), and the fullness of joy is found in His presence (Psalm 16:11).

Jesus, I am grateful Your will guides my future because I know You have never let me down and never will. Amen.

A CHANNEL OF BLESSING

It is more blessed to give than to receive.

ACTS 20:35

Do you realize that God's blessings to you are not actually meant to end with you? His desire is that you share them with others. This principle applies to every area of your life, including the gift of salvation, what He teaches you, and what He provides for you. The Lord graciously supplies what you need—and even what you want—in order to fulfill His plans in your life and shine His light to others.

The thought of giving to others may intimidate you somewhat because so many people have so many needs. But be assured: sharing your blessings with others will never lead to deprivation—especially when God is leading you. On the contrary, giving to others makes you a channel of His unending flow of provision. In fact, the Lord promises to "make all grace abound to you, so that always having all sufficiency in everything, you may have an abundance for every good deed" (2 Corinthians 9:8). He enriches you in response to your generosity.

Therefore, be confident that you can never outgive the Lord. Demonstrate God's goodness in your life by meeting someone else's need. Don't let His generous provisions end with you. Pass them on and discover the joy of His never-ending cycle of blessings.

Jesus, lead me in sharing my blessings with others and being Your loving representative. Amen.

GREATER SUPPLY

To the LORD your God belong heaven and the
highest heavens, the earth and all that is in it.
DEUTERONOMY 10:14

God doesn't meet your needs according to *your* resources—the gifts and talents you have, or some other measure of ability, worth, or wealth. No, the Lord answers your needs according to *His* great supply—and His riches are immeasurable, indestructible, and inexhaustible—beyond our imaginations in size, scope, and magnificence.

Everything that exists—seen or unseen—is owned by, governed by, and available to God at any given moment. He is in absolute control. Likewise, He can create out of nothing, so even if what is required does not yet exist, He can bring it into being.

Let this comfort you. As a Christian, you are living in union with the Creator. And you've been promised that He "will supply all your needs according to His riches in glory in Christ Jesus" as you follow Him in obedience (Philippians 4:19). There is no challenge or obstacle you could face that is anything to Him. There is nothing you can need that He cannot provide from His unlimited storehouse. You are united with God in His fullness, and that means that when you're walking in His will, you will never fall short.

Jesus, thank You for supplying everything
I need! I walk in Your will, grateful that
I need never be afraid. Amen.

ACCEPTED

He made us accepted in the Beloved.
EPHESIANS 1:6 NKJV

Sometimes we can feel we just aren't enough—regardless of what we do, we have the impression that we'll always fall short of what God wants. We try to earn His approval because we want our Father in heaven to be proud of us and love us.

Let me assure you today that God approves of you—and it has nothing to do with how many hours a week you volunteer or the pious things you do to be considered a "good Christian." Your heavenly Father loves you on the basis of what Jesus did for you on the cross, not on the basis of what you do for Him.

Yes, God desires that we respond to Him out of love and devotion. When you truly love someone, you will actively and joyfully show that person you care in ways you know they value. That's far different from doing things out of fear or obligation to win another person's acceptance.

The same is true for your relationship with God. He already loves you, is proud of you, and approves of you. Nothing you do will change that. So be freed by that truth, and love God by responding to Him in obedience as He leads you.

Jesus, thank You for accepting me. Help me to obey out of genuine love for You. Amen.

TOO BUSY

*"In repentance and rest you will be saved, in
quietness and trust is your strength."*
ISAIAH 30:15

A re you overly busy? You may well have legitimate reasons for having a full schedule. You may have to work long hours to meet the needs of your family or care for a loved one. But sometimes, people fill their lives with activities in order to shut out the Holy Spirit's promptings. They stay busy, running around all day. When they get home, they immediately turn on the television, computer, music—or what have you—and always have something playing so they can avoid the quietness.

Is this you? Are you either consciously or unwittingly trying to avoid the Lord? As I so often say, our intimacy with God determines the impact of our lives. So we should never let busyness rob us of our chance to know the Savior better, because our relationship with Him is what truly makes our lives worthwhile and a difference that lasts.

So how do you overcome the busyness in your life? Begin by bringing your fears to God—whatever it is that keeps you from approaching Him. Then ask Him what is truly essential and express your desire to choose His best. He will strengthen you, showing you what to keep and what must be cut out.

**Jesus, forgive me for the ways I've avoided
You. I repent and rest in You. Amen.**

TRUST HIS DISCIPLINE

He disciplines us for our good, so that we may
share His holiness.

HEBREWS 12:10

When God disciplines you, you can be assured that He does so out of love and for good purposes. This may be difficult to accept, especially when you are facing painful trials. However, always remember that the Father loves you and is on your side. He is never against you.

Even in times of correction, the Lord is working for your good. He uses the discipline to refocus your life when you've drifted from His path or when you are refusing to submit an area of your life to Him. He is not punishing you; on the contrary, He is giving you the gift of teaching you how to live a godly life. Therefore, 1 Peter 5:6 admonishes, "Humble yourselves under the mighty hand of God, that He may exalt you at the proper time." Submit yourself to the Father's authority so that you can eventually experience the overflow of His blessings.

Of course, the greatest benefit of discipline is the potential for intimacy it brings between you and the Lord. Therefore, greet your adversity with humility. Listen to the Father so you can obey. Submit yourself to Him because He will lift you to new heights at the proper time.

Jesus, I submit myself to Your loving discipline.
Help me love and obey You more every day. Amen.

HEART PROBLEM

Watch over your heart with all diligence, for from it flow the springs of life.

PROVERBS 4:23

The words of your mouth will reveal what's really in your heart. You can try to control what you say. However, when you're pressed, your emotions will escalate, and what flows from your mouth will betray what's truly inside of you.

All of us have experienced times when we've said hurtful things to others and felt bad for doing so. This is why David wrote, "Let the words of my mouth, and the meditation of my heart, be acceptable in thy sight, O LORD" (Psalm 19:14 KJV). We must fully submit ourselves to God to purify our thoughts and emotions so that what flows from us builds up others and glorifies Him.

Thankfully, when our minds and hearts are transformed by Jesus, what proceeds from us will be characterized by the fruit of His Spirit: "love, joy, peace, patience, kindness, goodness, faithfulness, gentleness, self-control" (Galatians 5:22–23). Then even in difficult times, the words we say will reflect the character of our Savior.

So consider, do you have trouble with your words? If so, you're suffering from a heart problem. Turn to God and allow Him to cleanse the source of your trouble as only He can.

Jesus, forgive me for what I've said to others out of the sinfulness of my heart. Purify me so I may glorify You with my words. Amen.

A CHANGE OF COURSE

If we confess our sins, He is faithful and righteous to forgive us our sins and to cleanse us from all unrighteousness.

1 JOHN 1:9

I n Christ, you are forgiven of the penalty of all your sin—past, present, and future—forever. However, you are called to confess your sins because there are still parts of you that aren't submitted to God—areas where your fellowship with Him is hindered and you're not living in His freedom. So when you repent, you're agreeing with Him that you've been doing things wrong and want to do things His way.

Often, people feel sorry for what they've done but live in defeat because they don't really understand that the purpose of repentance is to change course. If this is you, then take heart. God will empower you to change. And it starts by acknowledging He has a right to teach you what to do.

So if you have sins you need to confess, take full responsibility for your actions. Be honest with Jesus and obey whatever He says—even when He does the painful work of rooting out the attitudes and behaviors that incited the transgressions in the first place. Because then you can enjoy open lines of communication with your Savior and experience the freedom He died to give you.

Jesus, I repent. Teach me how to walk in Your ways. Amen.

KEEP LISTENING

*Do not be afraid . . . for the LORD your God is the
one who goes with you. He will not fail you or
forsake you.*

DEUTERONOMY 31:6

T he choices before you today may feel overwhelming—as if
they represent a precarious crossroads on which your whole
future hinges. You may feel as if a wrong decision could ruin everything. But take heart: these choices are a part of God's bigger picture
for you. It's unnerving to ask Him for guidance and not hear Him
immediately. But I can testify today that the Lord who created you is
more than able to teach you what to do and keep you on the path of
His will when you seek Him.

This is why Scripture often repeats the command that you should
not fear. Anxiety can blind you to God's guidance, can cause you to
lose heart and make bad decisions, and may even dishearten you to
the point you give up completely.

Therefore, set your heart to reject fear. Do not be afraid that you
are unworthy of knowing His will. Jesus makes you worthy (Romans
8:31–34). Do not fear that you won't or can't hear God. He created you
and can break through to you. Keep listening for Him.

Jesus, I know You will speak at the right
time and in a powerful way, so I won't
be afraid. I will trust You. Amen.

WHAT ARE YOU SEEKING?

"Do not be worried about your life, as to what you will eat or what you will drink; nor for your body, as to what you will put on. Is not life more than food, and . . . clothing?"

MATTHEW 6:25

I n Matthew 6, Jesus spoke to people who were in deep need. Many of those who listened to Him were simple people who lacked basic necessities, such as food, clothing, and shelter. They also had the same emotional and spiritual needs we do—to be loved, respected, and accepted.

Like many of us, some of the people listening to Jesus were guilty of striving to meet their needs without seeking God's help, and they were frustrated, anxious, and filled with worry because of it. Jesus said to them, "Seek first His kingdom and His righteousness, and all these things will be added to you" (Matthew 6:33).

How do we get beyond a spirit of fear, striving, and merely surviving to the point where we are thriving—with a spirit of total trust in the Lord? Jesus told us how: we must turn our minds away from acquiring earthly security and fulfillment and focus on God and His kingdom. We shift our priorities about what we think about, and everything else is added to us.

Jesus, I know I sometimes focus on the
wrong goal. Show me how to seek You
and Your kingdom first always. Amen.

AUGUST

CHOOSE HIS SPIRIT

The flesh sets its desire against the Spirit, and the
Spirit against the flesh.

GALATIANS 5:17

Today, understand that some of the struggles you are experiencing with God are because of your self-will and insistence on controlling your own life and path. Your flesh will fight against God's Spirit for rulership, driven by the desire to soothe the profound hungers within you. With your mind, you may very well acknowledge, "Yes, the Lord knows what is best," but in practice, you continue to strive for independence and self-determination. Sadly, the biggest problems you face will usually occur in the same areas where you insist on having control—unaware that your efforts are actually making things worse rather than better.

Friend, do not fear handing your life over to God. What you must ask is, "Would God deny me anything that is truly good for me? Would Jesus—the Savior who gave His life on the cross—really say no to something that would truly bless me, build me up, or strengthen me?" I hope you realize the answer is "Of course not!" If God says "Wait" or "No" to something you've been praying for, it is because He has a good reason for it. Therefore, stop fighting, trust Him, and walk by His Spirit.

Jesus, reveal the fleshly areas I'm still
trying to control and help me to be free. I
choose to walk by Your Spirit. Amen.

HEALING IN BROKENNESS

He will beautify the afflicted ones with salvation.
PSALM 149:4

Are you feeling broken today? One of the main reasons the Lord allows us to go through great trials and seasons of brokenness is that He is liberating us of our self-will. He is revealing the hurt we cause ourselves and our unhealthy dependencies on people and possessions that cannot last.

Therefore, if your Savior is in the process of working in some area of your life, take heart. Jesus knows what it will take to meet that deep longing within you. He's identified what must be healed if you're going to become what He has created you to be and reach your full, most meaningful, soul-satisfying potential. Likewise, He may reveal that what He desires for you is different from what you're working for. This is not because He wants to deny your heart's desire. Rather, it is because He realizes that what you're seeking won't make you happy—and He wants to give you what truly will.

So surrender yourself fully to your heavenly Father, and allow Him to heal you. Acknowledge that He knows what's best. Because as He promises, if you delight yourself in Him, He will fulfill the most profound desires, hopes, and dreams within you.

Lord Jesus, I submit to Your will and Your methods of accomplishing them. Thank You that I can always trust You. Amen.

CONFORMED

Do not be conformed to the former lusts which
were yours in your ignorance, but . . . be holy.
1 PETER 1:14–15

How do we change from business as usual to walking in God's will and becoming people who exalt Him? Today's verse admonishes us, "Do not be conformed." The Greek word for *conformed* here is *syschematizo*, which means to adapt yourself—your mind, character, and behavior—to another's pattern. It can mean being stamped by the likeness of something. If you've ever seen a chameleon jump from green grass to a brown branch, you've seen this concept in action. The chameleon almost instantly changes to blend in with its new situation—it protects itself by conforming, by avoiding standing out. And that's what we do.

It is interesting to note that Peter does not attribute our sinful acts to being enlightened to worldly ways—but to our ignorance. We don't know any better but to protect ourselves as the chameleon does. However, because we know Jesus as our Savior, we don't have to keep being blinded to what we are doing that undermines our well-being. We can be pressed into His likeness instead. However, that means we must take what He says seriously. Regardless of what He addresses in our lives, we obey and allow Him to transform us into His image.

Jesus, conform me to Your image.
I follow You. Amen.

PURPOSE IN PRAYER

"They themselves are in the world, and I come to
You. Holy Father, keep them in Your name . . . that
they may be one even as We are."

JOHN 17:11

I f God has a plan, knows all things, and is in control, why does He ask us to pray? It is because through prayer, He brings us into what He has purposed to accomplish. The Lord desires to involve us in the work that He is doing around the world. And in today's verse, Jesus asks that the disciples would be one in purpose with Him by the power of His name.

God could certainly build His kingdom without our input or help. But when we join Him in His work, our relationship with Him develops depth and intimacy. We mature as well. Praying and working alongside our Lord grows our faith, establishes our character, and strengthens our trust in His power.

Interacting with the Lord is a privilege. He created you to love Him and be loved by Him, and prayer is how that connection with Him gets nurtured and matures. So when your heavenly Father beckons you to pray, let Him draw you close. Listen to His heart and accept His call to join Him in building His kingdom. Be one with Him and experience the power and glory due His name.

Jesus, teach me to genuinely commune with You so
I may be one with You and Your purposes. Amen.

NOT ALONE

The God of peace will soon crush Satan under your
feet. The grace of our Lord Jesus be with you.
ROMANS 16:20

A t times you may feel utterly alone in the world because of the struggles you face and deep-seated feelings of failure or insignificance. The Enemy will try to discourage you with thoughts of isolation—that the reason you are suffering it is because you are singularly unworthy of God's help and intervention. But nothing could be further from the truth. In fact, Peter affirmed this, saying, "Be of sober spirit, be on the alert. Your adversary, the devil, prowls around like a roaring lion, seeking someone to devour. But resist him, firm in your faith, knowing that the same experiences of suffering are being accomplished by your brethren who are in the world" (1 Peter 5:8–9).

You are not alone. Your pain, feelings, and insecurities are not unique, wrong, or evidence of disqualification. Rather, your situation is something God has handled repeatedly throughout the ages, because adversity is a common tool the Lord uses to teach His people how to walk with Him. So don't be afraid. You are not alone, abandoned, or forgotten. Your life matters to God, and He sees a great deal worthy of developing in you. Therefore, resist the Enemy, take heart, and don't give up.

Jesus, thank You so much that I'm not alone,
but You are always with me. Amen.

228

THE RIGHT TO LOVE

"Pray for those who mistreat you."
LUKE 6:28

We hear many people talking about rights these days. Sadly, the attention given to human entitlements hasn't brought about any increase in personal freedom. Instead, most people are increasingly imprisoned by feelings of jealousy, greed, and bitterness.

This is why instead of focusing on the privileges due us, Scripture admonishes us to consider others better than ourselves, love our enemies, and forgive those who persecute us. That doesn't mean we invite people to trample on us. Rather, we're simply more concerned about showing God's love than about demanding what we're due.

Jesus is our example in this. He was betrayed by His friends, persecuted by His people, and crucified for our sins. Yet He said, "Father, forgive them; for they do not know what they are doing" (Luke 23:34). His awe-inspiring capacity for love and forgiveness are available to us through His Spirit, who indwells us. When we choose to honor Him even in mistreatment, God's power and care can flow through us.

You will never lose when you show the boundless love of Christ to others. Not only will you be blessed by God for representing Him well, but others may accept Him as Savior because of your example.

Jesus, I want to forgive and love as You do. Help me pray for those who've hurt me. Amen.

INSIDE OUT

We all . . . are being transformed into the same
image from glory to glory, just as from the Lord,
the Spirit.

2 CORINTHIANS 3:18

As soon as you accept Jesus as your Savior, a transformation begins in you, conforming you to His likeness. But how are you actually being changed? After all, if this metamorphosis is supernatural, then it's not something you can enact on your own. It's what Jesus does in you.

Romans 12:2 teaches that it happens by the renewing of our minds. So the key to transformation is changing *what* and *how* we think. But understand that what Jesus changes is not merely your opinions or system of beliefs. Sometimes we assume that's what religion is—you change the name of the deity, the sacrifice, and some of the rituals, but that's all there really is to it. But there's more God wants to do in us—and that is revolutionize us from the inside out.

In fact, the word Paul uses for *renewing* comes from the root word *anakainóō*, which means "to make new" or "to be changed into a new kind of life." Therefore, we know that when Jesus transforms our minds, it means He even changes the way we process information. So let Him. And join Him in the process by being in His Word every day.

Jesus, transform me into Your likeness from the inside out so that You can receive the glory. Amen.

THE IMPORTANCE OF PRAYER

Devote yourselves to prayer, keeping alert in it with
an attitude of thanksgiving.

COLOSSIANS 4:2

P rayer is the lifeblood of your relationship with the Lord. But perhaps you wonder how important it really is. Will you miss God's plans if you don't pray? Will you lose His favor or blessing?

While the Lord is not dependent on our prayers to achieve His plans, we miss out terribly when we don't pray. It is through prayer that He reveals Himself to us, heals our wounds, teaches us our identity, and involves us in His work.

So, in a sense, your prayer (or lack thereof) can impact what God does. There are times when His purposes are set and nothing can change them, of course—such as the promises He's given. But at other times, our lack of communication with Him means we're missing the blessings He has for us. James 4:2 even tells us, "You do not have because you do not ask." Your prayers can have a tremendous impact on your own faith and well-being—as well as others.

You have an awesome privilege to kneel before your all-powerful heavenly Father and know that He listens and will respond. So don't waste that blessing. Learn from God and receive what He longs to give you.

Jesus, teach me to take full advantage
of the wonderful privilege of prayer.
I want to know You. Amen.

WAIT FOR HIM

Wait for the LORD; be strong and let your heart take courage; yes, wait for the LORD.

PSALM 27:14

Today you may be thinking, *I just don't know if I really have confidence that God will help me. I feel like I need an answer right now.*

I understand feeling this way. However, I would point out that there are many aspects of your life that you entrust to others. You trust doctors with your health, financial advisers with your retirement, and accountants with your taxes—and you'll wait until they finish their work. No matter how skilled and trustworthy these experts are, is not God even more so?

It's crucial for you to grasp how reliable the Father is to lead you, because you are making your choices based on what you believe about Him. Though it's true that sometimes the people you count on will let you down or make judgments without all the facts, the Lord never will. God does not cheat, fail, or forsake you as others might. Rather, if He is delaying on giving you an answer, it is for a worthy reason that is for your ultimate good.

So as today's verse says, wait for Him. Listen for His answer. Do not despair. God will answer in His perfect time, in a manner that will genuinely bless you.

Jesus, I wait for You, trusting in Your perfect timing and plan. Amen.

GOD'S GOOD WILL

The LORD is gracious and merciful; slow to anger
and great in lovingkindness. The LORD is good to
all.

PSALM 145:8–9

Romans 12:2 tells us that the will of God is "good and acceptable and perfect." It doesn't say that the Lord's will for you will be unbearable, that you'll hate it, and that it will ruin your life. On the contrary, what the Father envisions for you is absolutely wonderful and praiseworthy.

Therefore, today think about the fact that *God's will is good*. The Lord's plan is morally honorable, excellent, and beneficial to you. It may not always appear to be so at first. There have been times in my own life when I told the Father that the trials and pressures He was allowing seemed far from good. However, we always have to remember the promise of Romans 8:28: "We know that God causes all things to work together for good to those who love God, to those who are called according to His purpose."

The Father is very careful about what He permits to touch your life. Why? Because He Himself is good. Why would we ever expect the will of God to be anything other than beneficial and honorable when both the nature and character of our heavenly Father are good? Therefore, today, rejoice in the fact that His will for you is wonderful.

Jesus, thank You for Your good
plans for my life. Amen.

GOD'S ACCEPTABLE WILL

Offer up spiritual sacrifices acceptable to God through Jesus Christ.

1 PETER 2:5

As we saw yesterday, God's will is "good and acceptable and perfect" (Romans 12:2). But what does it mean that *His will is acceptable*?

I believe many Christians struggle with how the Father views us and whether or not we're pursuing the best course in His sight. If finding acceptance and worth is so difficult with people, how can we ever hope to measure up to God, who is faultless in all His ways?

But understand that the Lord receives you on the basis of what Jesus did on the cross. Once you've received Christ as your Savior, you are accepted before the Father forever. And because of the presence of the Holy Spirit in you and the Word of God to guide you, you can live in a manner well pleasing to the Lord. In fact, Philippians 2:13 asserts, "It is God who is at work in you, both to will and to work for His good pleasure."

The Father patiently teaches you how to walk with Him—leading you in offering the spiritual sacrifices that delight Him. So not only is it possible to live in an acceptable manner before Him, but God is committed to helping you do so.

Jesus, thank You for teaching me to walk with You and to offer acceptable sacrifices to Your matchless name. Amen.

GOD'S PERFECT WILL

The LORD will perfect that which concerns me;
Your mercy, O LORD, endures forever.

PSALM 138:8 NKJV

For the previous two days, we've been studying the Lord's "good and acceptable and perfect" will (Romans 12:2). Today, we will look at what it means that *God's plans for you are perfect.*

When we read the word *perfect*, we may be daunted by thoughts of having to maintain a flawless walk with the Lord, but that is not what is intended by the word there. The Greek word *teleios* that is used is better translated as "finished," "brought to maturity," "enabled to reach the goal," or "needing nothing for completeness." In other words, the Lord already has a comprehensive and trustworthy strategy for leading you all the way to the victory.

Friend, the Father has no half-baked schemes—especially when it comes to your life. You may not know His full plan, but He does. In fact, He knows "the end from the beginning" (Isaiah 46:10 NKJV), and He can and will bring it to absolute completion. So there is never a need to worry about whether or not God's plans will work out. They will. Therefore, do not fear. Entrust your life to Him, and He will lead you to triumph.

Jesus, thank You for bringing Your perfect plans to completion in my life. I will trust You every step of the way. Amen.

BACK ON THE ALTAR

The godly may trip seven times, but they will get up again.

PROVERBS 24:16 NLT

As we've seen the last few days, the Lord's will is good, acceptable, and perfect. Why wouldn't anyone want to serve a God like that? Yet we know how difficult it can be to stay on the path when circumstances are both confusing and painful. As living sacrifices (Romans 12:1), we're tempted to crawl off the altar and run for the hills.

Presenting your total being completely to God is never easy. In fact, there's nothing more challenging in life than that. For this reason, it's important for you to understand that offering yourself as a living sacrifice is not a onetime experience. I wish it were. But that's not a reality of our fallen human nature or the world we live in. As long as we exist on earth, we will be tempted to take back control.

So when you fail, do not despair or run from God. Instead, renew your commitment to Him. Climb back on the altar and set your will on allowing Jesus to work in your mind, heart, and life. Because the true test of godliness is not in avoiding falling but in getting back up again. So rise up and give Him everything you are and hope to be.

**Jesus, I present myself to You completely.
I am Yours, Lord. Amen.**

INEVITABLE

"You will seek Me and find Me when you search for Me with all your heart."

JEREMIAH 29:13

When considering God's will, one of the questions I frequently run into is that of inevitability. Is it absolutely inescapable that the Lord's plan will be accomplished? No doubt this is on your mind as you strive to make choices that honor Him. If the Lord is completely in control of everything, then does it really matter what you decide?

In order to discern what God desires for you, it's helpful to understand that His will has two aspects. First, His *determined* will includes those parts of His plan that are unchangeable—events that absolutely will happen, such as the fulfillment of prophecy. Second is God's *desired* will, which is subject to your free will—to your choosing to obey Him. We will discuss these two aspects further in the next few days.

However, whether you're operating in the Lord's *determined* or *desired* will, realize that God wants to help you walk in His plan (Philippians 2:13). He is motivated to reveal the path. Therefore, the moment you set your heart to obey Him, you set yourself up for success. So don't be afraid. The Lord *will* show you His will. Seek Him with all your heart, for you will certainly find Him.

Jesus, I want Your will, and I will choose to obey You. Keep me in the center of Your plan. Amen.

FULFILLED PROMISES

The LORD of hosts has sworn saying, "Surely, just
as I have intended so it has happened, and just as I
have planned so it will stand."

ISAIAH 14:24

The first aspect of God's plan we will look at is His *determined* will, which is what will absolutely, unfailingly be done because He is the Sovereign of the universe. We must begin with this foundation because it is the basis for understanding how God keeps His promises. It is fully within His ability to accomplish anything that He says will come to pass.

For example, the Lord God promised to send us a Savior (Jeremiah 31:31–34). He faithfully accomplished this and did so with a detailed list of specifications—such as what family Messiah would belong to (Genesis 12:3, 49:10; 2 Samuel 7:16), where He would be born (Micah 5:2), when He would live (Daniel 9:25–26), what He would do (Isaiah 61), the location of His ministry (Isaiah 9:1; Matthew 4:12–17), and how He would redeem us from our sins (Isaiah 53). And each of these promises was miraculously fulfilled in Jesus.

This is why you can always count on God to keep His wonderful promises to you—His awesome, all-encompassing sovereignty. Absolutely nothing is too difficult for Him, but all is faithfully accomplished out of His perfect, sacrificial love for you.

Lord, You are the all-powerful God! Thank You for keeping Your promises. Amen.

YOU MATTER

He made from one man every nation . . . having
determined their appointed times and the
boundaries of their habitation, that they would
seek God.

ACTS 17:26–27

God's *determined* will is what He's going to do, and what you and I must understand is that He doesn't make such plans exclusively for world events or nations. Rather, He also makes such plans for individuals. He makes them for you (Psalm 139:15–16).

We can know for certain that there are aspects of our lives that are part of God's *determined* will. For example, today's verse tells us the Father chose where, when, and to whom we would be born. God actively chooses our personalities, talents, and abilities. Likewise, the Lord creates and equips us with His purposes in mind.

So take heart that you are not a mistake. Understand that there are certain aspects of your life that are part of God's sovereign, determined, unchangeable plan that *will* happen. Of course, this may raise questions for you—especially when thinking about the hardships you've experienced and even the unfortunate decisions you've made. But do not lose sight of the fact that He planned your existence, and your life matters immensely to Him. Therefore, look for His good purposes in every part of His plan for you.

Jesus, thank You for Your determined plan
for me. To You be the glory. Amen.

CHOICES

Who is the man who fears the LORD? He will instruct him in the way he should choose.

PSALM 25:12

The second aspect of God's plan is His *desired* or *permissive* will. This is where the Lord has expressed His will and we have the opportunity to honor Him or go our own way. The Lord's *desired* will is neither irresistible nor unconditional. Rather, God gives you choices so you can exercise your free will in obeying Him. He does so for the purpose of having a genuine love relationship with you.

For example, consider Adam and Eve in the garden of Eden. Why did the Father leave them with the one prohibition? For the simple reason that the Lord wanted to give them an opportunity to love and respect Him freely through their obedience to His command. Without free will—without a choice to make—Adam and Eve would merely have been under obligation to the Lord God, like slaves under compulsion or robots programmed to carry out certain tasks.

Our loving heavenly Father is not honored by forced, unwilling, artificial submission. Rather, He is pleased and exalted when we obey Him because we know He is trustworthy, wise, and always acts in love toward us. So love and obey Him from the heart.

Jesus, I want to demonstrate my love to You through obedience. Show me the path I should take. Amen.

WALK WITH HIM

The LORD God is a sun and shield; the LORD gives
grace and glory; no good thing does He withhold
from those who walk uprightly.

PSALM 84:11

Whereas the Lord's *determined* will is inevitable, the Father's *desired* will for your life is knowable in the circumstances you experience and through what He's revealed in His Word. However, both God's *determined* and *desired* will require you to walk with Him and to make a decision about who He is to you.

The Lord wants you connected to Him in an intimate relationship continuously (1 Thessalonians 5:17). Of course, that doesn't mean God is going to reveal every detail to you, but you can certainly know what He wants you to do in the choices that are before you as you walk with Him. He will not keep His plans secret unless you refuse to seek Him (Jeremiah 29:13).

This is important because there are times when we come upon crossroads and make decisions that we don't realize are setting the course of our lives. No matter how vigilant we are, we are simply blind to their significance or impact on us and others. But when we are walking consistently with Christ, He always makes sure to direct us in the right way. There is no way to lose when you obey God.

Jesus, I walk with You. Thank You for leading me perfectly in the center of Your will. Amen.

THE CIRCUMSTANTIAL PLAN

Receive forgiveness of sins and an inheritance among those who have been sanctified by faith in Me.

ACTS 26:18

We've been studying God's *determined* and *desired* will. But what happens to His plans for us when we mess up? Because the truth of the matter is that no one—other than Jesus—can say he or she has always done God's will.

But no matter what you've done or who you've hurt, when you acknowledge that you were wrong, you repent of your sins, and you submit yourself to God, He sets in motion a plan for you to get back on track (1 John 1:9). This does not necessarily mean that you get back on the path of His *original* will for you. If God calls you to preach when you're eight years old, but you ignore Him until you are eighty, naturally you won't be able to experience or accomplish all He initially intended for you.

However, it doesn't matter if you're eight, eighteen, or eighty-eight—your heavenly Father always has a *circumstantial* plan for you—assignments for you to fulfill on your particular place on the path. He picks up the broken pieces of your life, and with the glue of His love and forgiveness, He puts you back together and gives you a wonderful purpose.

Jesus, thank You for forgiving me and getting my life back on track to serve You. Amen.

THE FATHER AWAITS

"This son of mine was dead and has come to life again."

LUKE 15:24

The Lord's attitude toward you can be seen through the father in the parable of the prodigal son (Luke 15:11–32). Perhaps you remember this story about a young man who asked his father for his share of the inheritance. The young man left home, wasted his money, and found himself in deep destitution.

The father in the parable never gave up on his son—just as your heavenly Father never gives up on you. Yes, God's heart is grieved when you turn away from Him. But your departure saddens Him because He understands that sin can only lead you to increasing disillusionment and despair. So, like the father in the story, He watches and waits for you to realize that what you're doing isn't working.

Eventually, when the prodigal returned home, the father saw him and ran to meet him. In the same way, the heavenly Father forgives and welcomes you home when you repent of your sin and return to Him (1 John 1:9). And because of your Father's great love, you still have a future. So don't continue to make the same mistakes by demanding your own way. Instead, run into His arms, accept His mercy, and acknowledge that His path for you is best.

Jesus, I repent and return to You. Thank You
for receiving me with open arms. Amen.

ACCEPTING NO

I hope in You, O LORD; You will answer, O Lord my God.

PSALM 38:15

At times, God will answer "no" to what you ask of Him. Do not despair. Instead, be willing to accept His response with full confidence that He is sovereign, omniscient, and always has your absolute best interest at heart. Take courage in these facts:

First, the Lord knows what is best for you and for others. God knows what your future can be and will say no to things that would not truly satisfy your heart or that would impede you from reaching your full potential. *Second, be assured that God can fulfill His promises to you.* So if He says no to one option, it's because He has another that's better. He has all power and authority, so even when your situation seems impossible by human standards, the Lord can still triumph. *Finally, the Lord is never too early or too late.* It may feel like your time is past; however, your God knows exactly when and how to accomplish His plans perfectly.

Friend, it hurts when God says no. But remember, He always acts with wisdom and love toward you. He knows what is best for you—so trust Him fully. Soon enough, you'll rejoice in His yes.

Jesus, I thank You for telling me no, knowing that Your best for me is still to come. Amen.

THE LORD ALONE

You alone, LORD, are God.

ISAIAH 37:20

Babylonian king Nebuchadnezzar set up an image of gold and ordered that all the people in the land bow down and worship it. However, three Hebrews, Shadrach, Meshach, and Abed-nego, had been taught from birth to worship the Lord God alone—so they refused to comply. Nebuchadnezzar threatened to have them thrown into a fiery furnace, but they replied, "Our God whom we serve is able to deliver us from the furnace of blazing fire; and He will deliver us out of your hand, O king. But even if He does not . . . we are not going to serve your gods or worship the golden image that you have set up" (Daniel 3:17–18). What a great proclamation of faith!

This is the attitude the Lord desires of all who believe in Him. Because there will be times when the roar of evil will be so great that you'll feel helpless to overcome it. But that is always the time to say, "My God is able to deliver me! But even if He doesn't, I will stay faithful!" You continue to exalt the Lord as the only true God. That is the faith He honors, which will ultimately lead to your deliverance—just as it did Shadrach, Meshach, and Abed-nego.

Jesus, only Your name is worthy of my worship. Despite the pressure to conform, I will stay faithful. Amen.

IMPROVING PERCEPTION

The LORD is compassionate and gracious, slow to anger and abounding in lovingkindness.

PSALM 103:8

How do you view God? Do you see Him as kind, holy, and loving toward you? Or do you perceive Him as harsh, judging, and unkind?

Many believers buy into the idea that the Lord is cruel and unforgiving. Their stance before God is like that of a person who is about to be hit by someone who is much bigger and stronger. He or she cowers and cringes, anticipating the blows that are coming.

But why is this false perception of God so prevalent when He's so graciously offered us salvation? Often, it's because of persistent misconceptions about God's purposes and love. People don't understand why the Lord doesn't allow certain behaviors or give particular blessings. They translate that into vindictiveness and judgment rather than His protective care and desire to set us free.

However, the antidote for this is to look into the face of our heavenly Father. Because when we do, we find ourselves peering into eyes filled with overflowing love. When we know Him through prayer and His Word, we increase in our love for the One who gives us all things—including our most precious blessings. We discover the One who created us and continuously works to set us free.

Jesus, I praise You because You are always loving, wise, and good. Amen.

LET HIM IN

*The creation was subjected to futility, not willingly,
but because of Him who subjected it, in hope that
the creation itself also will be set free from its
slavery to corruption into the freedom of the glory
of the children of God.*

Our inability to experience God's love is much like our inability to experience the fullness of the Lord's power working in us; we haven't yielded ourselves to Him. We have closed ourselves off to His work. Of course, that doesn't stop Him from loving you or from attempting to heal the wounded places of your heart. And He does so through the circumstances of life that break your dependency on the fleeting identity, security, and worth this world offers you.

Even in the struggles you face, friend, realize that your heavenly Father is calling out to you today, saying, "I love you; I'm not going to hurt you. I can heal you and set you free." God is not out to destroy you, but to woo you to Him. He desires to give you what would truly satisfy the deepest parts of your soul. So stop shutting Him out. The very things you are depending on are keeping you in bondage to your most profound wounds. Let Him in and allow Him to give you exactly what you truly need.

> Jesus, I invite You in. Heal me, my
> Savior. I trust You. Amen.

OVERCOMING

"In the world you have tribulation, but take
courage; I have overcome the world."

JOHN 16:33

Realize that as you go through difficult times, God will actively strengthen you to endure and overcome if you'll allow Him to. In today's verse, describing future afflictions, Jesus said so to His disciples. There will be times of hardship and suffering, but you can actively partake of the victory Christ gives you.

Therefore, when trouble strikes, that's the time to burrow into God. So many people run away from the Lord, blaming Him for their afflictions or assuming He has rejected them in some way. However, what they're really doing is distancing themselves from the true Source of their strength. So the more immense the challenges you face, the greater your need to be with the Lord. You may be very busy, but find the time to spend with Him. His presence energizes you for your work, makes you swift for the task, gives you endurance, and supplies the wisdom you need at every turn.

Realize that eventually, you will outlast this trial. Certainly, no trouble lasts forever—and this one is no exception. Your challenge is to be standing in faith, declaring that Jesus is Lord over all when it ends. Because that is your witness to others. And it is the true victory that overcomes this world.

Jesus, help me to remain firm in You
until Your triumph comes. Amen.

REFINED

You have been distressed by various trials, so that the proof of your faith, being more precious than gold which is perishable, even though tested by fire, may be found to result in praise and glory and honor at the revelation of Jesus Christ.

1 PETER 1:6–7

G old must be refined to remove any embedded impurities. That is, it must be melted by fire so that any pollution can float to the top and be skimmed from the surface.

The Christian life is frequently compared to this process. When we face struggles, God is purifying us like a precious metal, digging deep into our lives to eliminate all the pollution—our dependencies on anything other than Him. The Lord does not put us through this process because He sees us as worthless; on the contrary, it is because He sees the treasure in us. He doesn't do this to hurt us but to preserve the best parts of us and bring out what makes us truly beautiful.

Going through the fire is never pleasant, of course. But it is necessary and ultimately good. It not only brings out the best in you but increases your faith and your value to the kingdom of God—because you shine as a beautiful, unclouded reflection of Christ to others.

Jesus, give me that faith that is more precious than gold, resulting in praise and glory to You. Amen.

GOD IS IN CONTROL

Their own arm did not save them, but Your right
hand and Your arm and the light of Your presence.
PSALM 44:3

There was time I was struggling terribly with discouragement, doubt, fear, and loneliness. I spent many evenings having long conversations with a close friend, who listened patiently. Many times, during these talks, my friend would stop me and say, "But remember, God is in control."

God is in control. This statement became an anchor in my life. No matter how hard the winds of affliction blew or how much the adversity intensified, I was able to remain steady because of the simple truth of the Lord's sovereignty over all things. I could face whatever terrifying obstacle or insurmountable challenge with the assurance of the Father's complete power and wisdom to overcome it on my behalf.

This is what I pray for you today. Nothing that is happening to you is beyond His reach or strength to conquer it for you. Yes, you may feel the full impact that this trial is too big for you. But that is so you can know for certain that it is the Lord who delivers you. So do not lose heart or be afraid. God is in control. And He will undoubtedly help you.

God, You are in control of everything that concerns me! I will not fear but will praise Your name forever. Amen.

SUSTAINED UNDER PRESSURE

*Cast your burden upon the LORD and He will
sustain you.*

PSALM 55:22

One of the ways Jesus dealt with the pressures He faced was by stepping away from the furious pace of His world to be with the Father. Matthew 14:23 reports, "After He had sent the crowds away, He went up on the mountain by Himself to pray." He understood that those quiet moments of communion were absolutely essential. If they were crucial to the Savior, who is God in the flesh, how much more imperative are they for us?

Therefore, when stress builds and there's no relief in sight, we need to take Jesus' example and find a quiet place to be alone with Him, because that opens us to His presence, wisdom, and power. We cast our burdens onto Him, acknowledging Him as our sufficiency. He can carry the weight that accompanies any stressful or painful situation we face.

Many people struggle because they feel guilt over past sin and believe God won't hear their prayers. But the Father is waiting with unconditional love and forgiveness for us to approach Him—always willing to set us back on the right course. So never hesitate to take your afflictions and pressures to God in prayer. He knows everything you need even before you ask and longs to spend time alone with you.

**Jesus, thank You for loving and sustaining
me in times of burden and stress. Amen.**

THE PATH TO PEACE

*The LORD will give strength to His people; the
LORD will bless His people with peace.*

PSALM 29:11

W herever you are in life, you can experience God's peace
deep within your soul. Such tranquility comes when you
acknowledge your trust in the Lord and release control of your situation to Him. This does not mean you avoid responsibility; it means
you acknowledge that you need the Lord to help and guide you.

How do you do so? There are four essentials to experiencing God's peace. *First, express your total dependence on the Lord.*
Acknowledging God as your strength and refuge shifts your focus
from your finite abilities to His infinite power. *Second, pray.* Prayer
and meditation on God's Word are essential to experiencing true
peace because they are the key to having intimacy with Christ—your
Prince of Peace. *Third, speak out and demonstrate faith.* Hold on to
the fact the Lord has promised never to leave or forsake you and can
get you through anything you face. *Finally, focus on God.* Because
certainly, He will give you the wisdom, strength, and the peace you
need to withstand whatever happens.

Friend, the Lord is glad to give you His peace. Therefore, stop
worrying, give Him your concerns, and trust Him to lead you.

Jesus, thank You for Your peace and for
delivering me through all circumstances.
I praise Your name. Amen.

POWER IN PRAYER

The heartfelt and persistent prayer of a righteous man (believer) can accomplish much [when put into action and made effective by God—it is dynamic and can have tremendous power].

JAMES 5:16 AMP

Do you sometimes find it difficult to pray? Does it seem as if there is a battle going on in your mind—with thoughts bombarding you as you try to focus on God?

Nowhere does the Bible suggest that prayer is going to be easy. In fact, a struggle ensues when you bow before the Father. The Enemy will attack you—harassing you with doubts and attempting to convince you that God would never listen to someone like you. But the Devil does so because he knows how dangerous you are when you're on your knees before the throne of grace.

Today's verse illuminates this fact. Your prayers have tremendous power because of the One you appeal to. When you ask God for His answers to the challenges before you, He makes known solutions that are beyond imagination and carries them out on your behalf—freeing you and glorifying Himself. The Enemy hates that because it means his defeat.

So keep on praying. Push through. Cling to God and expect Him to act. Don't ever give up. Because in prayer is the sure path to victory.

Jesus, pray through me and help me persevere in prayer so that Your will is done in all things. Amen.

HIS HANDIWORK

We are His workmanship, created in Christ Jesus
for good works, which God prepared beforehand so
that we would walk in them.

EPHESIANS 2:10

Today's verse clearly tells you how Jesus sees you—you are precious to Him, His masterpiece, and a vessel of His important work.

What does it mean that you are God's *workmanship*? That word in Greek means "a person of notable excellence." You are a prized example of the Lord's creative genius—fit to reflect His glory and grace.

But notice you are *God's* workmanship. It is the Lord who knows the reason you exist, why He gave you certain weaknesses and strengths, the full potential of your giftedness, and all that is possible through you. It is also God who works through you. This is why He gives you His Holy Spirit when Jesus becomes your Savior—so He can train and empower you to be the person He envisions.

People need to see and know the living God. The good news is He wants to reveal Himself to them through you. Therefore, each morning, say to God, "I'm Yours, Lord. Lead me by Your Holy Spirit. Show me how to live for You—acting and thinking as Jesus would. Help me to glorify You today. Amen."

Yes, Jesus, I am Yours and exist for Your glory.
Lead me and work through me today. Amen.

SEPTEMBER

LISTEN TO HIM

Draw near to listen.

ECCLESIASTES 5:1

T hink about your interaction with someone you truly love. If you do all the talking, it isn't really a relationship, is it? True communication is a two-way street. You express yourself, and then you listen to the other person. He or she discloses something to you, you process what you hear, and you respond accordingly.

This is the process through which decisions are reached, consensus is built, agreements are forged, problems are solved, secrets are divulged, dreams are shared, vulnerabilities are revealed, information is exchanged, attitudes are influenced, encouragement is offered, and advice is given and received. A sense of intimacy develops through it all.

However, if you spend all your time telling the Lord about your problems, hopes, needs, feelings, desires, and doubts, you are missing out on hearing His wisdom, His dreams for your life, His provision for you, and His work in the world. Even worse, you will miss out on hearing about how God feels about you.

Friend, don't make that mistake. You have the privilege of having a relationship with the Sovereign of all creation. Show Him how much you love Him by taking time to listen to all He wants to tell you. You'll be glad you did.

Jesus, I draw near to listen to You. Thank You for loving and leading me. Amen.

MAKE THE DIFFERENCE

It is time for judgment to begin with the household of God.

1 PETER 4:17

I f you are wondering why the world and the church are in such a mess today, we can trace the problem to the fact that many believers don't see why knowing God and doing His will are that important. Many Christians actually comprehend so little about the Lord that they couldn't fill one side of a sheet of paper with facts about Him. And even if they could, they couldn't tell you how those facts apply to their lives, circumstances, or relationship with Him. If they go to Him, it's with a list of requests rather than to know the One who created them and glorify Him.

But you can make a difference. You can *know* God. You can become so intimately acquainted with Him that you can perceive how He is moving in your life and do His will in the world. You may think, *Oh, that's just for pastors, preachers, prophets, and missionaries.* But no, it is not. This kind of intimate relationship is His will for you. The Lord answers whoever will seek Him and reveals Himself to those who long to know Him. And He wants to work through you. So spend time with Him in the Word and in prayer, and let Him change the world and the church through you.

Here I am, Jesus—work through me. Amen.

HE IS LORD

At the name of Jesus every knee will bow, of those
who are in heaven and on earth and under the
earth, and that every tongue will confess that Jesus
Christ is Lord.

PHILIPPIANS 2:10–11

We may think of Jesus as our wonderful Savior and gifted Teacher. And He absolutely is. However, one of the most frequently used titles for Jesus in the New Testament is *kurios* or *Lord*—one possessing authority, power, and control. The Word of God describes Jesus as the Head of the church, the Ruler over all creation, and the King of kings (Colossians 1:18; Revelation 3:14; 17:14). Christ's reign covers everything in existence—whether in heaven or on the earth. No one—not even those who deny Him—will be free of His authority.

Although the Enemy and the world may try to convince us that liberty is found in doing what we want, true freedom is acquired only through submission to Christ's loving lordship. You are either working with His power or against it. And when you are submitted to Christ and joined with Him in His purposes, you are more than a conqueror with Him.

So have you submitted to Christ's rule over you? Choose Him as the Lord of your life and rejoice as His kingdom is established in you.

Jesus, You are my Lord! Rule in me and help me serve You better every day. Amen.

GOOD OR EVIL?

There is a way which seems right to a man, but its
end is the way of death.

PROVERBS 16:25

Maybe today you are wondering why it is that God calls some behaviors and attitudes sin that feel so natural to you. This paradox goes back to the fall. If you recall, the Father instructed Adam and Eve not to eat from a certain tree in the garden of Eden. We know they eventually disobeyed and ate of the Tree of the Knowledge of Good and Evil despite the Lord's command and warning (Genesis 3).

What ensued was that Adam and Eve received a great deal of information that they were unequipped to handle without God's guidance. Good and evil were put on equal footing. Yes, there were certain actions that they knew to be immoral from the beginning—such as murder and stealing. But because their sin caused them to die spiritually, they lost the capacity to discern right from wrong as they would have learned if they had allowed the Lord to teach them.

This is why we sometimes don't realize that the ways we are filling our needs are actually causing us to feel emptier and more destitute. It takes a relationship with Christ to truly understand how to have those needs met—that is, what's God's will for us and what isn't.

**Jesus, please teach me to walk in Your
wisdom and freedom. Amen.**

WHOLEHEARTED OBEDIENCE

Whatever is born of God overcomes the world; and this is the victory that has overcome the world—our faith.

1 JOHN 5:4

When you serve God, do you do so wholeheartedly or only partially? It's important for you to be aware that to the Lord, partial obedience is actually disobedience.

For example, when the armies of Aram threatened to attack Israel, King Joash went to see the prophet Elisha. Elisha told Joash to shoot an arrow out of the eastern window because, he proclaimed, "This is the LORD's arrow, an arrow of victory over Aram . . . Now pick up the other arrows and strike them against the ground" (2 Kings 13:17–18 NLT). In other words, Elijah challenged Joash to shoot the remaining arrows into the earth as a sign of his trust that God would win the battle. Sadly, Joash shot only three of the arrows and held the rest back, demonstrating that he didn't really believe the Lord's provision. And because of his lack of faith, he failed to achieve a complete victory over the enemy armies.

Don't make the same mistake. When God tells you to do something, have faith and do it thoroughly. With wholehearted obedience comes not only the fullness of His blessing but complete victory.

Jesus, I will trust You and obey You wholeheartedly. Thank You for the victory. Amen.

WHAT'S ON YOUR MIND?

As he thinks within himself, so he is.

PROVERBS 23:7

Have you ever considered what an amazing creation your mind is? Who you are and what you become are largely affected by how you think—because from your thoughts flow your feelings, words, attitudes, and behavior.

This is why you must guard against the world's influence—so you don't find yourself squeezed into its destructive mold. This is also the reason God calls for "the renewing of your mind" (Romans 12:2)—allowing your deliberations to be aligned with His Word and controlled by His Spirit. When the Lord has authority over your thinking, He will teach you discernment, empowering you to look beyond the surface of issues and see situations as they really are. This allows you to distinguish beyond right and wrong to what is His very best for you.

Your renewed mind begins with surrender to the Savior. Until you give Jesus full authority over your thoughts—taking them captive to Him (2 Corinthians 10:5)—you'll have no power to clear out the clutter that hinders you from living in the fullness of His will. But as you yield to Him and fill your mind with His Word, He'll transform your life for good.

Jesus, I take my thoughts captive to
You. Speak to me through Your Word
and guide by Your Spirit. Amen.

UNSHAKABLE

His voice shook the earth then, but now He has
promised, saying, "Yet once more I will shake not
only the earth, but also the heaven."

HEBREWS 12:26

When God speaks, everything shakes. And if your life is quaking today, it is because the Lord is communicating with you. He is allowing instability in your life so you will understand that the foundations you're standing on for your safety and worth are unstable. God is ridding you of all that doesn't give you any real security—shaking it to loosen its grip on you and so you can see it's not working.

The Lord also shows us what's absolutely unwavering—His character, Word, and kingdom. As Christians, we know that our eternal relationship with God and our future are secure in Jesus. As David wrote, "I have set the LORD continually before me; because He is at my right hand, I will not be shaken" (Psalm 16:8).

Understanding this should change how we operate. Why would we devote our time to what is doomed to fail? Instead, we should expend our energy on that which will last forever. As Hebrews 12:28 admonished, "Since we receive a kingdom which cannot be shaken, let us show gratitude, by which we may offer to God an acceptable service." Therefore, serve Him. Put your full hope in Christ. And in so doing, you will stand firm.

Jesus, my trust and hope are in You forever. Amen.

NO DOUBT ABOUT IT

"You shall love the Lord your God with all your heart, . . . soul, . . . mind, and . . . strength."

MARK 12:30

D o you realize there are aspects of God's will you never need to pray about—that you know with 100 percent certainty are always the Lord's plan for you? We see that in the Ten Commandments and the Sermon on the Mount (Exodus 20; Matthew 5–7). We are to love one another, forgive, and remain faithful to the Lord.

The greatest commandment, of course, is to love God above everything and everyone else. We put Him first, learn to listen for His voice, and watch for His path to open up before us. We are patient in our love for Him and others. We don't demand our way or rights. Instead, we surrender to God regardless of what He asks because that is the devotion He deserves as our Savior and Lord.

Likewise, we are to be grateful. In 1 Thessalonians 5:18, Paul reminds us, "In everything give thanks; for this is God's will for you in Christ Jesus." We praise God for His goodness toward us. We are no longer focused on what is wrong or our own feelings of inadequacy. Instead, we love Him with everything we have—and this puts us in the center of His will.

Jesus, I love and thank You with everything in me. You are all I have and all I need. Amen.

POWER IN FORGIVENESS

Do not be overcome by evil, but overcome evil with good.

ROMANS 12:21

Yesterday we saw that there are facets of the Lord's will you never need to pray about, just carry out. One of those—perhaps one of the most difficult and painful ones—is forgiveness. It is *always* God's plan for you to give up the hurt, resentment, and bitterness that have come about because of other people's actions.

This is why Paul wrote, "Do not grieve the Holy Spirit of God . . . Let all bitterness and . . . slander be put away from you, along with all malice. Be kind to one another, tender-hearted, forgiving each other, just as God in Christ also has forgiven you" (Ephesians 4:30–32). Paul admonishes you to forgive because instead of distressing and offending the Holy Spirit—and allowing evil a foothold—you're clearing the path for Christ to transform you and those who hurt you supernaturally. You become a powerful vessel of good for Jesus to work through.

The truth is, we don't have a right to be unforgiving toward anyone—not after all Christ has pardoned us. But when we forgive, we're acting like Jesus—releasing the matter so He can do the miraculous through it. So do it. Even when it's difficult, let it go. And allow the Lord to have His perfect way in the situation.

Jesus, help me forgive so Your miraculous plan can be accomplished. Amen.

REST

*"Come to Me, all who are weary and heavy-laden,
and I will give you rest."*

MATTHEW 11:28

The pressure to be perfect can be overwhelming. In the early years of my ministry, I felt that if I wasn't preaching or following up with church members, I was going to fail. There was always something I needed to be doing. And it wasn't just the number of activities I was engaged in that wore me out—it was the pressure I placed on myself to do them all perfectly.

I did not live a balanced life and, as a result, my physical health and the overall well-being of my mind and emotions suffered. Perhaps you can relate. We often impose standards on ourselves that the Lord never meant for us to bear. To Him, perfect obedience doesn't mean that we're always busy. Rather, what He desires of us is complete obedience out of love and trust. And that includes time to rest (Mark 6:31).

The more intensely you engage in your work and ministry, the more you need extended time apart from the pressure. Therefore, trust God to take care of the details. Set meaningful time aside for Jesus to restore your soul. He will reenergize you, rejuvenate your mind, refresh your relationships, and take your walk with Him to a new level.

Jesus, I need rest. Show me how to disengage so I can spend meaningful time with You. Amen.

FENDING OFF ATTACK

Do not give the devil an opportunity.
EPHESIANS 4:27

We hear about conflicts and attacks taking place all over the world, but they often seem very distant. But the truth is that every believer faces a war each day—we battle the Devil. Unfortunately, many people don't recognize his assault in their struggles of everyday life.

Our Enemy camouflages himself so he can attack undetected, and he is very deliberate in the way he strikes us. He goes for our minds first—making us focus on what we lack and what's wrong rather than on what God has given. We begin to fantasize about having our hungers fulfilled, triggering a chain reaction of thoughts and fantasies that eventually take us down the path of sin. Then, when confronted with the temptation, it's already too late. From there, our bodies turn in the direction our minds are already facing.

Therefore, to win the battle against Satan, we must be aware of how he attacks and instead bring our thoughts under the control of the Lord Jesus (2 Corinthians 10:5). Jesus reminds us to be grateful for what we have, heals the pain that we're trying to cover over, and gives us the right tools to resist the Enemy successfully. Certainly, when we recognize Satan's deception and depend on Jesus' strength to repel him, we can be confident of victory.

Jesus, help me recognize a satanic attack and resist it with Your truth. Amen.

LISTEN CLOSELY

Pray without ceasing.

1 THESSALONIANS 5:17

Sometimes it can be difficult to hear God when so many other voices clamor for your attention. But you can train yourself to listen to the Lord in any circumstance. You always have the ability to think about Him, meditate on His Word, and receive His counsel no matter what is happening.

This is actually why you have the presence of the Holy Spirit indwelling you and taking every step with you. This is also what it means to pray without ceasing. God is intimately present within you and always available to you—closer than even the sound in your ears. Therefore, you don't have to allow anything to crowd Him out but can always communicate with Him in the deepest part of your soul.

Jesus can and should be involved in everything you're doing, and you should pursue His perspective on everything you encounter. So even when the other voices are roaring, set your heart to seek God's presence at every turn. Because there is something exceedingly wonderful about coming to the end of a day when you've been aware of Christ's guiding presence with you moment by moment. It makes the most awesome difference in your life when you experience His energy, peace, and fulfillment every step of the way.

Jesus, I want an intimate, step-by-step walk with You. Teach me to listen to You closely and obey Your every prompting. Amen.

TRUST AND OBEDIENCE

To obey is better than sacrifice.

1 SAMUEL 15:22

God isn't looking for us to check off a list of sacrifices—He wants us to trust Him. This was certainly true when the Lord instructed Saul to go to Gilgal and wait seven days for the prophet Samuel to join him. The two would make a burnt offering together, and then Saul would be free to engage the Philistines in battle.

As the seventh day approached, however, Saul became increasingly restless. His soldiers were running away out of fear of the vast enemy army. Believing he needed to make an offering to have God's favor before fighting, Saul did so without Samuel. Sadly, 1 Samuel 13:10 tells us that "as soon as he finished . . . Samuel came." Saul thought the sacrifice was important, but really, it was his ability to trust God despite the pressure that mattered. And because of Saul's lack of faith, the Lord tore the kingdom from him.

Take this to heart today. God doesn't promise that you'll understand why He asks you to do certain things, and He doesn't need you to convince Him to bless you through sacrifices. Instead, you are to submit to Him moment by moment, trusting Him to implement His plan in His time. So wait on Him in obedience, with confidence that He knows exactly what He's doing and will lead you well.

Jesus, I wait on You. Lead me, my Savior. Amen.

REJECTING UNBELIEF

He did not waver in unbelief but grew strong in faith, giving glory to God.

ROMANS 4:20

Today's verse is about Abraham, the father of the nation of Israel. Over the decades he waited for God to give him a son, he did not falter in *unbelief* or grow discouraged that his body was too old to produce an heir. He kept trusting the Lord even when earthly hope was gone.

None of us wants to struggle with unbelief, but it is "the sin which so easily entangles us" (Hebrews 12:1). Either we don't really believe in God's existence, or we don't truly trust His character—that He's good and rewards those who seek Him (Hebrews 11:6). We do this on a practical level—relying more on the evidence we gather by our senses than on what He says is true. That's when we fall into the wrongful thinking that it's all up to us—we must find our own way because we don't trust Him to provide what's best.

Don't make this mistake. Unbelief will not only hinder you but can actually destroy you. Therefore, be like Abraham. Lay aside your doubts and make the conscious choice to believe God exists, and He rewards you with His best when you seek Him. Keep trusting the Lord when your earthly hope is gone, because that's when He receives the glory.

**Jesus, I believe You. Drive out
my unbelief, Lord. Amen.**

OPINIONS AND OBEDIENCE

By faith Noah . . . in reverence prepared an ark . . .
and became an heir of the righteousness which is
according to faith.

HEBREWS 11:7

When we read about Noah in Genesis 6–8, we see a clear picture of obedience. When God called him to build the ark—a task that seemed both impossible and illogical—Noah obeyed the Lord despite what other people thought of him.

Often, we may think that when we obey God, everyone will support us and cheer us on—especially other believers. However, that's not always the case. When you choose the path of obedience, others may react negatively. People may criticize you because they simply don't understand what the Lord is doing through you. They may also be angry you're doing things His way and serving His agenda instead of theirs. So it won't always be popular for you to obey God. But remember that His thoughts and ways are higher than ours, and He is always right (Isaiah 55:8–9).

Therefore, when the Lord tells you to do something, don't focus on the circumstances or other people. If Noah had listened to his critics, he would have been swept away with everyone else. Instead, he chose to submit to the Lord and was saved. Trusting God is always the wisest course of action.

Jesus, Yours is the only opinion that
matters. I will obey You. Amen.

SURRENDER

"Bring them here to Me."

MATTHEW 14:18

Right now, as you sit contemplating how you are going to accomplish everything you must do, stop and give it to God. Surrender all of it. The reason it all feels so overwhelming for you is because you keep wrestling with Him for control. So He continues to introduce new interruptions, burdens, and responsibilities until you realize this was never yours to manage in the first place.

When all the disciples had were five loaves and two fishes, and Jesus called them to feed the five thousand men, plus all the women and children, the task seemed absolutely impossible (Mark 6:30–44). The disciples were already hungry and tired. Even though they wanted to obey the Lord Jesus, what He was asking was far beyond them. But it was an easy task for God—so much that He produced an extra basketful for each of the disciples to take with them.

Your burdens are easy for God as well. So let it all go. Submit yourself to God. Tell Him you trust Him to show you how to get everything done step-by-step. He makes the time, provides the resources, gives you the strength and wisdom, and even makes you swift for the task. Fix your eyes on Jesus, take a deep breath, relax, and let Him lead.

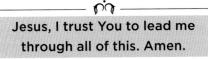

**Jesus, I trust You to lead me
through all of this. Amen.**

EMBRACE THE WORD

Faith comes from hearing, and hearing by the word of Christ.

ROMANS 10:17

D o you need something to hold on to when challenges arise? Would you like hope for your soul, a balm for your wounds, and answers to your deepest questions? God's Word provides just what you need. During any season, but especially in difficult times, His promises can be a very powerful anchor for your soul—giving you wisdom and enabling you to be courageous to face life's storms.

If you are unaware of all that the Father guarantees you in Scripture, it is no wonder you struggle during times of adversity. Faith is a gift from God, and it grows and matures as you hear, understand, and embrace His Word. It is through Scripture that He opens your spiritual eyes to see His reality and coming victory.

So take hold of the countless assurances you're given in Scripture—guarantees of protection, hope, counsel, and guidance, to name a few. And as you read God's Word, ask the Holy Spirit to point out applicable promises for your life. Study, memorize, and meditate on them. Your Father wants you to claim these truths. Then, when trials arise, you'll have a rock-solid foundation on which to stand because you'll trust that He will do all He says.

> Jesus, give me promises to hold on to, and help me understand and love Your Word more every day. Amen.

CLOSER AND DEEPER

*Do not hide Your face from Your servant, for I am
in distress; answer me quickly. Oh draw near to my
soul and redeem it.*

PSALM 69:17–18

D o you find yourself with an emptiness in your life that you just cannot seem to fill? Is it as if the life you're living just isn't enough? That is the Lord calling you to Himself—to a deeper, more meaningful level of relationship with Him.

I have often, in such instances, found myself praying, "God, draw me closer to You. I know You are all I need." Because only He can truly satisfy. Intimacy with the Lord is the only answer to our most profound needs. And we must come to a place of abiding in Him without wavering and without any obstacle to the flow of His Spirit into our lives. When we reach that place of deep intimacy with the Lord, we experience the joy, peace, and overflowing sense of love that we long for. Nothing on earth can equal it.

You will either move to the next level with the Lord, or you will continue to feel the emptiness—because nothing can fill it as He can. So allow Him to draw you closer. Relinquish whatever is standing in the way, and allow Him to satisfy your soul.

Jesus, draw me into deeper intimacy with You
and answer this profound emptiness in my
heart. You are enough. Fill my soul. Amen.

HE WILL FULFILL

*The vision is yet for the appointed time . . . Though
it tarries, wait for it; for it will certainly come, it
will not delay.*

HABAKKUK 2:3

Timing is everything. You see it in war—attacking at the wrong
instant could cost the battle. In the operating room, mistimed
procedures can result in tragedy. In sports, financial investing, business
negotiations, and personal relationships, moving in haste can
mean disaster; while waiting until the right moment can result in
victory. The most essential area for timing, however, is in your walk
with Jesus and His plan for your life.

You see it throughout Scripture—saints such as Abraham,
Joseph, Moses, and David were all developed, matured, and strengthened
in the seasons they waited on God. And at the perfect time, God
made all His promises come to pass (Joshua 21:45).

I know it can be very frustrating and wearying if you've been
praying for something for a very long time. Because it hasn't happened
yet, it may feel like it never will. But if the vision you have is
truly from God, there's absolutely no reason to fear. He will certainly
keep His word to you as He's always done (Isaiah 55:10–11). Stop
fretting and trust He's moving in the unseen and will fulfill all He's
said at the perfect time.

**Jesus, I trust Your timing and plan. Help
me be patient and faithful. Amen.**

CONTENTED IN HIM

*I have learned to be content in whatever
circumstances I am.*

PHILIPPIANS 4:11

A re you contented? Is there a sense of peace and fulfillment in your life that nothing can shake? For most people, the answer would be no. This is because contentment has nothing to do with material things, relationships, or achievements. In fact, making any of those the source of your security usually creates problems and turmoil.

Instead, only the Lord Jesus can bring about true contentment in a person's life—as can be seen in today's verse by the apostle Paul. However, what is important to understand is that Paul was not only strengthened when he was struggling, suffering, hungry, or abased. Christ supported and comforted Paul in all states—including when he was full, abounding, safe, and without adversity. This is important because Paul never attributed his well-being to anything other than Jesus. This is why, when other things were missing, Paul's contentment remained. Because Christ never left him.

True contentment doesn't rest in having earthly sources of worth and security, but in knowing that you are accepted, loved, and valued, despite what you may or may not have. Therefore, ultimate contentment is rooted in relationship with Jesus Christ and in Him alone. And because He never lets you down, you can always have peace.

**Jesus, You are my peace and contentment.
I set my heart on You. Amen.**

THE LEADING WORD

Send out Your light and Your truth, let them lead me.

PSALM 43:3

You know the Lord speaks to you and shows you what to do through His Word. He answers your questions, shows you what step to take next, and gives you understanding. This is why Psalm 119:105 says, "Your word is a lamp to my feet and a light to my path." You can know the Lord's plan because He reveals it to you through Scripture.

However, we can make the mistake of thinking of God's Word as a flashlight that passively sits in our hands—we point it in front of us to make sense of what's ahead. But the light of Scripture functions more like when God led the people of Israel out of Egypt as a pillar of fire (Exodus 13:21). The Israelites did not direct Him; rather, He actively led them.

You see, when you're using a flashlight, you can miss the path entirely if you don't know where to point. But when God is a pillar of light ahead of you, He makes turns that often don't make sense but that ultimately get you on the right road. Therefore, never treat your time in Scripture as passive. Instead of saying, "Lord, how can I solve my problem?" ask, "Jesus, lead me." Then you can follow His light wherever He takes you, certain you're on the right path.

Jesus, lead me. Illuminate the path through Your Word. Amen.

THE PROTECTIVE WORD

Be careful to listen to all these words which I
command you, so that it may be well with you . . .
for you will be doing what is good and right in the
sight of the LORD your God.

DEUTERONOMY 12:28

Throughout His Word, God is clear—His commands are meant to safeguard us from danger. You see, at times we may see something or someone we want and cannot imagine why our longings could be contrary to God's will. But the Lord perceives the dangers associated with it, and He doesn't want us to destroy ourselves. Rather, He wants us to take hold of His plan for our lives.

So God's commands are not meant to prevent us from enjoying life. On the contrary, they are meant to lead us to life at its very best. This is why the Lord told Joshua, "Be careful to do according to all the law which Moses My servant commanded you; do not turn from it to the right or to the left, so that you may have success wherever you go" (Joshua 1:7).

Therefore, trust what God tells you through His Word. Even when it seems restrictive or doesn't make sense, heed His warnings so that all may be well with you and you'll do what's good and right in His sight. Because that always results in blessing.

Jesus, I trust what You tell me, and I obey.
Thank You for keeping me safe. Amen.

THE CONVICTING WORD

I would not have come to know sin except through the Law; for I would not have known about coveting if the Law had not said, "You shall not covet."

ROMANS 7:7

Have you ever been doing your quiet time or reading the Word and felt the pang of conviction in your heart? If there's anything that can identify, convict us of, and uproot sin in our lives, it is the Holy Spirit working through Scripture. He speaks straight to you, convicting you of what you never even realized was wrong.

The Word not only shows us our faults but is also our weapon against sin (2 Corinthians 10:5). In other words, through Scripture, the Holy Spirit reveals not only the sin we are committing but also the consequences it is producing, why it has such a hold on us, and the root of error causing it. With such understanding and the knowledge of our true identity in Christ we find in the Bible, we are equipped to win a lasting victory over the bondage.

Therefore, when you're reading Scripture and feel conviction, don't ignore what the Lord is saying. Instead *confess* your sin, which means agree with God about it, and *repent*—or turn from your path to the one He shows you. And know He is making you free indeed (John 8:32).

Jesus, thank You for Scripture and for convicting me of sin so I can be free. Amen.

THE HEALING WORD

The word of God is living and active . . . piercing as far as the division of soul and spirit . . . and able to judge the thoughts and intentions of the heart.

HEBREWS 4:12

At times, we can be hesitant to read God's Word because it effectively pinpoints the areas the Father wants to work on—and that can be painful. But friend, it's absolutely worth it.

Scripture pierces as far as the soul and spirit. The *soul* is the seat of our senses, desires, affections, and appetites—what makes us who we are. The *spirit* gives us the ability to have an intimate relationship with God—it's how He interacts with, teaches, enables, grows, and empowers us. So Scripture helps us differentiate what originates in us and what's coming from God Himself. Likewise, through the Word, the Lord judges the thoughts and intentions of our hearts. Scripture reveals the forces driving us in the most profound places—not just *what* we're thinking, but *why*. God does this so He can apply the truth in our innermost parts and set us completely free (Romans 8:2).

So even when reading the Word is daunting or painful, keep at it! God sees you. He knows your burdens, wounds, and everything that steals your rest. Nothing is hidden from His sight, and none of it is beyond His reach. He can heal you. Let Him.

Jesus, heal me through the power of Your Word. Amen.

THE REVIVING WORD

"It is not an idle word for you; indeed it is your life."
DEUTERONOMY 32:47

As we've seen over the last few days, God's Word is not like other writings. It is different because it "is living and active" (Hebrews 4:12). It has vital power that's alive not merely in an earthly sense but also in an everlasting manner. Isaiah 40:8 tells us, "The word of our God stands forever." In other words, Scripture works to give you life—here and eternally.

How does it do so? The Bible guards what is sacred within you, feeds you as you mature, nourishes you when you're weary, comforts and strengthens you when you struggle or mourn, purges what is destroying you, brings you healing, and so much more. It's amazing how the Father will bring to mind the perfect verse when you're hurting, counseling others, needing wisdom, or requiring encouragement to endure difficulties. The Holy Spirit works through Scripture to reveal Himself, teach us how to walk with Him, conform us to Christ's image, minister to others, and breathe resurrection life into us.

With other writings, you bring your conceptions to them. But the Word of God brings the Lord's wisdom and understanding to you. And in that is life—abundant, everlasting, fulfilling life. So don't ignore it. Read it and live.

Jesus, my living Lord and Savior, revive me through Your living Word. Amen.

THE WORD OF WORSHIP

Ezra blessed the LORD the great God. And all the people answered, "Amen, Amen!" . . . then they bowed low and worshiped the LORD.

NEHEMIAH 8:6

H ave you ever been reading Scripture and the Holy Spirit touched your heart in such a powerful way that you began to worship God? We see this happen when Ezra opened God's Word and began to read it to the inhabitants of Jerusalem. When the people realized the Lord's awesome provision for them, they fell on their faces in adoration.

At times, we come before the Lord, and it's possible we're not really certain of what is causing the struggles we're living with. But then God reveals something very personal and private to us—some way He is healing or providing for us. This leads us to understand how deeply and intimately God loves us and cares for the issues closest to our hearts. He speaks directly to our most cherished hopes and answers the deepest questions of our souls through His Word in ways we've never imagined possible. And it causes us to worship Him.

If you've never experienced that, I pray the Lord will open Scripture to you in that way. Because God's Word reveals who He is and how much He loves you in a manner nothing else can. And that can change everything for you.

Jesus, I love You. Lead me to worship You through Your Word. Amen.

PAY ATTENTION

*We must pay much closer attention to what we
have heard, so that we do not drift away from it.*

HEBREWS 2:1

Today, your anchor is within reach. The ability to endure every-thing that assails you is within your ability to grasp it. You may feel as if you're drifting toward the edge of the abyss—so much is failing, unsure, unknown, and out of control. But hope is within reach. So how do you take hold of it?

Today's verse tells you how: *pay close attention to what you've heard from God.* Fix your eyes on Him. Remember that no matter how everything might look at the moment, it does not reveal the full story or take into account everything that's really going on. For example, Hebrews was written to Jewish Christians who were being persecuted. However, God worked through the persecution to scatter those early believers throughout the Roman Empire. This resulted in the gospel spreading like wildfire throughout the realm. What looked like a terrible situation was actually part of the Lord's great plan to save multitudes.

The same is true for your situation. God is always in control and always has a purpose. But taking hold of what Jesus has for you requires devotion. So don't allow the drift to dishearten you. Pay attention to the Lord and grab hold of hope.

**Jesus, my focus is on You. I hold on, knowing
You always give me hope. Amen.**

A PROTECTED MIND

Let us be sober, having put on . . . as a helmet, the hope of salvation.

1 THESSALONIANS 5:8

Have you ever considered why Scripture admonishes you to wear your salvation as a helmet? It seems a strange directive until you consider that soldiers would wear those helmets to protect their heads—and, more important, their ability to think and function. Certainly, we know that the brain keeps all our systems running and allows us the capacity to reason, make decisions, and process the information we receive through our senses.

But this is also why it's so necessary for us to guard our minds with the reality of the amazing gift Jesus has given us. It makes a difference as we interpret what's happening to us, make choices, and keep moving forward. Unfortunately, we can reduce our salvation to merely having heavenly housing insurance. But it is so much more than that. Being spiritually alive and indwelt by the Holy Spirit, having a relationship with the Father, belonging to His kingdom—these are all wonders we could ponder forever.

So today, carefully consider all your salvation means. Really think about all Jesus has done for you and make it a habit to guard your mind with it. It is the protection you need for all the earthly and spiritual battles you'll encounter.

Jesus, protect my mind with the fullness of Your salvation. Amen.

YOUR HEAVENLY CALLING

Holy brothers and sisters, who share in the
heavenly calling, fix your thoughts on Jesus.
HEBREWS 3:1 NIV

You have a heavenly calling—plans for your life that originate from the throne of grace. The Lord raises you up to be everything He created you to be. You are a member of the great assembly of witnesses, with supernatural empowering for all He calls you to accomplish. And you have authority—all things are subject to God's plan for your life as you obey Him.

What is past is gone. The Lord is doing a new thing in you. This is why Paul says, "Forgetting what lies behind and reaching forward to what lies ahead, I press on toward the goal for the prize of the upward call of God in Christ Jesus" (Philippians 3:13–14). Yes, you may feel pulled downward by the circumstances of your life, but your call from Jesus is ever upward.

Therefore, leave the past behind. Let it go and look up to pursue your victorious heavenly calling. Take hold of God's plan by fixing your thoughts on Jesus. You don't have to figure it all out or be in control. Rather, you focus on Christ—continually drawing nearer to Him spiritually, relationally, emotionally, intellectually, physically, and psychologically. And when you do, He takes care of the rest.

Jesus, I fix my eyes on You—pressing on to
take hold of all You have for me. Amen.

DAILY ENCOURAGEMENT

Encourage one another day after day, as long as it is still called "Today," so that none of you will be hardened by the deceitfulness of sin.

HEBREWS 3:13

So often, our unbelief arises as a result of discouragement. It comes from not seeing God's hand in our situation or the promises He's given us fulfilled. Somehow, the delays and disappointments remind us of the ways others have let us down. We confer their untrustworthiness to the Lord.

This is why it's so important to share our testimonies of God's faithfulness and encourage one another with the truth that He always keeps His word. Unfortunately, we do the opposite at times. Rather than recount all the blessings He's given us, we get together and complain. And the disbelief spreads.

Therefore, if we want to take hold of the promises God has for us, we must be on the lookout for unbelief—both in us and in others—and we must root it out. We must encourage ourselves daily in the Word and remind others of how the Lord has come through for us in the past. Because circumstances will arise that will make us doubt. But if we have a community of faith to support and reassure us, it will lessen the blow and make our trials an encouraging testimony for all involved.

Jesus, show me who I can encourage daily and who will do so for me in return. Amen.

OCTOBER

LETTING GO OF BITTERNESS

*Forgive anyone who offends you. Remember, the
Lord forgave you.*

COLOSSIANS 3:13 NLT

There may be people in your life who can immediately make your blood boil. At the mention of their name, you become tense. Perhaps it's someone who hurt you or cast you aside—treating you unfairly. Or maybe it's someone who has given you so much grief throughout your life, you just can't take it anymore.

When other people wound us, bitterness can creep into our hearts and create a stronghold. We are admonished to forgive those who injured us, but far too often we ignore this wisdom. Instead, we either strike out at them directly or undermine them in the eyes of others—seeking ways to wound them as they did us. But this doesn't actually achieve anything positive—certainly not justice for you. On the contrary, as long as you hold on to the hurt, you will continue to sink into the mire of pain, self-pity, and bondage. Stop that immediately.

Yes, it's right and good to have boundaries with those who are abusive—and you should. But stop trying to get retribution by holding on to your anger. Instead, forgive. Let go of the bitterness and give your wounds a chance to heal.

Jesus, help me let go and forgive. I need
You to heal me, rebuild my identity, and give
me grace for those who hurt me. Amen.

FREEDOM FROM FALSE GUILT

The sorrow that is according to the will of God produces a repentance without regret, leading to salvation.

2 CORINTHIANS 7:10

I f God is so gracious toward us, why does a feeling of guilt continue to plague so many believers? From where do the feelings of condemnation originate?

If you are experiencing random feelings of judgment that have no real basis in your life, understand that they may be coming from false beliefs about God or yourself. You know these are feelings of *false* guilt because they continually bombard, imprison, and depress you rather than leading you to repentance and freedom.

But understand, Jesus is not in the business of making you feel guilty; rather, He is working to clean up your life so you will no longer have to wrestle with shame and unworthiness. So if you would like to be free from the false feelings of condemnation that hold you captive, you must accept one very important fact: *Jesus has already forgiven you; therefore, you are accepted by God forever.* You must take it to heart that He knows your life from beginning to end—every trial and triumph, every fear and failure, every stumble and every success—and He accepts you *completely for eternity.* Don't fight it. Let Him set you free.

Jesus, if there is any sin in me, reveal it so I can repent. I receive Your forgiveness and love. Amen.

MOVING GOD'S WAY

On God my salvation and my glory rest . . . my refuge is in God.

PSALM 62:7

Today, intentionally move toward God. He most certainly is drawing you to Him. Tell the Lord how you feel, what you desire, where you hurt, and even why you believe there is pain in your heart. Then read God's Word with your eyes open to the ways the Lord wants to speak to you personally.

At times, you may feel as if God is answering the very questions of your heart as you spend time in Scripture. This is the Holy Spirit working in and through you. You are likely to discover the wise counsel you need, so read the Word with your heart open to the work God desires to do in you.

As the Lord reveals areas of woundedness, sin, improvement, challenge, or what have you, ask Him to lead you to the life He has for you. Be aware that He doesn't usually address issues at the symptom level; rather, He will go for the root—the profound ways He desires to transform you. Therefore, be willing to be open and transparent in the Lord's presence, to repent, and to do whatever He asks. Because this is the way to take hold of the hope He has for you.

Jesus, my heart is open to all You will say. Draw me near. Amen.

THE SOLUTION OF EVERY AGE

Do not be conformed to this world, but be transformed by the renewing of your mind.

ROMANS 12:2

After we accept Jesus as our Savior, aspects of how we operate must change. However, as we consider whether to make the change He's asking of us, we may think, *I thought this was natural— the reality of how people function and what feels right.* So we're continually tempted to remain trapped in our sins because we think it's how we're wired.

But we're admonished not to conform to "this world," which can also be translated as "age" or "time period." Of course, one of the main complaints we hear against the Bible is that it is old-fashioned. Nothing could be further from the truth. We may have a unique expression of the human struggle with sin today, but the underlying problem is the same as it has always been. Since the fall, people have always wrestled with issues of identity, acceptance, worth, and the rest. Most cope with their felt needs by turning to the accepted behaviors of the age, which promise to be new and improved. What people fail to understand, however, is that like every other man-made solution, those behaviors can only dull the pain they feel temporarily, because they don't reach down into the true source of the hurt as only Jesus can.

Jesus, I will do as You say. Transform me and set me free. Amen.

BLESSED BY HIS LOVE

I pray that the eyes of your heart may be
enlightened, so that you will know what . . . are the
riches of the glory of His inheritance in the saints.

EPHESIANS 1:18

D o you realize that you're the heir to an unimaginable inheritance that will never fade? If you're a believer, God has incredible blessings for you that are based not on anything you've done but on whose you are. No one can take your inheritance, because the Lord has guaranteed it to you by sealing you with His Holy Spirit of promise.

Of course, a great deal of it is available to you now—such as the indwelling Holy Spirit and your spiritual transformation, whereby you're conformed to the likeness of Jesus (Romans 8:29). Much of it, however, is beyond earthly comprehension. For example, one day, your mortal body will be changed into an imperishable, glorious one that is absolutely free from sin and death (1 Corinthians 15:42–54).

Why has the Lord done all this for you? Amazingly, He says it's so that throughout eternity He can show you "the surpassing riches of His grace in kindness" (Ephesians 2:7). He does it to show you His love. Let that encourage you today. And in gratitude for such amazing goodness, show Him you love Him in return by serving Him.

Jesus, thank You for Your great gifts to me.
You are so good, and I praise You! Amen.

UNFAILING

The LORD God, my God, is with you. He will not
fail you nor forsake you.

1 CHRONICLES 28:20

Do you struggle with inadequacy? Are you afraid that you will be unable to succeed in what you have been given to do? The fear of failure is one of the most debilitating but common anxieties people experience. Throughout the years, I've counseled many people who could not move ahead in their careers, relationships, or personal goals because they were afraid of being unsuccessful. Unable to trust God's strength, they looked at their own human frailty and concluded there was no hope.

I am convinced that this is why so many people struggle to rest completely in the Lord's provision—they believe He will let them fail. But understand, God will never call you to accomplish something in His name and then leave you to work out the details by yourself. Instead, He is personally involved in every aspect of your life and takes full responsibility for your needs as you obey Him.

As a believer, you have access to the wisdom and strength of almighty God. So renounce any feelings of doubt or fear. Instead, rejoice that the Lord works in you to do "far more abundantly beyond all" you can ask or imagine (Ephesians 3:20).

Jesus, You are my strength, wisdom, and
adequacy. Thank You for accomplishing
all You call me to do. Amen.

CHOOSING OBEDIENCE

"We must obey God rather than men. The God of our fathers raised up Jesus, whom you had put to death by hanging Him on a cross."

ACTS 5:29–30

After Jesus was resurrected, multitudes of people accepted Christ as their Savior through the ministry of the disciples. Miracles were happening on the streets of Jerusalem, and the Lord was being glorified. Sadly, because of jealousy, the scribes and Pharisees demanded that the disciples cease from preaching. However, we read the disciples' response in today's verse. They would continue preaching. Although the authorities killed Jesus on the cross, the Father raised Him up again! Whatever punishment the high priest could inflict, it wasn't permanent. But what God was doing through them was eternal.

I hope you're inspired by their example. Consider the millions of people who received eternal life because those disciples were faithful and counted obedience to God more important than their fear of man. In fact, if you think about it, you and I are saved today because they didn't give up testifying to the truth. Like them, we have a choice whether we'll acknowledge God's sovereignty and trust Him or turn away when there's pressure. So let's imitate their example and commit to following our heavenly Father wherever He leads.

Jesus, give me the courage to always obey You no matter the pressure. Amen.

UNIQUE PURPOSES

"I have filled him with the Spirit of God in wisdom, in understanding, in knowledge, and in all kinds of craftsmanship."

EXODUS 31:3

Have you experienced the joy, fulfillment, and inspiration of doing what the Lord created you to do? Often, when you discover the purposes for which God formed you, you know it because it fits you in a manner nothing else can. There is a freedom and pleasure in your work because of how the Holy Spirit flows through you to accomplish it.

This was certainly the case for Bezalel, the man God enabled to build the Old Testament tabernacle. The Lord gave him the artistic ability to follow and carry out all of His instructions, including understanding how to work with the special wood, metals, fabrics, and precious stones of the sanctuary.

God has created you with special giftings as well, and I pray you've had the joy of walking in what you were created to do. But if you've not yet discovered what it is, pay attention to what you do that feels like you're worshiping God, because that will tell you exactly what it is. Then trust the Holy Spirit to empower you, because He'll fulfill His mission through you in ways that will fill your heart.

Jesus, thank You for the unique purposes
You've created me for. Lead me in expressing
and glorifying You through my gifts. Amen.

ENTER HIS REST

Let us fear if, while a promise remains of entering
His rest, any one of you may seem to have come
short of it.

HEBREWS 4:1

Today's verse may seem strange, considering that Scripture often tells us not to fear. After all, in Isaiah 41:10, the Lord says, "Do not fear, for I am with you; do not anxiously look about you, for I am your God." Likewise, Deuteronomy 31:8 teaches, "The LORD is the one who goes ahead of you; He will be with you. He will not fail you or forsake you. Do not fear or be dismayed."

But Scripture is clear that we are to be wary of missing God's rest. The Greek word for *rest* is key to understanding this admonition. Yes, it means a cessation of activity, but in the ancient world, it also carried the understanding of overthrowing an oppressive force from power. The idea here, therefore, is that you depose earthly forms of rulership from the throne of your life, recognizing that the Lord is, indeed, the One in control.

Entering into God's rest means you don't have to strive or feel helpless or unworthy anymore because you accept the Father's leadership, provision, and protection. He fights the battles for you. So don't miss out. Instead, "in all your ways acknowledge Him, and He will make your paths straight" (Proverbs 3:6).

Jesus, take Your place on the throne of my life. You are my Lord. Amen.

WARFARE PRAYER

Take up the full armor of God, so that you will
be able to resist in the evil day, and having done
everything, to stand firm.

EPHESIANS 6:13

As believers, we face a very real adversary and spiritual warfare that can affect us in untold ways. Ephesians 6:12 confirms, "Our struggle is not against flesh and blood, but against . . . spiritual forces of wickedness in the heavenly places." Of course, to do battle in a spiritual war, you have to fight with spiritual armaments such as we see in the armor of God. And one of our greatest weapons is prayer.

Through prayer, God prepares you to resist the Devil, sin, and temptation. How? First, He helps you avoid the traps and the pitfalls the Enemy sets for you. Second, the Lord identifies the triggers the Enemy uses to entice you to sin and uproots them. Third, God builds up your spiritual strength and defenses to oppose the Devil. Finally, the Lord defends you by sending the shield of Scripture to mind when a temptation arises.

The point is, through prayer, God enables you to use the spiritual arsenal He's given you and leads you to victory. So don't miss what He is saying. Fight your battles—both earthly and spiritual—on your knees. Because when you do, you win every time.

Jesus, I fight these spiritual battles in prayer to You. Lead me to victory, my Commander. Amen.

WAIT IN PRAYER

*"Do not be afraid, Daniel, for from the first day
that you set your heart on understanding this and
on humbling yourself before your God, your words
were heard, and I have come in response."*

DANIEL 10:12

Sometimes it will take time for the Lord to respond to your requests. The point is, *keep praying* because God *will* answer you. We see this in a wonderfully vivid way in Daniel 10. Daniel had seen a vision from the Lord but didn't understand it. So for weeks, he prayed without ceasing.

Perhaps you understand Daniel's desperation at not receiving a response. The Lord allows trials to assail your life, but there's no explanation, so sorrow fills your heart. You may never know why it is that God delays—it may be because He is engineering your circumstances or teaching you to trust Him despite your situation. Likewise, there may be forces standing in the way of God's will for you that you couldn't possibly imagine—as there were in Daniel's case. However, eventually, God sent a messenger to answer Daniel, which you see in today's verse. Certainly, He will respond to you as well.

The key is that, like Daniel, you must wait patiently for the Father. *Be diligent and do not give up.* Because God is working in the unseen and will certainly triumph on your behalf. Pray in faith and wait on the Lord.

Jesus, I wait in faith on You. Amen.

GOOD SOIL

"The seed in the good soil, these are the ones who
have heard the word in an honest and good heart,
and hold it fast, and bear fruit with perseverance."

LUKE 8:15

D o you ever wonder what it takes to grow in Christ? In the parable of the sower, Jesus explains the kind of heart that's receptive to His Word. He says we must:

Hear the Word. We don't allow the teaching of Scripture to merely pass through our ears; rather, we listen to and apply it. We're willing to have any area sifted, refined, and liberated by His truth.

Be honest—open, transparent, and genuine with the Lord.

Be good—which means *turned toward God.* We know this because when the rich young ruler called Jesus a good Teacher, Jesus replied, "Why do you call Me good? No one is good except God alone" (Mark 10:18). So we must be people who seek to have His character and purge all things that oppose Him from our lives.

Hold the Word fast—keeping possession of it. We never let go or doubt God—even when we don't understand our circumstances.

Bear fruit—being productive and examining the fruit of our lives regularly.

And *persevere*—staying the course always, because that's how we become mature and produce a great harvest for His name.

**Jesus, make my heart good soil for Your Word,
and make it abundantly fruitful. Amen.**

ALL TO APPROACH

"Their burnt offerings and their sacrifices will be acceptable on My altar; for My house will be called a house of prayer for all the peoples."

ISAIAH 56:7

When the priests would enter the tabernacle, the first thing they would see is the altar of sacrifice. Have you ever considered why? We would be correct in saying that sin had to be atoned for—that the priests had to be made clean internally before they could serve God. They surrendered sacrifices to destruction in order for that to be possible.

But those offerings actually carried an even deeper meaning. In fact, the book of Leviticus often uses a word for *sacrifice* or *offering* that comes from a root that means to "approach" or "go near"—as in becoming personally involved in a relationship with someone. In other words, the priests would make the offering first in order to say, "I would give anything to draw near to You, Lord."

This is why Jesus became the sacrifice for us. So when we say, "I would give anything to draw near to You, Lord," Jesus can tell us, "I gave *everything* so you *could*—always." He wants us to be in relationship with Him even more profoundly and passionately than we do. So don't deny Him. Appreciate His sacrifice, draw close, and love your Savior.

Jesus, thank You for giving everything so I can draw close. Amen.

RECEIVE HIS LIGHT

*God, who said, "Light shall shine out of darkness,"
is the One who has shone in our hearts to give the
Light of the knowledge of the glory of God in the
face of Christ.*

2 CORINTHIANS 4:6

T he road ahead may seem very veiled and dim for you. But realize that Jesus came to illuminate your path. You see, sin not only condemns the unbeliever to death but also darkens our vision, blinding us to divine things and working despondency and ruin in us. This is the gloom we can feel when we lack understanding of God and His ways, unwittingly engage in behaviors that lead to our destruction, and don't know what to do.

This is why Jesus came. He is "the true Light which, coming into the world, enlightens every man" (John 1:9). He not only provides us with salvation but instructs us and gives us understanding. You may be feeling some darkness about your situation, and you wish you knew what to do. Jesus desires to make the path clear.

Therefore, even though shining the light on your darkest places is humbling, allow Christ to expose the areas where sin is defeating and blinding you. He will reveal what keeps you in bondage and set you free. So listen to Him. And receive the light you need.

**Jesus, You are the Light of my life. Illuminate
the way, and I will obey You. Amen.**

HIS POWERFUL NAME

*"Whatever you ask in My name, that will I do, so
that the Father may be glorified in the Son."*

JOHN 14:13

As a believer, you can pray in Jesus' name—which signifies your relationship with Christ and your right to approach His throne of grace because of what He's done for you on the cross. Jesus sits glorified at the right hand of God, where He intercedes for you and serves as your High Priest (Hebrews 4:16; 7:25). He has instructed you to approach and ask for whatever you need from your heavenly Father, knowing you have an Advocate in Him.

However, to pray in Jesus' name means agreement with His holiness, purpose, and plan. Some have misunderstood this verse, interpreting it as a license to ask God for anything and believing that the Lord is then bound to give it. What Jesus is really saying, however, is that by calling on His name, you're making your request according to His will and character (1 John 5:14).

Praying in Jesus' name is a serious matter and a matchless blessing. His name is your assurance that He will shape your prayers in His image and that you have assurance of an answer. You can be absolutely certain that your prayers will be heard and that God will respond.

**I praise You, Jesus, for the power in Your
name! I pray in agreement with You. Amen.**

THINK ABOUT OTHERS

*Let us consider how to stimulate one another to
love and good deeds.*

HEBREWS 10:24

Have you been caught up in your own worries and fears? Has your focus been on yourself? You probably realize that doesn't really help your situation (Matthew 6:25–34). Certainly, you know your attention would be better spent on what God would have you do, which is "seek first His kingdom and His righteousness" (Matthew 6:33). And you do that by loving others in His name.

Understand that the Enemy will tempt you to dwell on your problems because it stops you from taking part in the body of Christ. But can you imagine if the apostle Paul had gotten mired in worry and self-pity when he was in prison? He wouldn't have written so much of the New Testament. But instead, because he stayed faithful in encouraging others, Paul would hear good news about how the churches were growing and how believers were stepping out in faith, and could say, "This is all worth it."

So instead of entertaining thoughts about what is wrong, think about how you can help others grow in their faith and mature in their giftedness. In other words, focus your energy on helping others be more like Jesus. Because that is certainly worthy of your attention.

Jesus, give me opportunities to help other
believers grow in their faith for Your glory. Amen.

NOT KNOWING, BUT TRUSTING

By faith Abraham . . . obeyed by going out to a
place which he was to receive for an inheritance . . .
not knowing where he was going.

HEBREWS 11:8

It's frustrating when God doesn't tell us what our destination will be. We want to know where we're going so we'll know how to prepare. But Scripture gives us Abraham as an example of the complete trust we can have in the Lord when our vision of the future is incomplete.

Abraham left everything he'd always known, and he was not told where he was going. He had no idea if he'd know the language or customs or would be able to find the provisions he needed along the way. But Abraham obeyed God immediately. Without complaining or questioning God's wisdom, he went forth. And the Lord honored Abraham because He could count on him to do whatever He asked—which is the definition of faith.

The Lord doesn't give maps, just steps to obedience. Yes, being blind to what's ahead and being out of control is uncomfortable. But faith means stepping out without the details, trusting the One who sends you. So do what He says, and believe God will not only get you to the destination but will ready you for it before you get there.

Jesus, I believe You and will do all You say. Amen.

A GOOD WORD

He who gives attention to the word will find good,
and blessed is he who trusts in the LORD.

PROVERBS 16:20

If you need a good word today, remember that the Bible always has something worthy, edifying, and profound to say to you. I have often found that God leads me to exactly the right passage just when I need it the most. He also reminds me of principles He's already taught me so that I'll be able to apply them in the circumstances that arise throughout the day.

The wonder of God's Word is that through it, the Holy Spirit reveals countless layers of insight and meaning to you and can address an infinite number of areas in your life. But the most important thing the Holy Spirit does through Scripture is grow your relationship with Christ—the more you comprehend His character and ways, the better you trust Him. Likewise, you mature in your understanding of who He created you to be.

God's Word is always a sure and absolute foundation for you. It doesn't change even when the storms blow and the world around you is shifting, confusing, and unstable (Matthew 7:24–25). Therefore, go to Scripture for the good word you need, receive the insight and strength you seek, and build your life on the foundation that never fails.

Jesus, thank You for Your wonderful Word!
Speak to me through it, Lord. Amen.

ACTIVE WAITING

Wait for the LORD and keep His way, and He will exalt you.

PSALM 37:34

A re you waiting on God today? Understand that was not meant to be a passive undertaking. Yes, you are to be *still* in the sense that you take your hands off your situation and allow the Father to work through your circumstances. But you are also to be *active* in growing spiritually. As you discover God's will, you actively claim His promises and continue obeying Him step-by-step.

Think of it like this: just as we work on our physical muscles in a gym, a time of waiting is an opportunity to develop our spiritual muscles—our faith, character, and perseverance. We do so by incorporating Scripture into our lives and expressing our faith that the Father is working on our behalf. We take hold of the promises He's given, vigorously set our hearts to believe Him, and energetically obey whenever He calls. And as we make the active choice to trust His promises, our hope grows, and we learn to face the time of delay with expectant endurance.

Thankfully, because the Sovereign God of the universe has never faltered in fulfilling His word, we are absolutely assured He will not fail us now. Our active resolve to trust Him is part of the process that leads to blessing.

Jesus, I resolve to actively trust in You as I wait. Lead me step-by-step, my Savior. Amen.

THE BEST PATH

You will make known to me the path of life; in Your presence is fullness of joy

PSALM 16:11

Today, express your faith that God will lead you in the absolute best path for your life. The Lord is the only One who has all the facts, who knows the full truth about you and your future, and who can guide you unwaveringly to what is right and good every time. The sovereign, omniscient God is the only One completely capable of accomplishing whatever He promises you. He is going to have His way no matter what happens. Therefore, it is *always* wise to listen to Him, to include the Lord in all your decision-making, and to entrust Him with every aspect of your life.

So even when details of God's plan remain mysterious to you—even when you don't understand what's going on or know what to do—trust Him and obey inch by inch and step-by-step. Choose to submit to and have faith in the God who loves you unconditionally. He has the best plan for your life, has equipped you to accomplish it, and will enable you to fulfill all His awesome purposes for you as you walk with Him.

God, I trust You in all the unknowns, fully confident that You are working in the unseen. I have absolute faith that You are leading me in the very best path. Amen.

UNDERSTANDING HIS DISCIPLINE

*All discipline for the moment seems not to be
joyful, but sorrowful; yet . . . it yields the peaceful
fruit of righteousness.*

HEBREWS 12:11

God is working in you and on you today because He desires to work *through* you. Take that to heart, regardless of what you're facing. His love for you hasn't changed. Even if you don't feel His presence as you once did, He still cares for you deeply.

However, understand that the Lord has a great plan and purpose for your life—and that takes discipline and training. Like an athlete preparing for an Olympic game, it takes instruction, work, and refinement. God is doing something good in you.

So why do you keep feeling as if you're being punished? Understand that the issue probably isn't with Jesus—He loved you so much He died for you. Rather, the problem may be your perception of the Father. If you have a wrong attitude about Him, you aren't going to hear what He wants to say to you.

Therefore, today, ask God to make sense of the challenges you're facing, and root out any misperceptions you have of Him. Certainly, He will show you His love and how He's working for your good.

**Jesus, help me accept Your love and all
You are doing in my life. Amen.**

AS HE SEES YOU

LORD, You have searched me and known me . . .
You understand my thought from afar.

PSALM 139:1–2

Today, listen to your thoughts. Think about what you think about. This will show you what is truly dominating your mind. Because if you're continually saying, "God isn't going to speak to me," "I don't deserve His love," or any variation of those messages, then no matter how loudly He speaks to you, you won't believe it. You may even be afraid to listen to God. You may feel so condemned that you don't want to hear how else you fall short.

But friend, you must see yourself as the Lord sees you—as His beloved, blood-bought child who needs His divine guidance and grace every day. Jesus has forgiven your sins and made you acceptable and worthwhile. He has sealed you with His Holy Spirit and made you His representative in this lost world. He could have taken you home to heaven immediately after you accepted Christ as Savior. But He didn't because you have a story to tell. You've had your sins forgiven. And there are others who need to hear how profoundly God has set you free. So embrace who you are and fight any feelings of inferiority and guilt with the truth of Scripture.

Jesus, thank You for loving me and
having a purpose for my life. Help me
see my life as You do. Amen.

WAIT IN STILLNESS

Cease striving and know that I am God.
PSALM 46:10

Today, the pressure to move forward may be overwhelming. But if God has not spoken to you, stay where you are. It is inherently dangerous to act in haste. You may feel tempted to reason everything out in your mind and figure out all the unknowns—as if it depends on you to engineer a solution. But the Lord does not need your assistance.

In fact, the adage, "God helps those who help themselves" is not biblical. Instead, what Scripture says is, "Trust in the LORD with all your heart and do not lean on your own understanding. In all your ways acknowledge Him, and He will make your paths straight" (Proverbs 3:5–6). God sets your course. So stop wrestling with Him for control. Instead, as today's verse instructs, cease striving and trust His all-powerful, all-knowing, unconditionally loving plan.

The Father knows that you cannot help yourself in this situation. He realizes the pressure you feel and how important all of this is to you. But as long as you're trying to orchestrate a solution, you will miss what He is doing. So be still and quiet in His presence. Lay down your efforts and simply trust Him. Not only will He direct your path, but He will do so in ways beyond what you can imagine.

> Jesus, You are God. I wait in stillness
> for Your wise direction. Amen.

Keep Praying

"Always pray and never give up."
LUKE 18:1 NLT

There is a vital element in prayer that most people overlook, which is persistence. So if you've been praying for something for a long time, keep at it and do not lose heart. At times, God will delay answering our requests, even if they are His will for us. Why does He do so?

First, the Lord will postpone if you're not ready for His response. If He sees sin, bitterness, unforgiveness, or unhealthy habits in your life, He will straighten that out first. A second reason for God's delay is to build your faith. Do you trust the Lord and respect Him as God even when you don't see His answer? Remember, faith means you believe He exists and that He rewards you when you earnestly seek Him (Hebrews 11:6). Make Him your delight, keep believing Him, and be confident that He will provide the best for you. Finally, God sometimes delays His answer to develop your patience. What you desire may require perseverance once you receive it, and persisting in prayer will train you to endure.

So keep on asking, seeking, and knocking. Don't give up. Hang in there—even when you don't see any evidence that God will answer your prayer, because, eventually, you will see His provision in your situation.

Jesus, I believe You will answer me, so I continue to pray and trust You. Amen.

LEAVE HIM ROOM

Never take your own revenge, beloved, but leave
room for the wrath of God, for it is written,
"Vengeance is Mine, I will repay."

ROMANS 12:19

A t times, when someone wrongs you or a loved one, you may feel tempted to become an arbiter of justice and take matters into your own hands. However, remember that your charge is always to be a representative of Christ. As believers, our duty isn't to get revenge or prove a point. Our responsibility is to represent Jesus so that others will be saved. We can do so because God is already a good and faithful Judge, and we don't have to do His job.

In fact, today's verse is a quote from Deuteronomy 32:35—a warning to Israel about seeking forms of security other than God. In that passage, Moses prophesied that Israel was going to chase after other deities for prosperity, guidance, and security. So God warned them, saying, *I am your Protector. If you run to one of these false gods, then My vengeance will turn from your enemies to you.*

The same is true for us. When we turn to our forms of vengeance against another person—whether with gossip, politics, or manipulation—we're getting in God's way. This is why Paul admonishes us to leave room for His justice. Remember that. Forgive and give the Lord space to work.

Jesus, I trust Your judgment.
Help me forgive. Amen.

CLOSED DOORS

*Rejoice in the Lord. I never get tired of telling you
these things, and I do it to safeguard your faith.*

PHILIPPIANS 3:1 NLT

It can be confusing when you face a closed door, sudden tragedy, or loss. You may wonder, *How can any good come out of this?*—especially when your circumstances are painful or disheartening. However, often what appears to be an ending is actually a new opportunity God has for you if you'll trust Him in it.

This was certainly true when Paul was arrested and imprisoned for doing the very thing the Lord had called him to—preach the gospel. Paul could have easily become discouraged and thought, *God, why did You allow this to happen? I thought You had a plan for my life.* But he didn't. Instead, Paul used the time he spent in jail to write Galatians, Ephesians, Philippians, and Colossians. And God has worked powerfully through Paul's writings to encourage believers throughout history.

So today, if you are facing losses that you don't understand, realize God is positioning you for an open door of purpose and blessing. Stay on course, keep your eyes on Him, and trust that what He is doing is good. Certainly He will use everything in your life for His greater purposes.

Lord, I will rejoice in You and trust Your good
purposes regardless of closed doors. Amen.

EXPECTANT WAITING

*I wait for the LORD, my soul does wait, and in His
word do I hope.*

PSALM 130:5

Waiting on the Lord doesn't mean you are stagnant and inactive—or that He is either. God is always moving and orchestrating His plans. Still, the temptation to move forward without receiving direction from Him may be great because of external pressures that are very real and stressful.

Remember that God is greater than all the circumstances that assail you. But it's of utmost—and maybe even eternal—importance that you pause until you receive further instruction from Him. This means you are actively pursuing *Him*. You are still in motion; however, your direction is toward *God*, not the thing you're waiting for. You decide not to act on any decisions until the Lord gives you clear direction.

Never fear about whether or not God has a plan for the next stage of your life. As believers, we can get to the point where we wonder if the Lord is done with us, but He never is—not for eternity. And He won't leave you to guess what He desires of you—not as long as you're seeking Him. Rather, He desires that you remain connected to Him through an intimate relationship. So it's essential that you listen to Him and wait—actively, with great expectation and hope.

**Jesus, I wait on You with hope and
expectation. My focus is on You. Amen.**

ON THE ALTAR

"Take now your son, your only son, whom you love, Isaac, and . . . offer him."

GENESIS 22:2

This was the first time the word *love* was used in Scripture—when the Lord asked Abraham to offer Isaac. If you recall, Abraham was one hundred years old when God gave him a son so he could become a great nation (Genesis 15:1–6). But Isaac wasn't just the fulfillment of the promise to Abraham—he *loved* his son. So to sacrifice Isaac must have been excruciating.

We tend to think that telling God how much we love something will force Him to do as we wish. But often, what we're really saying to Him is, "If You take this away or refuse to give it to me, I won't believe in You anymore." We are actually betraying that what we want is more important to us than He is.

That is why the Lord will say, "I'm making sure that nothing stands in the way of you placing your full trust in Me." For Abraham, that meant putting both Isaac and the promise on that altar. But for you, that may mean submitting your own desires in order to do God's will. It's difficult, friend, but worthwhile. Because just as He honored Abraham's obedience and provided for both him and Isaac, He will do so for you—above and beyond what you can imagine.

Jesus, I completely surrender. I trust You to provide. Amen.

HEMMED IN

"Stand by and see the salvation of the LORD which
He will accomplish for you today."

EXODUS 14:13

As God led the people of Israel out of their bondage in Egypt, He made it seem as if the Israelites were confused in order to tempt Pharaoh into chasing them. This resulted in the people of Israel being trapped between the Red Sea and the powerful Egyptian army. Certainly, this was a perplexing situation for Israel. Had the Lord brought them all this way just to abandon them?

The same may be true for you today. You may feel caught in a situation that has no earthly solution. And you may be wondering why God would bring you so far just to corner you in these adverse circumstances. But remember, the miracle of parting the Red Sea—by which God saved the Israelites—stopped the Egyptians from ever pursuing them again. In much the same way, the Lord has hemmed you in to reveal His glory and provision to you.

So take heart. God has not forgotten or failed you. He led you here to this place for a reason—and it certainly isn't for destruction. Rather, it is to show you freedom in an area where you haven't experienced it previously. So do not fear. Stand by, trust Him to work, and watch for His deliverance.

Jesus, only You can solve this. I trust You to
show me Your powerful salvation. Amen.

TIME TO LISTEN

"The LORD will fight for you while you keep silent."
EXODUS 14:14

Most people, when in high-pressure situations, want to talk out their troubles, complain, and poll others about what to do. You can almost imagine the conversations the Israelites were having as they came to the Red Sea, pursued by the Egyptian army. "What are we going to do? Should we fight? Should we give up? Can you swim?" However, all the discussion in the world could not help them. No, it was time for them to stop speaking and start obeying.

In your own troubles, understand it's not necessary to continually rehash your worries, opinions, and misgivings to the Lord. Yes, you should "pray without ceasing" (1 Thessalonians 5:17). But that doesn't mean you do all the talking, and it certainly doesn't mean you can intercede instead of obeying. God doesn't need you to figure this out; He wants you to trust Him.

The Israelites had no way of knowing the Lord would part the Red Sea to save them, and you probably won't be able to guess how God will help you. So cease from agonizing over your problems. Stop talking and start listening to your Commander. And no matter what He says, obey. Because He will certainly open the way before you.

Jesus, help me to listen to and obey You, and keep me in the center of Your plan. Amen.

DESTROYING STRONGHOLDS

We are destroying speculations and every lofty
thing raised up against the knowledge of God.

2 CORINTHIANS 10:5

When the Enemy has a stronghold in your life, he's established a pattern of thinking or behavior from which he can assault your inner being. Therefore, it's crucial for you to tear down the Enemy's strongholds so you can enjoy the freedom Christ has purchased for you. However, understand that you cannot fight the Enemy by ordinary means.

First, you must restrict the Enemy's work and influence by bringing every thought captive to Christ. Second, rid yourself of any objects that belong to Satan. If you have any astrological or occult paraphernalia, destroy it at once (Deuteronomy 18:10–14; Galatians 5:16–25). Third, pray in Jesus' name for the stronghold to be shattered. Finally, ask Christ to lead you to Scripture that will arm you for the battle and replace the error in your thinking with His truth.

You're not the one crushing the Enemy's influence in your life. Rather, you triumph through the name of Jesus, because Satan cannot stand in the presence of the Son of God. Therefore, your liberation lies in humble faith in Christ. Jesus came to set you free, so claim that freedom today by submitting to His battle plan.

Jesus, thank You for shattering every
stronghold by the power of Your blood!
I claim Your freedom today. Amen.

November

RESURRECTION POWER

*There was born even of one man, and him as good
as dead at that, as many descendants as the stars
of heaven in number.*

HEBREWS 11:12

Our God is absolutely brilliant at bringing what is dead back to life when we place our faith in Him. We know the Lord brought a child to Abraham and Sarah—when both of them were hopelessly far beyond their childbearing years.

The Lord—the Giver of Life—can breathe life into dry bones and even nations (Ezekiel 37). Throughout Scripture, we see His resurrection power—bringing back to life the widow's son through Elijah (1 Kings 17:17–24) and the Shunamite's son through Elisha (2 Kings 4). During His earthly ministry, Jesus raised Jairus's daughter (Mark 5:35–42), the widow of Nain's son (Luke 7:11–15), and Lazarus (John 11:1–44).

Of course, the greatest resurrection in history was Christ's, because He showed His ultimate victory over sin and death—never to die again. And you're promised that same resurrection power that raised Jesus from the grave works in you (Ephesians 1:18–21). So never fear that hope is dead to you. Trust God, who breathes His resurrection life into all that concerns you.

**Jesus, I can't see how this difficult
situation will work out, but I trust
Your resurrection power. Amen.**

JESUS FIRST

*"Everyone who has left houses . . . or farms for My
name's sake, will receive many times as much, and
will inherit eternal life. But many who are first will
be last; and the last, first."*

MATTHEW 19:29–30

Every day, we have a choice to make about what kingdom we're
serving—either God or ourselves. When we put ourselves and
our desires first, that means we're putting Him last—and He will
return the favor in His kingdom. So we should not seek great things
for ourselves here, but do as God asks us, making Him our priority.

Because the truth is this life is a breath, and there's far more
coming than we can imagine. Remember: "We must all appear before
the judgment seat of Christ, so that each one may be recompensed . . .
according to what he has done, whether good or bad" (2 Corinthians
5:10). For the believer, this is not unto salvation, because if you've
accepted Jesus as your Savior, you are assured heaven. However,
what's being evaluated are the rewards for how we served Christ
here—and that will shape how we live in heaven.

The challenge for you is to realize that right now you are setting
the tone for eternity—the authority and privileges you'll have forever.
So put Jesus first. Humble yourself now, and He will lift you up.

Jesus, You are my priority. Lead me
in how to serve You well. Amen.

FORGIVE

Whenever you stand praying, forgive, if you have anything against anyone.

MARK 11:25

Sometimes the insensitivity and selfishness of others will astound you—especially if you've tried to be kind and they've hurt you in return. Even after the initial shock wears off, you may find it difficult to erase the incident from your mind. How can you overcome the disappointment and discouragement?

First, refuse to allow the actions of others to hinder your relationship with God. You may wonder why the Father allowed it to happen. However, He never fails you, even when others do. God continues to provide you with perfect love, wisdom, strength, and support.

Second, forgive the person who wounded you. Harboring bitterness only hurts you and is never the Christlike thing to do.

Third, draw consolation from the Great Comforter, the Holy Spirit. You know that the Lord works all things together for your good. So allow Him to turn your pain into something beneficial.

The next time you're failed by others, release it to God and pray for the people who disappointed you. Don't let their actions destroy you; rather, let the Father turn it into an opportunity for your blessing.

Jesus, help me turn to You so I can forgive, heal, and be blessed. Amen.

DRAWN OUT

*She named him Moses, and said, "Because I drew
him out of the water."*

EXODUS 2:10

When the people of Israel became numerous in the land of Egypt, Pharaoh grew anxious that they would join forces with enemies to overthrow him. So to stop their population growth, he enslaved the Israelites and gave the evil, devastating decree that they should throw their newborn sons into the Nile (Exodus 1:22). Don't read over that as if it's just a story. The persecution and agony experienced by the Israelites were just as real as any pressures you feel today.

But consider what God was teaching us through this. Death was by water, but the Lord—through Pharaoh's daughter—drew Moses out of the Nile to deliver the people of Israel. God reversed the situation to bring good to His people.

There's an important principle here. When God delivers you, He will use the very challenge you face to raise up a blessing in your life. True, it's not until you're beyond the ability to save yourself that the Lord receives the glory for rescuing you—and that can be unnerving. But you can always count on Him. So when you face a situation that appears beyond your control, don't fear. Instead, rejoice. Because that means God is at work and, in some way, He will use it for your good.

Jesus, thank You for taking my difficulties and
working through them for blessing. Amen.

A REGENERATED MIND

*He saved us . . . by the washing of regeneration and
renewing by the Holy Spirit.*

TITUS 3:5

Take note of who it is that saves and regenerates you (Romans
8:29). Of course, it is God's own Spirit who does the work. You
learn to leave the world behind as you're completely sanctified by the
internal influence of the Holy Spirit. Paul explains:

It is written, "Things which eye has not seen and ear
has not heard, and which have not entered the heart of man,
all that God has prepared for those who love Him." For to
us God revealed them through the Spirit . . . For who has
known the mind of the Lord, that he will instruct Him? But
we have the mind of Christ. (1 Corinthians 2:9–10, 16)

In other words, with a natural, unredeemed mind, we could
never perceive the great plans God has for us or how to live in them.
But as believers, we have a completely different mind—one that's
much greater because we have the very thoughts of God through the
presence of the Holy Spirit. We have "the mind of Christ" (v. 16). That
is astounding! The Lord regenerates us by the renewing of our minds
so we can walk in the center of His will.

**Jesus, thank You for regenerating me by Your
Spirit and giving me Your mind. Amen.**

COMPLETE TRANSPARENCY

You desire truth in the innermost being, and in the
hidden part You will make me know wisdom.

PSALM 51:6

Are you completely transparent before God when you pray? If not, you may not be experiencing the intimacy with the Lord that's possible for you. Humility and honesty are crucial for growing closer to Jesus.

Thankfully, Jesus was an excellent model of this throughout the Gospels. For example, in the garden of Gethsemane, Jesus transparently expressed His anguish about the crucifixion with the Father. Knowing He would carry the sins of the whole world on His shoulders, Jesus was "grieved, to the point of death" (Matthew 26:38).

If Christ can admit that, so can you. Of course, it's possible that you don't share yourself with God because you want to have control—handling things on your own. You may also shut the Lord out because you're ashamed of what you really think and feel. But realize that your heavenly Father already knows what's in your heart, loves you as you are, and desires for you to be yourself before Him. So as a sign of genuine faith, lay your heart bare before Him. Open up to Jesus, show Him you truly trust Him, and allow Him into your innermost places so He can give you peace.

Jesus, I open my heart to You completely.
Cleanse me from sin and help me to be
transparent before You. Amen.

IN THE STORM

You have been a defense for the helpless . . . a
refuge from the storm.

ISAIAH 25:4

Whenever storms roll in accompanied by violent winds, there is always the possibility for electrical lines to go down and for transformers to be rendered useless. At such times, darkness is the inevitable result, as the power connection is lost.

The same is true when tempests batter your life. God created you to live in the light of His wisdom and love, with a continuous link to Him. However, when your eyes are on the ferocity of the rain and winds, rather than on the Lord, you can unwittingly surrender that powerful connection to Him. So if you feel helpless, and everything looks dark right now, you know why.

What's important at such times is not that you beat yourself up for failing to cling to God as you should but that you return to Him immediately. Restore the connection by getting back into the Word, praying, and submitting yourself to whatever He tells you. Wait out the storm in His care, confident that He will light your way, empower you for whatever you face, and be a steadfast refuge. The Lord your God can silence the thunder and shield you from the gale. So look to Jesus and find the shelter your heart longs for.

Jesus, I trust You to give me light and empower me in this storm. Amen.

WATCH YOUR WORDS

*Death and life are in the power of the tongue, and
those who love it will eat its fruit.*

PROVERBS 18:21

In 2 Samuel 23:13–17, the Philistines had captured Bethlehem, David's birthplace, and had established a stronghold there. As David plotted to take the city back, he expressed a desire to drink water from the well there. Three of his men heard him, crossed enemy lines, and risked their lives to bring a cup of Bethlehem's water back to David.

We might envy David's power and the loyalty of his men. But when David saw what they had done, he was humbled. He refused to drink the water, choosing instead to pour it out as a drink offering to God. You see, although David was grateful for his men, he recognized that only the Lord was worthy of such devotion. And that with the authority he carried, he had to be much more careful with his words, lest he put others in unnecessary danger.

We must be wise as well. Our words carry power, and we must be careful how we use them. Therefore, be careful not to use your authority to feed gratuitous desires or in a manner that would harm others. Rather, be humble and make sure that even in your words, you are submitted to God.

**Jesus, I want to glorify You with my words.
Help me always speak life. Amen.**

ONLY THE WORD

The Berean Jews were of more noble character . . .
for they received the message with great eagerness
and examined the Scriptures every day to see if
what Paul said was true.

ACTS 17:11 NIV

On what do you base what you believe? If you say the way you were raised or what a certain denomination, church, or pastor teaches, then your belief system could be faulty. Scripture needs to be the basis for the principles and doctrine you hold dear, because it is the only true revelation of God.

This is why I often say to read the Word—because it is Christ alone who can truly lead, comfort, heal, convict, and instruct you. When you regularly study Scripture, you are tapping in to His infinite wisdom, power, and direction. The Holy Spirit works through the Bible to reveal how He is actively involved in every aspect of your life and applies the truth to edify you.

It is true that sometimes the Word will be difficult to understand, but don't let that stop you—God is a good and able Teacher. He will answer your questions, help you understand His truth, and show you how to apply His principles. He will also sift through what you believe to show what is man-made and unhelpful. So get into the Word, and expect Him to speak to you.

Jesus, thank You for the power of Your
Word. Help me understand it. Amen.

INNER REALITIES

*You are just in all that has come upon us . . . You
have faithfully.*

NEHEMIAH 9:33

A s the Jews returned to Jerusalem after the Babylonian captivity, they found their city in ruins—with the protective outer wall and temple destroyed. The homeland they dreamed of was as devastated as they were. However, it was not until Ezra stepped out and read God's Word aloud to them that they really understood their problem. The outer reality of Jerusalem's devastated condition reflected their inner condition due to sin.

Their response was overwhelming—they wept in repentance and relief. The Jewish people immediately confessed their sins, understanding their hardships were a result of their actions. Israel's rebellion against God had led to spiritual, emotional, and physical bondage. But the Lord was calling them back out of His love for them.

Certainly, not all the adversity we experience occurs as a result of sin—some hardships are the result of our fallen world. But it's important for us to realize that outward devastation often reveals an inward reality we must submit to God. Thankfully, while there are consequences, there's also hope and forgiveness when we return to the Lord. So today, examine your heart and turn back to God so He can rebuild whatever has been broken.

**Jesus, reveal any sinful way in me so I can
repent and return to Your path. Amen.**

PERSIST IN PRAYER

He continued kneeling on his knees three times a day, praying and giving thanks before his God, as he had been doing previously.

DANIEL 6:10

How much does it take to dissuade you from spending time in prayer? Are you easily distracted by the sound of the phone, errant thoughts, or tasks that suddenly arise?

As an exile in Babylon from Judah and prominent counselor to the king, Daniel was constantly under attack by those who wanted him removed. Eventually, his enemies convinced the king to "give orders that for the next thirty days any person who prays to anyone, divine or human—except to you, Your Majesty—will be thrown into the den of lions" (Daniel 6:7 NLT). They targeted Daniel's relationship with God, knowing this was the only way to defeat the wise Jew. However, not even the threat of being eaten by lions deterred Daniel from his daily habit of spending time with the Lord. To Daniel, his relationship with God was more important than anything else.

In the end, the Lord delivered Daniel, and he endures as an example of how important prayer should be to us. So don't let minor issues distract you from meeting with the living God. Make prayer a priority, and don't allow anything to stop the Lord's wisdom and power from flowing through you.

Jesus, I want to spend time with You as Daniel did. Create in me a tenacious passion for prayer. Amen.

SPIRITUAL SIGHT

He gave sight to many who were blind.

LUKE 7:21

When was the last time you learned something new about God that changed your life? Whether you realized it or not, until that point, you had a spiritual blind spot. It was not until the Lord gave you understanding that you received insight into that particular area of your life and could function differently. In a spiritual sense, it parallels what happened when Jesus healed the man born blind.

This is the spiritual transformation Scripture talks about, wherein the truth sets you free. You learn to see things as Christ does. Of course, you may feel some fear when this happens because you're unsure of how to proceed. You may even beat yourself up for not previously seeing what the Father showed you. But what's important to remember is that no matter how long it's taken for you to get your sight, you should rejoice that you finally have it. Second, the God who gave you the insight can teach you to walk in it.

If the Father has revealed a spiritual blind spot to you, you've experienced a miracle. Do not be afraid or focus on yourself. Instead, continue to watch for what the Lord is doing, and He will continue to transform you.

Jesus, thank You for this new insight. Help me walk in it and keep my focus on You. Amen.

INSIDE INTERCESSION

He who searches the hearts knows what the mind of the Spirit is, because He intercedes for the saints according to the will of God.

ROMANS 8:27

Many times, when you come before the Father in prayer, you may feel completely in the dark about what to say. You may not even know what to ask for or how to approach Him with the questions in your heart. If you cannot form the words to describe what you are feeling, how can you possibly communicate with the Father effectively?

But remember, this is the very reason God gives you His Holy Spirit. He knows exactly what is going on inside of you. And often, the reason you cannot put what you feel into words is because the Lord Himself is working on something so deep inside of you that it transcends human understanding.

So today, rather than feeling fearful or frustrated, believe that the Lord wants to communicate with you in prayer—even helping you understand what you feel. This is why James 1:5 instructs, "If any of you lacks wisdom, let him ask of God, who gives to all generously and without reproach, and it will be given to him." The Father wants to interact with you and make sense of what you're experiencing. Because that's how He leads you in the very best path possible.

Jesus, I will listen to You and trust how You lead. Amen.

THOUGHT REIGN

Do not let sin reign in your mortal body so that you obey its lusts.

ROMANS 6:12

Today, realize that the Holy Spirit is committed to guarding your life—especially your heart and mind. So why is it that we can still be tempted and fall? Even though God defends you from evil, He also allows you the free will to choose what you'll think and do. This is often why we get into trouble. Instead of fixing our eyes on Jesus to bring us joy, peace, and stability, we entertain our appetites and cravings—doing more harm to ourselves than we can imagine. Sooner or later, our errant deliberations lead to sinful behavior.

Sin begins its reign in your mind, which is why it's always crucial to examine what you're thinking. It is not the passing lustful thought that's sinful; rather, it's when you dwell on it—imagining what it would be like. As long as you reject those thoughts, you'll do what God has called you to do and walk in the light and freedom of His truth.

So watch your thoughts. Rebuke the temptation to dwell on things that are not worthy of who you are as a child of God. Instead, train your mind on Jesus and you will be the victor.

Jesus, I know I dwell on sinful thoughts. Help me stop them so I can obey You. Amen.

PROMISES AND PURPOSES

No matter how many promises God has made,
they are "Yes" in Christ.

2 CORINTHIANS 1:20 NIV

Have you claimed a promise of God? At times, we may come to a passage of Scripture that we know is true, but we have difficulty believing, in a practical sense, that it can actually apply to us. At its core, this is because we don't fully understand what the Lord is doing in us, which is conforming us to the likeness of Jesus. So it's important to realize that while God is our loving Provider and desires only the best for us, He does not exist to do things our way or fulfill all of our wishes. Rather, His desire is to teach us to act and respond as He would.

Therefore, when we think about God's promises, we must always keep in mind that they're given for the fulfillment of *His* ultimate purposes—developing our character, carrying out His plans, and empowering us to be His light in the world. This is why Psalm 37:4 says, "Delight yourself in the LORD; and He will give you the desires of your heart." When Jesus is our goal and joy, He is actively shaping our lives and what's important to us. And when that's the case, we can know for certain that His promises will be fulfilled for us.

Jesus, thank You for Your promises and
fulfilling Your awesome purposes. Amen.

GET ALONE

When you pray, go away by yourself, shut the door
behind you, and pray to your Father in private.
MATTHEW 6:6 NLT

It can be difficult to hear God among the cacophony of voices that compete for your attention. Even when you're seeking Him, you'll be surrounded by countless people in need of your attention and who will seek to shape your path. With all the distractions, is it any wonder that God may seem distant at times?

This is why truly seeking the Lord requires solitude. If you don't make an effort to get away from the demands of your daily life, your ability to hear God's voice will be hindered. Jesus was well aware of this need for seclusion. In teaching the disciples how to pray, He told them to go into their rooms and close the door behind them. He knew that it was vital to take a break in order to truly worship and fellowship with the Father.

This is especially true today, when it is increasingly difficult to escape all the ways people can contact us, the demands of technology, and the pervasiveness of media. Therefore, you must be intentional. At some point today, turn everything off and set aside some time for Jesus. Make a decision to be alone with the Lord, get quiet, and listen.

Jesus, I need You. Help me to stop, listen,
and hear Your voice today. Amen.

Secure Forever

*"I give eternal life to them, and they will never
perish; and no one will snatch them out of My
hand."*

John 10:28

D o you realize that you are eternally secure in your salvation with Jesus? This is because nothing in all creation has
the power to take anything out of the omnipotent grip of God—
including you.

We may have doubts or fears, we may make mistakes and even
sin, but we cannot lose our salvation—we simply do not have that
power. Once we've truly trusted Jesus as our Savior, we are safe in His
hand (John 10:27–30). This is because along with receiving forgiveness of our sins, we've also received Christ's life. He promised that
He would not leave us as orphans, fending for ourselves, but instead,
He would send us the Holy Spirit to be with us forever (John 14:16).
And through the Holy Spirit, who seals us for the day of redemption
(Ephesians 4:30), Jesus abides with us and dwells within us to help
us live the Christian life (John 15:4; Galatians 2:20).

There's not a verse anywhere in Scripture indicating your
redemption lasts only for a season. Of course, that isn't a license to
sin. Rather, it's a reason to rejoice, to praise God, to walk holy before
Him, and to obey Him out of gratefulness.

**Jesus, thank You for keeping me secure forever! I
rejoice in Your awesome provision and love. Amen.**

GET SPECIFIC

Your ears will hear a word behind you, "This is the way, walk in it."

ISAIAH 30:21

As you wait to hear from the Lord about how He wants you to proceed in the situations that concern you, listen especially for the specifics of what He's communicating. Not only will the Lord show you the *direction* in which you are to move, but He will also reveal *when* and *how* to carry out what He wants you to accomplish. You know by now that He likely won't give you *all* the details you desire, but He will certainly give you the information you need to take the next step in wisdom.

Likewise, as you proceed in what God is telling you to do, look for confirmation that you've heard Him correctly. That corroborating word may come as you read Scripture, through friends, in a Bible study, or as you listen to sermons. But ask God to verify what you've heard Him say so that you make no mistake in direction, methodology, or timing.

And take heart. Once you say to the Lord, "I'm trusting You to show me when and how to move," it is then the Lord's responsibility to prompt you to act. So do not fear or succumb to pressure to move ahead. You'll know exactly what to do when the time is right.

**Jesus, I trust You to show me when
and how to proceed. Amen.**

For His Glory

All have sinned and fall short of the glory of God.
ROMANS 3:23

At times you may feel doubtful of your calling because you feel inadequate, sinful, and unworthy of representing the name of Jesus. In fact, I have found that it is when people truly want to dedicate their lives to Christ that they go through some of the deepest times of brokenness.

If this is you, take heart. It is true that the closer you get to God, the more you will be aware of your mistakes and failings. But realize that the Lord does not reveal your faults to condemn you, but to heal you, forgive you, and cleanse you from all that keeps you bound so you can become all that you were created to be. He also wants to teach you that *He* is the One who accomplishes His will through you—not you—so you must depend on Him regardless of what He calls you to do.

Therefore, today, allow your brokenness and inadequacy to serve as a reminder that you reflect His glory—it does not originate with you. Rely on Him completely for any assignment He calls you to accomplish so that people will experience Him and be saved.

Jesus, the work You call me to is for Your glory—not mine. May people see You in whatever You call me to do. Amen.

HIS PRESENCE IN ACTION

The fruit of the Spirit is love, joy, peace, patience,
kindness, goodness, faithfulness, gentleness, self-
control.

GALATIANS 5:22–23

God wants you to be the physical manifestation of His presence in action today. He desires to bear the fruit of His Spirit and make a difference in the world through you. This means your life will be characterized by:

Love—all the other qualities associated with having the Holy Spirit flow from the presence of God's love in you. *Joy* is rejoicing in His work and possibilities in every situation. *Peace* is resting on the promises of God and expecting their fulfillment. *Patience* is waiting for God to reveal Himself to you and expressing grace to those around you. *Kindness* is reaching out to others in their need. *Goodness* is choosing to do what is right and good in God's eyes. *Faithfulness* is remaining true to Jesus and clinging to Him regardless of what happens. *Gentleness* is empathizing with people in need or pain. *Self-control* is actively resisting temptation.

As you embrace and manifest the fullness of God's love to you, these other character qualities are going to be expressed through your life. Therefore, say to your heavenly Father, "Work through me today, Lord. I want to be Your hands and feet."

Yes, Jesus, work through me to shine Your
light to whoever may need You. Amen.

MANIFESTING HIS QUALITIES

*Just as we have borne the image of the earthy, we
will also bear the image of the heavenly.*

1 CORINTHIANS 15:49

There are countless books and videos that will tell you how to be a positive, upbeat person. Most of these resources will give you techniques for becoming happy—repeating certain phrases to yourself, meditating on cheerful memories, or imagining yourself in pleasant environments. The emphasis is nearly always, however, on the outward things you can do.

Although some of these techniques can be helpful for temporarily relieving stress, the genuine and permanent joy, peace, and contentment that you desire are not feelings you can generate on your own. They are solely the work of the Holy Spirit in you. These qualities are developed and manifested in your life only as you receive, by faith, the love and freedom of God.

God's purpose in you from the moment you accept Jesus as your Savior, until you enter His presence to live with Him in heaven forever, is to produce the qualities of Christ within you (Romans 8:29). The key to taking hold of His attributes is to submit yourself to Him fully—regardless of whether His commands make sense to you. It is then He can do His supernatural work and change you permanently from within (Romans 12:2).

Jesus, I submit myself to You. Do Your awesome
work and transform me, my Savior. Amen.

Breaking Free in Praise

Paul and Silas were praying and singing hymns of praise to God . . . and suddenly there came a great earthquake, so that . . . all the doors were opened.

Acts 16:25–26

There is awesome, earthshaking power in praise and thanksgiving. Something amazing happens when we rejoice and give God the glory regardless of our circumstances. Not only does our gratefulness honor the Father in the manner He deserves, but it also sets us up for success—refocusing our attention on His ability to help us.

For example, when Paul and Silas were unjustly beaten and thrown into the Philippian prison, they did not allow their pain or situation to cloud the reality of who they belonged to and what He had called them to do. Instead of weeping and complaining, they sang God's praise. Their attitudes of trust and gratefulness were the perfect channel through which the Lord could show His power and work miraculously on their behalf.

Of course, if you're facing a painful season of trials and disappointments, this may be a difficult principle for you to practice. But that is why Paul encourages you: "Rejoice in the Lord always" (Philippians 4:4). He knows the awesome way it sets you free when you place your trust in God through praise.

Jesus, I worship You! No problem I encounter is as great as You are. Amen.

PROCLAIMING HIS BLESSING

*Willingly I will sacrifice to You; I will give thanks
to Your name, O Lord.*

PSALM 54:6

Do you ever wonder if your sacrifices *to* God are actually acceptable *to* Him? When Cain and Abel offered God sacrifices, Abel's offering was received favorably, while Cain's was not. Why?

When Cain gave God the fruit of his farming, it was as if he was saying to God, "Look what I've done. I'm giving You of *my* work." Abel, on the other hand, recognized that all life comes from the Lord by giving Him the firstlings of his flock. Abel was in effect saying, "You are the Life-giver. I am privileged to be a part of *Your* work, to tend the sheep You've given me."

There is a message in that for us today. God is the Source of all life, and He wants us to acknowledge that we do nothing on our own—that everything we have was given to us by Him to steward. Therefore, it is important to check our motives. Do you acknowledge that You are joining in His work—or do you still see it as only yours? Do your sacrifices proclaim that He is the Source of your life and blessings?

Jesus, thank You for the life and blessings You've
given me. I join You in Your work, proclaiming
Your goodness and provision. Amen.

HE IS WORTHY

The LORD of hosts, He is the King of glory [who
rules over all creation with His heavenly armies].
PSALM 24:10 AMP

Have you ever truly considered the seat of power you've been invited to approach as you go to God in prayer and thanksgiving? This is not an earthly chair that can be destroyed or overthrown, because the King of kings seated on it is unmatched, omnipotent, and everlasting.

You have been beckoned to the throne of the living God—the immortal, invincible, all-powerful, all-knowing Sovereign of heaven, earth, and all creation. The entire universe is spread out before Him.

Yet even as great as He is, His love for you is so profound that He pays careful attention to the smallest details of your life, even numbering the hairs on your head. He is so near to you that He catches your tears and hears your heart.

Do you realize to whom you are speaking? You are right when you kneel. Your God deserves your devotion and gratefulness—because every good thing you have comes from His loving hand (James 1:17). So today, truly think about your Lord and give Him the honor, power, worship, and praise He deserves.

Lord, You are God! Holy and wonderful are You—
deserving all my thanks, devotion, reverence, and
adoration. To You be all glory forever. Amen.

HE PRAYS FOR YOU

Christ Jesus is He who . . . is at the right hand of
God, who also intercedes for us.

ROMANS 8:34

Today, give thanks that when God hears your prayers, He has sent His Holy Spirit to search out the deepest groans of your inner self—the most profound needs and wounds there (Romans 8:26–27). Likewise, you do not pray alone, because Jesus "always lives to make intercession" for you (Hebrews 7:25 ESV).

Understand, Jesus does not pray powerlessly and is not bound by limitations. No, your Savior prays with authority and unmeasurable capability. This is the voice of the Great I AM—omnipotent in power and omniscient in wisdom. The voice that speaks for you is the same that masterfully and brilliantly called the heavens and the earth into existence. "When he spoke, the world began! It appeared at his command" (Psalm 33:9 NLT). He declared the onset of time, and the seconds, minutes, hours, days, months, and years started their count. He spoke and the sun, moon, stars, planets, and every other celestial body were formed and set on their galactic courses.

That is the voice that intercedes for you—that is working all things together for your healing, training, and blessing. So rejoice and give thanks for the One who hears and prays for you!

Jesus, thank You for praying for me! I know
You're working all things together for
my good and Your purposes. Amen.

CONSIDER HIS MERCY

In His love and in His mercy He redeemed them.

ISAIAH 63:9

Today, thank God for all the ways He has expressed mercy to you and those you love. He is tender toward you, forgiving, generous, and loving. It is important for us to think of and recognize this because we cannot truly worship God genuinely and wholeheartedly until we come to the place of recognizing how much He has blessed us and how gracious He's been to us.

We know this was certainly true for the apostle Paul. He wrote, "It is a trustworthy statement, deserving full acceptance, that Christ Jesus came into the world to save sinners, among whom I am foremost of all" (1 Timothy 1:15). Paul understood the grace the Lord had shown him, the incredible price that Jesus paid for us, and what a tremendous gift our salvation truly is. He realized that he did not deserve Christ's mercy or forgiveness and was always grateful for it.

No one can serve the Lord with real passion until they are persuaded of the everlasting and overwhelming kindness of God. So today, spend time considering what your life would be like without Him. Certainly, realizing all He has given you and forgiven you of will inspire your praise.

Jesus thank You for Your magnificent mercy
and love! You have redeemed me from so much,
and I will praise Your name forever. Amen.

HE ABSOLUTELY WILL

*"Ask, and it will be given to you; seek, and you will
find; knock, and it will be opened to you."*

MATTHEW 7:7

One of the many reasons God is worthy of our praise is because
He will move heaven and earth to show us His will. He is *fully*
invested in His whole plan for each of us.

If you are seeking God and have a heart to do His will, you can
know with absolute certainty that He *will* show you what to do. Jesus
Himself said, "Everyone who asks receives, and he who seeks finds,
and to him who knocks it will be opened" (Matthew 7:8). That is
God's heart toward you. As your heavenly Father, He wants you to
ask, seek, and knock so He can give, reveal, open, and provide what
is good for you.

That means that even when you're not clear about the choice
to make—if for some reason He keeps His will concealed—you can
take comfort in the fact that "it is God who is at work in you, both to
will and to work for His good pleasure" (Philippians 2:13). The Lord
takes responsibility for directing you through the fog. So thank Him
for leading you—step-by-step and from glory to glory (2 Corinthians
3:18).

**Jesus, thank You for moving heaven and earth to
show me Your will. I pray to You, Lord! Amen.**

IN EVERYTHING GIVE THANKS

In everything give thanks; for this is God's will for you in Christ Jesus.

1 THESSALONIANS 5:18

God's will is for you to be grateful regardless of what happens to you. So what truth can you focus on to help you give thanks when everything seems to be against you?

First, remember that God is always in absolute control, no matter how challenging things seem. This is the key to being able to endure emotionally and mentally during difficulties. Regardless of what pain you're experiencing, who has turned against you, or how you've failed—the Father is still in control and can lead you to overcome.

Second, count on the fact that "God causes all things to work together for good to those who love God" (Romans 8:28). If He's permitted some issue or challenge to touch your life, it is for a beneficial purpose. Of course, there may be some hardships you face that you will never comprehend this side of heaven. However, you can be completely certain that He still loves you and has your best in mind—and that is always cause for praise.

So today, thank Him that you're never helpless or alone. Your God can always handle whatever problems you face and will give you the strength, wisdom, and hope you need to endure.

Jesus, I praise You for being in control and turning everything for my good. Thank You, Lord. Amen.

THE FLOW OF FORGIVENESS

Be kind to one another, tender-hearted, forgiving each other, just as God in Christ also has forgiven you.

EPHESIANS 4:32

P erhaps, you've noticed that it's possible to attend church every Sunday and profess Christ yet not be able to express His love to others. Sometimes it's easy to embrace the intellectual aspects of Jesus' love but quite another thing to let that love flow through you to a needy world. What's important for us to realize is that one of the primary hindrances to the expression of His care can be traced to unforgiveness.

Often, when we're wounded, we may be tempted to build a wall around our hearts to protect ourselves from more pain. Unfortunately, that ultimately isolates us from others and imprisons us. Thankfully, we know from Scripture that Jesus came to set the captives free. And He does so not only through the divine pardon He's given us but through the way He empowers us to forgive others.

Jesus will enable you to forgive those who have wounded you deeply, if you're willing to accept His provision. So don't remain entrapped by resentment. Ask Jesus to help you root out the bitterness and experience, forgive those who hurt you, and allow the love of your heavenly Father to flow freely in and through you.

Jesus, give me the strength to forgive. And let Your love flow through me. Amen.

THE SUFFICIENT ONE

"I am El-Shaddai . . . Serve me faithfully and live a blameless life. I will make a covenant with you."
GENESIS 17:1–2 NLT

A prominent Hebrew name for the Lord is *El Shaddai*, which means the all-powerful, all-sufficient God. He is the God who is enough, regardless of what you might need. He is not just mighty as your Protector; He is also proficient as your Provider.

When the Lord led the Israelites out of Egypt, He showed them in vivid ways that He is *El Shaddai*. He guided them in a pillar of cloud by day and fire by night, gave them water and manna in the wilderness, defended them against enemy armies, and delivered the land of their inheritance to them. Yes, the Israelites had to go forward when He called, fight battles, and honor Him in how they lived. In other words, they had to submit to His commands. But they were exceedingly blessed whenever they did.

The best news is the Lord your God has not changed—He is absolutely sufficient for whatever you require today as well. And the manner by which you take hold of it is to obey Him. So do not fear whether or not you'll have enough. *El Shaddai*—the Sufficient One—is with you. Honor Him and He will be all you need.

Jesus, You are everything to me. Thank You for being my mighty Protector and my perfect Provider. Amen.

DECEMBER

FALLING AND RISING

When he falls, he will not be hurled headlong,
because the LORD is the One who holds his hand.

PSALM 37:24

Y ou may fail in your faith. You may fall to the temptations of this world, take matters into your own hands, and mess up completely. Do not fall for the Enemy's lie that the Father has rejected you because of it (1 John 1:9). Part of God's process of making you into Christ's image is helping you understand the unseen strongholds that are preventing you from giving Him full access to your life. He reveals an area of stubborn self-sufficiency in you and then sets about breaking your bondage to it.

So don't give up! Proverbs 24:16 instructs, "The godly may trip seven times, but they will get up again" (NLT). This is the difference between those who have a true relationship with God and those who don't—the ability to fall and get back up.

As someone who knows Jesus as your Savior, you always have Someone to help you up after you've fallen. You always have forgiveness and hope for a good future. Therefore, confess your sin, repent, get back up, and steady yourself on God. And take heart that He continues to work out all things in your life as you trust Him.

Jesus, thank You for always helping me back up. With You, I always have hope. Amen.

SUCCESSFUL WAITING

*You are my hiding place and my shield; I wait for
Your word.*

PSALM 119:114

A re you waiting for God to intervene in some area of your
life? One of the struggles we can face as believers is trying
to understand why the Lord delays in matters that are urgent to us.
Of course, the Father always has good reasons. However, there are
several adjustments that will be important for us to make if we desire
to wait successfully.

First, determine to focus on God. Do not center your attention on
your need, because that will only sustain and increase your anxiety.
This is crucial because, at times, the Father will delay until you get
your focus back on Him. He wants you to delight in Him, not just in
what He gives you. *Second, release your expectations.* You can cling
so tightly to a particular outcome that He must wait until you let go
of your preferences so He can give you His best. Stop fighting Him
and let Him work on your behalf.

*Finally, rejoice that while you are waiting, God is working in the
unseen.* The Lord sees the entire picture and is orchestrating everything in ways you cannot even imagine. So spend time with Him,
express your love for Him, and trust Him—because that's what will
ensure your success while you wait.

**Jesus, thank You for working in the
unseen. My hope is in You. Amen.**

LOVE AND AUTHORITY

Good and upright is the LORD; therefore He
instructs sinners in the way.

PSALM 25:8

O ften our difficulty in trusting God is rooted in the tension we see between His authority and His love. Some people think of the Lord as authoritarian—a cold and distant Ruler, moving us about as pawns. His laws seem harsh and His ways appear strange and uncaring. So they obey out of fear rather than loving reverence. Others imagine God as so tender that He merely nods at our failings because He understands we are weak. Because we're His frail children, He doesn't really expect that much from us.

Neither of these caricatures is accurate, of course. Rather, we must hold these two aspects of God's character—His authority and His love—in balance. Yes, His ways are higher and more wonderful than we can possibly imagine, and we should always obey Him because He is worthy of our respect. But He's also unconditionally caring toward us—so we can always trust His direction, even when we don't understand it.

Therefore, today, be certain that even God's most difficult commands are not heartless but given out of His deepest love for you and will ultimately lead to blessings. Yes, submitting to Him may sometimes be difficult, but He will always lead you to liberty and joy.

Jesus, You are God. Out of respect and
love for You, I will obey. Amen.

FOR RELATIONSHIP

*Many, O LORD my God, are the wonders which
You have done . . . there is none to compare with
You.*

PSALM 40:5

The Lord didn't save you just so He could have another follower.
Rather, He wants you to know Him and experience how deeply
He cares for you in relationship. He is your Creator, the One who
looks at you with tenderness and joy. And He longs for you to trust
Him as your God—as the One who walks with you on the mountains
of success and in the valley experiences of life.

The Lord wants you to understand His ways—the wisdom with
which He works in the world and the detailed manner in which He's
watching over you. He wants you to sense how deeply He loves you
and to feel the joy and purpose you were created for. So He engineers
circumstances—trials where you cannot help yourself—where you
can experience His work on your behalf.

Maybe you're facing such a challenge now. But understand, this
is so you can draw near to Him, experience His awesome power
poured out for you, and so you can realize how completely you can
depend on Him. So embrace the fact that Jesus is not just the Savior
of your soul but also your Friend, King, Defender, and Deliverer in
every moment of your life.

**Jesus, I worship You for Your goodness. Thank
You for being everything to me. Amen.**

STOP AND LISTEN

Incline your ear and come to Me. Listen, that you may live.

ISAIAH 55:3

You may be a person who prays a great deal. Perhaps you have a list of people you intercede for. Likewise, you share your heart with the Father—letting Him know everything that's bothering you. Yet something is still missing from your relationship with Him. You don't feel close to Him, sense His wisdom guiding your steps, or feel His resurrection power fueling your obedience to Him. Why?

The answer is simple. We all have friends who talk so much that we can never get a word in. Even when they ask us questions, they barely pause before they're off on another train of thought. Sadly, that's how most of us are with God. We talk and don't stop to listen. Oh, we may ask Him about His will or to give us wisdom, but we usually don't give Him much time to respond before we're giving Him our opinion of what He should do.

But if you really want to know someone, you have to listen—and that goes double for God. God's every word has meaning and impact. He does not speak merely to be heard. He speaks the very words of life that will absolutely transform you from the inside out. So stop and hear what He has to say.

**Jesus, I come before You to listen.
Speak, Lord, and I will obey. Amen.**

TRUE INSURANCE

Thanks be to God, who gives us the victory through our Lord Jesus Christ.

1 CORINTHIANS 15:57

It is human nature to want to plan and create safeguards against all eventualities. We want to feel sheltered and protected. However, we can never fully anticipate the onslaughts we'll face—either in this fallen world or spiritually. Our only complete defense is in Jesus. He is the only Defender against evil who will ever be truly victorious in every situation.

So there may be a specific problem on your heart today that you have no idea how to overcome or plan for—such as future financial security, what you will do if someone important is taken from you, or even the stability of the nation. It is wise to think ahead, but you cannot plan for everything. What you can and must do is seek the wisdom of the One who holds all things in His hand, and obey Him. Because when you do, the Lord prepares you for what you cannot see, carries you when you are helpless, and provides when you have no resources to draw from.

Your first line of defense, therefore, is to seek God and be sensitive to His guidance. Walk in the center of His will because that is always the safest and most victorious place to be.

Jesus, thank You that—no matter what—I am safest in the center of Your will. Amen.

DON'T MISS HIS BEST

*"Obey me, and I will be your God and you shall be
my people; only do as I say, and all shall be well!"*
JEREMIAH 7:23 TLB

Are you fearful of what God will ask you to do? You can try
to avoid Him, but realize that what you're really missing is
what you were created to accomplish—what you were *formed* to do
and what would give you the greatest degree of satisfaction and joy.
Instead, you are taking the dangerous risk of disobeying God and
living the rest of your life wondering what the Lord would have done
through you if you had obeyed Him.

Don't make that mistake. Don't turn a deaf ear to the Father's
call and His good, acceptable, and perfect purposes for you. Let go of
your fear toward God. Set your mind and heart on comprehending
how profoundly He loves you, and grow in your love for Him. Do
not fear His will; instead, respect what God says and honor Him by
obeying His leadership. Yes, He may call you to accomplish assignments that scare you. The issue isn't whether you fear; rather, it is
whether you do as He says, trusting that He knows what is best for
you. Because He absolutely does—and you don't want to miss it.

**Jesus, I will obey You. I know You always
lead me in the best way. Amen.**

HIS WAITING ARMS

I will go home to my father and say, "Father, I have
sinned against both heaven and you."
LUKE 15:18 NLT

Today, realize that you have not fallen so far that the Father will not receive you back (1 John 1:9). Remember the prodigal son. As he looked at the hogs he was feeding, he realized they were eating better than he was. He was at such a low point—with nothing of his own and no one to help him—that he was actually envying the pigs. The prodigal's future and prospects seemed absolutely lost. The only alternative he could imagine was to return to his father, in the hopes of finding mercy. Perhaps his father would accept him as a hired hand.

The prodigal didn't realize how his father yearned for him to return or that his father's arms would be open to him. But the same is true for you. No matter how far you are from God, He is longing to receive you back. God's grace is always available to you—to free you from sin, give you hope, and lead you to a victorious future.

So don't envy the pigs; rather, run back to the Father. He will restore you by His grace and fill your life with His goodness.

Jesus, reveal the areas where I've become
a prodigal, and help me come back to
the safety of Your love. Amen.

JOY ALWAYS

The joy of the LORD is your strength.

NEHEMIAH 8:10

Jesus promised to give you His joy. However, if you're facing challenges today, you may be wondering when your gladness will return. Because of this, there are some important things for you to understand about the joy Christ gives you.

First, the gift of joy has a spiritual source—the Holy Spirit within you. In other words, you can experience it at any time as you rely on His presence because joy exists independent of your circumstances. Therefore, focus on your relationship with Jesus. Nothing can separate you from Him or from His love now or in eternity. Second, watch for His transforming work in others. You can draw pleasure from what God is doing in those around you—rescuing people from sin and conforming them to Christlikeness. Third, serve whomever He sends to you. Obedient, loving care for others brings spiritual joy. Finally, meditate on God's Word. Through Scripture, you will receive His truth on which to build a fulfilling life.

The Holy Spirit desires to produce His gladness within you. Therefore, take a few minutes to ponder the wonder of your salvation, share someone's spiritual joy, serve as God directs, or receive guidance from His Word. And praise the Lord as His gladness pours forth from you.

Jesus, may Your joy always flow through me, regardless of what happens. Amen.

A GREATER HIGH PRIEST

We have a great high priest.

HEBREWS 4:14

The New Testament describes Jesus as your great High Priest. But what does that mean? In the Old Testament the priests represented the people as they made sacrifices before God, just as Jesus does for us. But whereas earthly high priests were often separated from the people because of their temple duties, we don't have that problem with Christ. Jesus is continually available to us.

Jesus is intimately acquainted with what we face—the suffering, hunger, thirst, weariness, betrayal, and all the human emotions we can experience. So not only does Jesus sympathize with our weaknesses—understanding why temptations are so difficult for us, as other priests might—but being sinless, Christ knows how to lead us to victory over them.

Likewise, Jesus is greater than all other priests because He "has passed through the heavens" (Hebrews 4:14). He knows what our eternal home in glory is like and what it will require of us. He has seen what the entire universe looks like from the throne of God and realizes what we need to do to be prepared for everlasting life there with Him.

Certainly, we can rejoice that we have the greatest High Priest.

Jesus, no earthly priest compares with You!
Thank You for Your ministry to me and for
representing me before the Father. Amen.

POWERFUL SERVICE

*When they had prayed . . . they were all filled with
the Holy Spirit and began to speak the word of God
with boldness.*

ACTS 4:31

After His resurrection, Jesus gave the disciples the incredible assignment of reaching the whole world with the gospel (Matthew 28:18–20). Do you think those uneducated fishermen knew what to do? Of course they didn't. They needed God's wisdom and power to proceed. So they prayed (Acts 1:14), and the Lord not only showed them what to do but empowered them mightily for the task.

Likewise, when other activities began to crowd their time, the disciples made a conscious choice, saying, "We will devote ourselves to prayer and to the ministry of the word" (Acts 6:4). They committed themselves to the purpose God gave them (ministry) and to the one activity that would ensure success in that mission (prayer).

The apostles regarded prayer as absolutely indispensable when carrying out Christ's commission. In fact, all of God's most effective servants have been mighty in prayer. Their gifts and backgrounds may have been different, but they were all committed to listening to the Father so He could guide and empower them for the tasks they carried out. This must also be true of you.

**Jesus, give me tenacity in prayer so I may
know Your will and power. Amen.**

A LIFE OF FAITH

We walk by faith, not by sight.

2 CORINTHIANS 5:7

W hat does it take to live a life of faith? It's not as difficult as
you might think.

First, know God and be known by Him. Walk in intimate fellowship with Him, and experience His unconditional love, unwavering
presence, and awesome plan daily.

Second, commit to obey Him. Submit to God without yielding to
feelings of doubt or fear—especially when it comes to moving forward on important decisions or facing serious challenges.

Third, be confident that God will fulfill every promise. Be willing
to trust Him even though His timetable may be different from yours.
Do not falter in unbelief as time passes. Remember that little faith
says, "God can," and great faith says, "God will." But perfect faith
says, "God has done it."

Finally, live a lifestyle of faith. Choose what you know would
honor Jesus rather than chasing after your personal desires.

Are you willing to trust God to see all He will do in your life? It is
when you do so that He rewards your faith with great blessing. So set
your heart to know God, obey Him, be confident He will fulfill His
promises, and live a life that honors Him. Because He will certainly
lead you to life at its very best.

**Jesus, help me live a life of faith that
honors and glorifies You. Amen.**

HIM THROUGH YOU

*"My grace is sufficient for you, for My strength is
made perfect in weakness."*

2 CORINTHIANS 12:9 NKJV

Never fall into the trap of thinking of ministry as *your* work *for* the Lord. The truth is that we're not even able to live the Christian life on our own—never mind make an impact for the kingdom of God. Even though we may genuinely want to honor the Lord, no matter how diligently we try in our own strength, we'll keep slipping back into bad habits and fall short of all He has for us. If we feel completely helpless to change our own hearts and situations, how can we hope to change anyone else's?

But the good news is that *you were never meant to live the Christian life or do ministry in your own strength.* The true Christian life is not so much that you live for Jesus. Rather, the Christian life is *Jesus living through you,* and you are thus empowered to do the work only He can do.

Friend, God has chosen you for the service before you so *He* can shine His power *through* you—so that when the work is accomplished, people won't look to you, they will look to Him. So do not despair about your inadequacies; rather, submit to Him and rejoice that His glory shines through you.

Jesus, thank You that ministry isn't
dependent on me but on You working
through me for Your glory. Amen.

ALWAYS WITH YOU

The Lord stood with me and strengthened me.
2 TIMOTHY 4:17

Nothing is more painful than being forsaken by those we trust during times of trouble. Of course, there are many reasons others may fail us: they may feel inadequate to help us, fear trouble or inconvenience, be jealous of us, or simply be self-centered and insensitive. Although examining the cause may not erase our pain, it can help us understand why we are always admonished to put our full trust in God.

Paul certainly understood this. As he sat in prison, facing a sentence of death, he wrote, "No one supported me, but all deserted me" (2 Timothy 4:16). The apostle who had sacrificed so much and poured his life into so many was bereft of earthly comfort or companionship. However, God never let him down.

The good news is that the Lord offers His strength and presence to you in the same way today. Even if no one understands your struggles or all others leave you, God is with you. So don't be discouraged. Love those around you and be there for them, but put your trust in the Lord. He will never leave you or forsake you and is always faithful to comfort and deliver you regardless of what you face.

Jesus, thank You for remaining faithful
when others fail me. I rejoice that because
of You, I am never really alone. Amen.

DAILY FILLING

"Give us this day our daily bread."
MATTHEW 6:11

When was the last time you heard God speak to your spirit? I believe the Lord desires to communicate with each of us as often as we need to hear from Him—which may be several times in a day. He always has a message for us that is timelier and more important than we may realize.

Unfortunately, when we think of prayer, very often we think about telling God what we want Him to do or voicing our opinions about His promises. However, I believe when we do so, we are wasting an incredible opportunity to speak with the One who best knows how to satisfy our souls.

As we see from today's verse, Jesus taught His disciples to pray for their daily bread; however, He was referring to more than the food one might consume for physical nourishment. *Bread* is a term that refers to everything that is necessary for wholeness in life—including the things we need mentally, emotionally, and spiritually.

So the next time you go to God in prayer, don't just go to talk. Your heavenly Father wants to satiate the most profound hungers within you. Allow Him to fill you up with everything you really need.

Jesus, thank You for fulfilling everything my soul truly requires. I am listening, Lord; show me how to honor You with my life. Amen.

A SACRIFICE OF LOVE

*"By this all men will know that you are My
disciples, if you have love for one another."*

JOHN 13:35

Your willingness to love others must never depend on their ability to give love back to you. Some people will never be satisfied with what you do for them. Others will never feel worthy of your care, no matter how much you encourage them or include them in your life. People may even reject you by their actions while saying that they love you with their words.

To love means risking the possibility of being rejected. However, the goal in loving is not to evoke a response from another person but to be a living example of Christ's love. Therefore, care for others by ministering to them—supporting them in a manner that is meaningful to *them* rather than how you would want to be ministered to.

However, if you find someone will not accept you despite your best efforts, then ask yourself, "Is God really asking me to show love to this person?" If so, then be assured that Jesus accepts your efforts, even if they don't—and that's all that really matters. He will reward you by sending you someone who can receive your love and who will love you in return in the ways and in the moments you need it most.

Jesus, I want to be Your disciple. Help
me love others with Your wisdom
and sacrificial grace. Amen.

LOVE AND HOPE

"Love one another, just as I have loved you."
JOHN 15:12

To love others in Jesus' name gives hope and meaning to your life. When you know you're making a difference in someone else's life, when you can see that your gifts are valued, when your words of encouragement fall on appreciative ears, and when your acceptance of another person creates a friendship or helps them mature in their faith, you have a sense of purpose in your life. You have a desire to love more and to extend yourself further because you see the good fruit it produces. And in that, there is hope. You look forward to tomorrow because you know God can work through you.

On the other hand, if you isolate yourself and turn inward, refusing to acknowledge the hands that are reaching out to you or rejecting the encouragement that others offer you, you will become increasingly depressed and may feel that your life is worthless and has no meaning. But it doesn't have to be that way.

Loving others is the most hope-filled thing you can do, because Jesus is actively working through you. So turn your focus outward and watch what He can do through your caring heart. You'll be amazed at how truly impactful your life can be.

Jesus, help me minister to others with Your love so I may find the purposes for which You created me. Amen.

SEEKING THE TREASURE

Wisdom is better than jewels; and all desirable
things cannot compare with her.

PROVERBS 8:11

Nothing you can acquire is as valuable as wisdom. One of the reasons God places such an emphasis on having understanding is because it changes the course of your life from the destructive track of the world (Proverbs 16:25) to His path of life (Psalm 16:11).

A wise life is characterized by six things. *Joy*—you have gladness based on the abiding knowledge that your life is blessed and has meaning given to you by God. *Confidence*—that comes from having faith that the Lord is with you at all times, regardless of your circumstances. *Worth*—which is the result of understanding that your Savior loves you with an everlasting, unconditional love. *Peace*—that is rooted in the knowledge that God is masterfully working all things for your benefit. *Maturity*—which is based on the Lord's transformational work of forgiveness, renewal, and growth. And *blessing*—God pours His spiritual, emotional, relational, and material grace and goodness into your life.

The person who walks in wisdom grows in Christ's character and experiences life at its best. Therefore, seek the Lord's insight and understanding in everything you experience, and you'll find a greater treasure than anything the world can offer.

Jesus, teach me Your wisdom and help me
walk in Your understanding. Amen.

RESTORATIVE MERCY

I was shown mercy . . . and the grace of our Lord was more than abundant.

1 TIMOTHY 1:13–14

Today you may be wondering, *Can the Father bring joy and meaning back to my life? Can He really heal me of all my regrets?* Absolutely He can. You may feel low about yourself, but we all need Christ's forgiveness. After all, remember what Paul said about himself: "Jesus came into the world to save sinners—of whom I am the worst" (1 Timothy 1:15 NIV). Why did Paul think of himself in this way? Because he'd persecuted the church, punishing those who followed Jesus. To him, there could be no worse crime than attacking the people and work of God.

Yet Paul also said this: "God had mercy on me so that Christ Jesus could use me as a prime example of his great patience with even the worst sinners" (1 Timothy 1:16 NLT). Paul was saying that when you feel low about yourself, you can look at the mercy and grace Jesus showed him and realize that Christ can turn your life around too.

So receive Jesus' forgiveness. And realize that it's not only imperative to forgive yourself, but you must also leave your former ways behind and accept God's new path for you. Because that's the path to true restoration—just as Paul received it.

Jesus, thank You for Your magnificent mercy and restoration. Amen.

REAL LOVE

"He who has My commandments and keeps them is the one who loves Me . . . and I will love him and will disclose Myself to him."

JOHN 14:21

From personal experience, you know it is easy to *say* you love someone, bear allegiance to that person, or trust him or her; but when it comes to putting that person's needs or desires over your own, it becomes far more difficult. However, as any soldier or parent knows, real love is sacrificial. We prove our love when we put the other's well-being above our own. As Jesus said, "Greater love has no one than this, that one lay down his life for his friends" (John 15:13).

In a sense, the same is true for God. We say we believe in and love the Lord, but do we trust Him more than we do ourselves? Are we willing to obey Him out of reverence because He is our Creator, Savior, and Lord? Our choices show whether we do or not. We either respond to Him in faith—acknowledging He is God by saying yes to Him—or in rebellion, choosing our own imperfect wisdom above His. This is up to us and ultimately reveals what we truly believe about Him.

Jesus, I believe You and want to honor You as God—not just with my words but with my actions. Reveal where I fall short and how I can love You more. Amen.

YOUR PERSONAL SAVIOR

*"Behold, the virgin shall be with child and shall bear
a Son, and they shall call His name Immanuel,"
which translated means, "God with us."*

MATTHEW 1:23

Throughout history, God has appeared to be far away to most people. Even when He came to dwell among the Israelites in a pillar of cloud and fire, then in the tabernacle and temple, they were still separated from His holy presence and had only a vague and impersonal understanding of Him.

But that all changed when Jesus came. The Lord was no longer distant; He was with us personally—living in flesh, suffering the same pains and weaknesses you and I experience, and understanding how we feel. Yet He also displayed His power as almighty God, healing the sick, casting out demons, calming the storms, and gaining the ultimate victory over sin and death. His very name—Jesus—means "the Lord is salvation." He is not only with us in our suffering but is also the actively working force of deliverance from it.

This is the Savior you celebrate this Christmas—Jesus, your Immanuel. Not a deity who is distant, unconcerned, or unaware of what you face. Rather, He is the God who is intimately with you and actively working to help you in His perfect power and wisdom. So know Him and rest in His care.

**Jesus, my Savior and Immanuel! I praise and
worship Your wonderful name forever! Amen.**

BEYOND THE EXTERNAL

She gave birth to her firstborn son; and she
wrapped Him in cloths, and laid Him in a manger,
because there was no room for them in the inn.

LUKE 2:7

The birth of Jesus shows us that you cannot determine a person's value by His surroundings. Many babies had been born in Israel and the surrounding Roman Empire at that time. Many sons and daughters of kings, rulers, military commanders, and dignitaries were delivered that year in palaces and places of great wealth and opulence. But none of them were God in human flesh.

No, when the Lord of all creation poured Himself out for us, His surroundings were the lowliest—fit for animals. He was not laid in a gold and jewel-encrusted crib, but a rough feeding trough. Yet here was Immanuel—God with us—our true Savior. Caesar could not save us. The armies of Rome could not deliver us from sin. No, only the Messiah could relate to us in our very worst, most impoverished and destitute moments.

Remember that. You cannot judge people or situations by how they appear externally. At times, the humblest, roughest wrappings hold the very greatest, most precious and powerful gifts.

Jesus, thank You for relating to me at my worst and for coming to be my Savior. In every person and situation, I will look past the outside appearances to what You are accomplishing within. Amen.

SEE THE FATHER

"He who has seen Me has seen the Father."
JOHN 14:9

Today, stop for a moment and consider that with the birth of Jesus, God Himself has come to earth as a Man. That means that in Jesus, we have a glimpse of what our Creator and Sustainer looks like. Of course, we do not see the full scope of who He is, because the King of kings has "emptied Himself, taking the form of a bond-servant" (Philippians 2:7). But we have the privilege of seeing Him interacting with people—teaching, healing, feeding them, and even dying on the cross to save us all.

What we see in Jesus is so telling. He did not compliment the religious leaders for their outward appearance of piety (Matthew 23:27); rather, He praised the centurion for his genuine recognition of Christ's authority (Luke 7:2–9). While the Roman soldiers were putting nails in His hands and feet, Jesus forgave them, recognizing, "they do not know what they are doing" (Luke 23:34). That is our God—loving, forgiving, and concerned more with our spiritual health than on what we look like from the outside.

So as you read about Jesus today, think to yourself, *This is how God would interact with me.* And take comfort in how wise and compassionate He truly is.

Jesus, thank You that through Your earthly life, I see how You interact with me as my God. Truly, You are worthy of praise! Amen.

LIGHT THE DARK

The Sunrise from on high will visit us, to shine
upon those who sit in darkness.

LUKE 1:78–79

We often say that Christmas is a time of joy and peace. But the truth of the matter is that the celebration of the birth of Jesus can often be obscured by many things. The stress of choosing the perfect gifts, traffic, traveling, and the myriad of preparations can dim the spirit of Christmas. Likewise, the anxiety of conflict, the sorrow and loneliness of missing those who are gone, the exhaustion of too much activity, and the depression of so many unmet expectations can make it a dark and difficult season indeed.

Thankfully, regardless of everything else going on, nothing can interfere with the light of God's eternal love for you. Regardless of what situations may arise in your life, the acceptance and worth Jesus gives you never change. And these flow through you most freely when you're showing love to others.

Much more than Christmas presents and parties, what people need from you is to know you care for them. So stop the scurrying and simply let people know God loves them and so do you. This will not only revive the spirit of Christmas in you but will shine the Light of the World to others as well.

Jesus, Your love is the real reason for
Christmas. Shine Your light through
me, wonderful Savior. Amen.

WRITTEN FOREVER

"For this is what has been written."
MATTHEW 2:5

Second to the crucifixion and resurrection, it is the most important event in history—wrapped in the humility of the lowliest setting. It was the moment that God came to earth to provide for our salvation. In that instance, a multitude of prophecies were fulfilled, prayers were answered, and hopes were realized.

The Savior had been foretold from the foundation of the world (Ephesians 1:3–5), affirmed at the fall of humanity (Genesis 3:15), reported by the prophets (Genesis 49:10; 2 Samuel 7:16; Isaiah 7:14; 9:6–7; Micah 5:2, etc.), and etched onto the very heart of Israel (Genesis 12:3). It could only be Jesus—only He fulfilled all that had been written. And when the time came for Him to be born, everyone in the known world was required to register their names for the temporary kingdom of Rome.

What people did not realize was that God was making a way for their names to be permanently penned in the Lamb's Book of Life. And when you accept Jesus as your Savior, what had been written from the foundation of the earth is inscribed in heaven eternally. You become part of His story forever. Therefore, you can have confidence that whatever He has written for you will certainly come to pass.

Jesus, thank You for fulfilling all that was written and for inscribing my name in Your Book of Life. Amen.

THE LOVE IN DISCIPLINE

Those whom the Lord loves He disciplines.

HEBREWS 12:6

God will *always* do what is best for you. If you really believe this, you'll trust the Lord even in your most difficult trials. The Enemy, who works to undermine your trust in Him, however, often takes advantage of adversity by calling the Father's motives into question. He whispers, "If God really loved you, He wouldn't have allowed this to happen." The Enemy wants you to associate the sting of spiritual discipline with a lack of divine caring.

However, the opposite is true. Jesus loves you with an unshakable, sacrificial, everlasting love, and His discipline is actually evidence of your membership in His family. The reason is clear: God cares for you so much that He will not allow you to stay as you are. Instead, He wants to transform you into the likeness of His Son and help you mature in your faith.

Always remember that the Lord is omniscient—He sees the end from the beginning and knows exactly what fruit will come from the challenges you face. Although you may not understand His reason for allowing certain hardships, your difficulties are evidence that God is still working on you and that the best is yet to come. Trust Him and don't lose heart.

Jesus, I know You love me and want me to grow. I believe, Lord; help me to persevere and grow. Amen.

HE KNOWS THE WAY

Oh, the depth of the riches both of the wisdom and knowledge of God!

ROMANS 11:33

In His unlimited knowledge, the Lord always knows what is in your very best interest and acts accordingly. Regardless of what your circumstances look like, God knows the optimal course of action in every situation you face and will act only in a manner that ultimately benefits you as His child.

Sometimes we look at our difficulties and think, *Lord, I know You are infinitely wise, but I think You've forgotten something here.* Be assured He has not overlooked a single factor that concerns you. In our limited understanding, we simply do not see our circumstances from God's perspective. The Lord alone comprehends the totality of every single factor and decision, and because He is infinitely loving and wise, He will never make a mistake when it comes to leading you. In other words, He knows what He's doing in your life.

While it can be frustrating and scary to lean on God and not your own wisdom, it is always the best way to live because His logic vastly exceeds your own (Isaiah 55:8–9). You *can* trust Him. Therefore, have faith that your infinite, all-wise, loving Lord and Savior knows the best action to take in your life and that He won't steer you wrong.

Jesus, I don't know, but You do. I will trust Your wisdom as You lead me. Amen.

AUTHORITY IN ADVERSITY

The LORD has established His throne in the
heavens, and His sovereignty rules over all.

PSALM 103:19

Today, take heart that the Lord has absolute authority over everything in creation. In other words, you can trust Him because
He is able to accomplish anything He promises you. He can protect
you and provide whatever you need.

This may be a difficult truth to accept because of the fallenness
of our world and the painful things that happen. However, we should
never doubt God because we lack understanding about our circumstances. Instead, we should surrender ourselves to Him, accepting
by faith that He is good and fully worthy of our devotion and trust.

Our lives belong to our sovereign, all-knowing, loving God,
and nothing can touch us except what He allows. Sometimes that
includes hardship and suffering, which may leave us wondering,
How can this possibly be good? Yet I've met many people who have
gone through tremendous trials who say, "I despised the difficulty
while I was going through it, but now, on this side of it, I can see
all the good God's done through it." So take comfort, realizing that
God has His purposes and, in His perfect way and timing, will bring
blessing from everything you face if you'll continue to trust in Him.

Jesus, I know that nothing that touches
my life is a mistake. To You be the
glory even in the trials. Amen.

NO MATTER WHAT

*Lord GOD! Behold, You have made the heavens
and the earth by Your great power and by Your
outstretched arm! Nothing is too difficult for You.*

JEREMIAH 32:17

When you truly understand that your loving heavenly Father is in complete control, your life and perspective will change forever. Because God is *sovereign*, you have full assurance that He will work out *every* circumstance in your life for good, no matter what happens. It may be painful, confusing, or seemingly impossible, but the Lord can and will use that situation to achieve His divine purposes for you.

Likewise, the Lord is *omniscient*—He can answer your most trying questions. He is *omnipotent*—He is strong enough to overcome your biggest obstacles. He is *omnipresent*—wherever you may go, He will be there with you. And you have the assurance that nothing can touch you apart from His permissive will.

Therefore, when something happens that is difficult or unexplainable, you can know that the Lord has allowed it for a purpose that will ultimately edify and benefit you. So step boldly into the future because you know that God will protect and guide your steps as you go. Regardless of what pain, trial, or tragedy comes your way, rejoice that your Father will be there to work it out for your good.

**Jesus, how great You are! Thank You for
working out all things for me! Amen.**

HEAVEN IN VIEW

"In My Father's house are many dwelling places . . .
I go to prepare a place for you."
JOHN 14:2

Isn't it wonderful to know that Jesus is preparing a place just for you? He's been working on your home in heaven for nearly two thousand years. You know it's going to be far better than anything you could ever imagine (Ephesians 3:20–21)!

But heaven is more than just an everlasting dwelling place. Rather, along with it comes some extraordinary hope. First and foremost, we will have the joy of being with God and our believing loved ones for all eternity. Second, there will be no evil, no darkness, no tears, no pain, and no more death or loss in heaven (Revelation 21:4). Finally, all that you've done in faithful service to Christ and others will be rewarded. "For God is not unjust so as to forget your work and the love which you have shown toward His name, in having ministered . . . to the saints" (Hebrews 6:10).

Certainly, that is all cause for praise! But understand that ultimately, that's what you're really working for when you serve the Lord. God's plan for you is not just building a kingdom here on earth but getting you and others ready for the heavenly one that is to come (1 Corinthians 3:12–15).

Jesus, thank You for my heavenly home! Help me serve You with heaven in view. Amen.

PREPARED FOR GREATER

*"I will do something new . . . will you not be
aware of it? I will even make a roadway in the
wilderness."*

ISAIAH 43:19

God is always doing a new thing in you—preparing you for His
great plans. You may be doing the same tasks you've done for
years, but He is still causing you to grow in your faith and talents
and mature in your character and depth. No one ever gets to the end
of their potential—no matter how old or experienced you may be.
There's always more that the Lord calls you to do, be, and experience.

Therefore, I challenge you to review the past year and identify
the areas where God has been growing you. If you find you are not
progressing, ask Him why that is and what is holding you back. There
may be an obstacle in your life that you need to face or a sin you need
to confess before you can move ahead.

So do it! There is a new year ahead of you, and God wants to
work through you and demonstrate His power and wisdom in your
life as you live out His purposes. Go into the new year with an attitude of freedom, hopefulness, and victory by taking hold of the new
things the Lord is doing in you.

**Jesus, may this new year bring even more of Your
awesome plans to fruition in my life! Amen.**

About the Author

Dr. Charles Stanley is the senior pastor of the First Baptist Church of Atlanta, where he has served for more than forty years. He is a *New York Times* bestselling author who has written more than sixty books, including the bestselling devotional *Every Day in His Presence*. Dr. Stanley is the founder of In Touch Ministries. The *In Touch with Dr. Charles Stanley* program is transmitted throughout the world on more than 1,200 radio outlets and 130 television stations/networks, and in language projects in more than 50 languages. The award-winning *In Touch* devotional magazine is printed in four languages with more than 12 million copies each year. Dr. Stanley's goal is best represented by Acts 20:24 (TLB): "Life is worth nothing unless I use it for doing the work assigned me by the Lord Jesus—the work of telling others the Good News about God's mighty kindness and love." This is because, as he says, "It is the Word of God and the work of God that changes people's lives."